Global Liberalism
and Political Order

SUNY series in Global Politics

James N. Rosenau, editor

Published by
STATE UNIVERSITY OF NEW YORK PRESS
ALBANY

© 2007 State University of New York

All rights reserved

Printed in the United States of America

No part of this book may be used or reproduced in any manner whatsoever without written permission. No part of this book may be stored in a retrieval system or transmitted in any form or by any means including electronic, electrostatic, magnetic tape, mechanical, photocopying, recording, or otherwise without the prior permission in writing of the publisher.

For information, address
State University of New York Press
194 Washington Avenue, Suite 305, Albany, NY 12210-2384

Production, Laurie Searl
Marketing, Michael Campochiaro

Library of Congress Cataloging-in-Publication Data

Global liberalism and political order : toward a new grand compromise? / edited by Steven Bernstein, Louis W. Pauly.
   p. cm. — (SUNY series in global politics)
   Includes bibliographical references.
   ISBN-13: 978-0-7914-7045-9 (hardcover : alk. paper) 1. International relations. 2. Legitimacy of governments. 3. Globalization—Economic aspects. I. Bernstein, Steven F. II. Pauly, Louis W. III. Series.
   JZ1308.G58 2007
   327.1—dc22

2006017858

GLOBAL LIBERALISM AND POLITICAL ORDER

Toward a New Grand Compromise?

Edited by

STEVEN BERNSTEIN
LOUIS W. PAULY

STATE UNIVERSITY OF NEW YORK PRESS

Contents

Preface		vii
Acknowledgments		ix

PART I
The Challenge of Crafting a New Grand Compromise

One	Introduction: Power, Social Purposes, and Legitimacy in Global Governance *Steven Bernstein*	3
Two	Global Markets and Global Governance: The Prospects for Convergence *John Gerard Ruggie*	23

PART II
Power and Authority in Global Governance

Three	Would Citizens Support a New Grand Compromise? *Robert Wolfe and Matthew Mendelsohn*	51
Four	The Politics of International Development: Approaching a New Grand Compromise? *Jean-Philippe Thérien*	71

FIVE	The United Nations in a Changing Global Economy *Louis W. Pauly*	91
SIX	Compromises of Embedded Knowledge: Standards, Codes, and Technical Authority in Global Governance *Tony Porter*	109

PART III
Integration and Fragmentation in Global Governance

SEVEN	Big Judgments, Elusive Phenomena, and Nuanced Analysis: Assessing Where the World Is Headed *James N. Rosenau*	135
EIGHT	Currency Blocs and the Future of Embedded Liberalism *Eric Helleiner*	143
NINE	Institutional Fragmentation and Normative Compromise in Global Environmental Governance: What Prospects for Re-Embedding? *Steven Bernstein and Maria Ivanova*	161
WORKS CITED		187
CONTRIBUTORS		213
INDEX		215

Preface

Some twenty-five years ago, John Ruggie coined the phrase "embedded liberalism" to describe the grand post-1945 political compromise between free-market liberalism and domestic political interventionism that legitimated and stabilized the multilateral economic order. After the traumatic three decades that began in 1914, it certainly seemed plausible that such a compromise in leading states, combined with US-led military alliances, provided the foundation for a remarkable period of systemic peace and widening prosperity. After the cold war ended, and in the face of widespread perceptions that social safety nets were fraying at the local level and that governing institutions were overwhelmed at the international level, the nature and persistence of that compromise became matters of serious debate among citizens, policy makers, and scholars. Ruggie himself had pointed to the risk that a resurgent ethos of global liberalism could destabilize a political order that necessarily remained only as strong as the political ties that bound together still-independent states. The rising influence of corporations and other non-state actors in our own day only complicates matters. So too does the rising challenge posed by deterioration of the natural environment.

This volume engages that debate. At its core is a fresh look at the idea of embedded liberalism and our current situation by Ruggie himself. A group of distinguished collaborators then explore various aspects of that situation in a series of original essays. Following several rounds of revisions, the volume focuses tightly on the contemporary foundations of political authority at the global level and on the prospects for adapting or renegotiating the grand compromise crafted so many years ago.

Acknowledgments

As with most collaborative projects, this one grew out of the work and intellectual input of a great many people. It originated as a workshop at the 2002 Canadian Political Science Association (CPSA) annual meeting in Toronto, co-organized by Steven Bernstein and Ron Deibert. The idea for the workshop was generated at a brainstorming session that included the editors, Ron Deibert, Janice Stein, and Ron Pruessen. CPSA, the Munk Center, the Center for International Studies, and the Departments of Political Science and History of University of Toronto provided financial support for the workshop. Generous assistance from the Social Sciences and Humanities Research Council of Canada allowed Steven Bernstein the time to write the introduction and oversee the initial round of editing for the volume. Much of that work occurred in 2004 while he was a Visiting Scholar at the Mortara Center in the School of Foreign Service at Georgetown University in Washington. After he returned from Georgetown, Bernstein continued to drive the project forward. In truth, the resulting book would never have emerged without his energy, dedication, and persistence.

We all owe a particular debt to Jim Rosenau, editor of the series in which this volume appears, who assisted Bernstein in many ways during his stay in Washington and who enthusiastically encouraged the collaboration to proceed. His long and continuing scholarly career remains an inspiration.

We benefited enormously from the constructive commentary of two anonymous referees. Erin Hannah provided invaluable assistance in putting the draft manuscript together and assisted in the final editing. Sarah Kim and Tina Lagopoulos helped us at the production stage. Michael Rinella of SUNY Press has been a patient and constant supporter from the earliest days of the project. We are also grateful for the hard work of Laurie Searl and the production team at SUNY Press.

Chapter 3 is a revised and updated version of an article that originally appeared in *International Journal* (59(2): 261–80); we are grateful to the *Journal* for permission to reprint.

LWP
Toronto, Ontario

PART I

The Challenge of Crafting a New Grand Compromise

ONE

Introduction

Power, Social Purposes, and Legitimacy in Global Governance

STEVEN BERNSTEIN

THIS BOOK IS ABOUT world order. It comes amidst deep challenges to the institutional and political foundations of the multilateral order created after World War II. Fissures have appeared in the Western alliance that underpinned its power structure, the fracturing of political authority accompanying globalization has put strains on its legitimacy, and growing material and ideological disparities among leaders, followers, and, for lack of a better term, takers of order have revealed the inadequacies of institutions designed to bridge those divides.

Looking back, the immediate post–cold war period marked an interregnum: a brief honeymoon of optimism for a renewed multilateralism and new global bargains among old foes as well as rich and poor. International economic institutions gained in authority, a host of global issues largely buried beneath cold war priorities began to receive a serious political hearing, and a new engagement with civil society in global affairs promised to extend the reach and legitimacy of institutions of global and regional governance.

Cracks in that vision appeared almost from the start. The debacle of Somalia and the failure to prevent genocide in Rwanda, among other failures of collective security and peacekeeping, exposed the limits of multilateral conflict management through the United Nations. The Asian financial crisis of the late 1990s similarly shook confidence in multilateral financial management. And, the rise of a global protest movement targeting international economic institutions pointed to a deeper systemic crisis of legitimacy.[1] As the transformative capacity of globalization began to crystallize in the collective consciousness of world leaders and ordinary people alike, the strains on institutions designed for another age became more and more obvious. To paraphrase John Ruggie in his contribution to this volume, the postwar order presupposed an *international* world in which sovereign state diplomacy and multilateral innovation could avert crises and manage the most pressing global problems. But a *global* world where transactions, ideas, and even human beings cannot easily be blocked at borders' edges, requires a reconstitution of multilateralism, at a minimum, and perhaps even a shift to a new paradigm of governance altogether.

Just when people began to turn their attention to this challenge, the shock of the September 11, 2001, attacks in Washington and New York jolted the system yet again. The George W. Bush administration responded with a turn away from serious efforts at reform, and toward aggressive initiatives to work through bilateral or coalition arrangements when multilateral institutions were perceived as inimical to short-term US interests. Whether or not this shift in policy reflects a secular trend in US foreign policy, the immediate consequence has been to highlight the precarious balance of norms and power that underlies the architecture of order.

The lessons E. H. Carr drew from an earlier interregnum—the interwar years—resonate very well with the current dilemma. They also capture the philosophical orientation of this volume. Carr's analysis pointed to the flaws in the utopian logic of global liberalism, while at the same time warning of the dismal alternative of pure power politics. This is not merely a matter of perspective, as Robert Kagan (2002) would have it. For Carr, as for the contributors to this volume, realism and utopianism are dialectical poles, in both policy and analysis.[2] A synthesis is especially needed in times of crisis, including today's when global institutions simultaneously face challenges to their legitimacy and increasing demands to widen their scope and authority in response to material and social forces associated with globalization. As Carr (1946) put it, "[W]here utopianism has become a hollow and intolerable sham, which serves merely as a disguise for the interests of the privileged, the realist performs indispensable service in unmasking it. But pure realism can offer nothing but a naked struggle for power, which makes any kind of international society impossible" (93).

In straddling that line, the contributors to this volume are engaged in what James Mittelman has called "critical globalization studies," anchoring assessments of the prospects for peaceful change with critical realist, historically grounded analysis (Mittelman 2004, 222). Unlike other books that document the breakdown of the old order or focus primarily on the limitations of the available conceptual and methodological arsenals to explain such changes, we pressed contributors to examine the foundations of the emerging global system.

Our starting point is the work of Ruggie, who coined the phrase "embedded liberalism" to describe the grand postwar political compromise of laissez-faire liberalism and domestic political interventionism that legitimated and stabilized a multilateral economic order for some fifty years. Some have predicted that the undoing of embedded liberalism could lead to chaos and disorder, while others expect a necessary adaptation to new global economic and political realities. To avoid simply assembling a collection of ruminations on possible futures of international order, this volume begins with a clearly articulated baseline of what has plausibly for many decades been the constitutive basis for global governance. We then asked contributors to assess what existing conditions suggest for that order and to explore the possibility of a new grand compromise. The volume's focus on the foundations of political authority at the global level establishes a basis for rigorously imagining the implications of success or failure of a new compromise for international economic order and political stability. Each author examines a different aspect of order or a particular issue area to assess whether the constitutive basis of governance is changing or could be replaced, and the implications of any such changes for political stability, internationally and domestically.

The remainder of this introduction first outlines the core constitutive elements of the embedded liberalism compromise to establish that baseline for the contemporary challenge. This discussion highlights the challenges to multilateralism, as well as responses put forward in contributions to the volume. Much of this discussion foreshadows Ruggie's own comprehensive statement on the contemporary situation in chapter 2. A second section examines two common themes addressed by contributors, the problem of legitimacy and the role of agency. A final section discusses contributions along two key axes of tension around which the book is organized, and that the original compromise was meant to mediate: authority/power and integration/fragmentation.

THE ORIGINAL COMPROMISE OF EMBEDDED LIBERALISM AND THE NEW CHALLENGE

The post-1945 order described by Ruggie as the compromise of embedded liberalism rested on three pillars: US power projection sufficient to provide security guarantees and arrest the expansion of the communist bloc, multilateralism in collaborative institutions required to build a sustainable international economy, and a commitment shared by the United States and its key European and Asian allies to the political autonomy required by each of them to intervene in internal markets and promote domestic social stability. Ruggie's formulation, building on the work of Karl Polanyi (1944), recognized that national autonomy was not an end in itself, but a necessary mechanism to embed more open markets in the broader values of still-distinct political communities. Over time, the willing deference of most citizens in those communities to the new global order would provide the essential test of its legitimacy, while that legitimacy, it was hoped, would underpin expanding prosperity and a durable peace. The challenge was to maintain those pillars or find substitutes for them as the dynamic system set in train after the war evolved. Over time, the very legitimacy of the order itself would come to be questioned as the security situation changed, as open markets came to be seen as truly global markets, and as national authorities confronted new constraints on their capacities effectively to address social and environmental dilemmas unanticipated in 1945.

Looking back, the United States employed enormous resources in the negotiation of the postwar economic order to entrench the principle of multilateralism in trade and finance and delegitimize discriminatory systems (Ruggie 1982). But the specific goals of openness in trade and collective intergovernmental management of exchange rates in finance comprised only pieces of a larger effort. American planners had nothing less in mind than a reconstruction of the institutional architecture of world order. Driven by antipathy to Nazi and eventually to communist models of bilateral and state-controlled trading systems, and also to preferential systems championed by their British allies, they made multilateralism, in the generic sense, the foundational principle of the new order (Ruggie 1993a). Characterized by general principles of conduct to which all states were bound, multilateralism acknowledged the sovereign authority of states but aimed at rendering the exercise of that authority open, interdependent, and accountable. Thus, even as the "deep structure" of the postwar system firmly entrenched sovereign state actors as the constituent units, the institutional architecture it supported was based on principled understandings of appropriate state-market relations and on a set of systemic decision-making norms (Ruggie 1998b, 20). State identities were secure, even if the governments of states were bound by interlocking sets of economic commitments and obligations.

Multilateralism, not coincidentally, fit very well with the historical shifts throughout the noncommunist industrial world associated with enduring perceptions of the Great Depression. It proved, in short, to be well suited to the exigencies of the modern welfare state. Perhaps there is no coincidence, then, in the fact that both the multilateral institutional form and redistributive policies characteristic of the welfare state would simultaneously come under pressure as a rawer version of global liberalism eventually returned. "Globalization" came then commonly to be linked to a sense of deepening crisis in the postwar order, truly a crisis of systemic legitimacy.

The embedded liberalism compromise first came under serious stress in the early 1970s, when market pressures for deeper economic integration coincided with an apparent fragmentation of political authority. States began having difficulty responding to internal social demands, and multilateral institutions designed for a more decentralized environment, especially one less hospitable to the free flow of capital, lacked the authority to intervene in meaningful ways in any but the poorest regions of the world. Market integration also put unprecedented performance pressures on multilateral institutions. Increased demands came not only from member states, but also, increasingly, from corporations and other actors in civil society, who expected greater responsiveness to their particular concerns. Not coincidentally, international economic institutions were becoming more visible just as governments were increasingly absolving themselves of responsibility for managing economies under their jurisdictions. Under such circumstances, legitimacy demands on the institutions themselves increased as ordinary citizens began to view them as the institutional embodiments of the deterritorialized process of globalization. Civil society increasingly looked, for example, to the International Monetary Fund and the World Bank to provide social justice and equity, not just economic stability (Devetak and Higgott 1999). As Ruggie argues in this volume, as *intergovernmental* institutions they were simply not designed to respond to these kinds of challenges to the very legitimacy of a fast-changing system.

The related threat to multilateralism as an institutional form stems, ironically, from its success. Institutional developments that went beyond the earlier model evidently created fears among a subset of American conservatives especially influential in the George W. Bush administration, dubbed the "new sovereigntists." Certainly by the late 1990s, perceptions of threats to US domestic autonomy and the supremacy of the US Constitution were given wide media attention.[3] The European Union model of pooled sovereignty, a possible harbinger of future world order, provoked particular ire. With the end of the cold war and the expansion of the European Union, the idea that state sovereignty itself was becoming more complex no longer seemed radical, even if it remained difficult to envisage the straightforward adoption of EU-style decision-making practices on a global level (Grande and Pauly 2005). The real target of American skeptics, however, appeared to be the proliferation of international norms and agreements in security and economic affairs to which the United States had not formally and finally assented. In particular, new sovereigntists raised alarms about norms related to human rights, the environment, and labor standards. They also seemed to resent the increasing influence of certain groups claiming to represent global civil society.[4] Whatever the intellectual merits of their arguments,[5] the skeptics did reflect concerns on both the conventional political Left *and* the Right about the potential reach of global institutions into policy areas formerly treated as realms of domestic autonomy.[6]

These challenges to the original compromise of embedded liberalism suggest a variety of possible outcomes. On the one hand, established institutions may need to be more inclusive of non-state actors and amenable to increasingly fuzzy boundaries between formerly distinct policy domains.

Such aspirations are now well entrenched not only in the writings of cosmopolitan political theorists, but also in official circles. On the other hand, a more thoroughgoing restructuring may be required. New public, private, hybrid, and networked forms of governance may come to replace earlier multilateral forms. A return to bilateralism as the primary institutional form of governance beyond the state may even occur, although the building of broader coalitions of the willing (or plurilateralism) seems more likely.

Not entirely impossible to imagine are more radical moves to rein in the authority of states, an outcome that, ironically, would conform with positions widely articulated on both the far Right and the far Left in advanced industrial societies. The far Right would like to see not only a rollback in international economic and social regulation, but also in domestic regulation as well. On the far Left, international institutions and their major member-states have long since come to be viewed as champions of neoliberalism, so any reining in would presumably be a good thing. The dilemma thereby posed is perhaps nowhere more evident than in the global justice movement, a loose coalition of groups most closely associated with what the media has labeled the "antiglobalization" agenda. Generally desiring greater social regulation of market capitalism, these groups have become increasingly suspicious of multilateral institutions. Yet engaging, and thereby shoring up the legitimacy of, multilateral institutions may be increasingly required under globalization for the global justice movement to achieve its goals (Smith, forthcoming).

The desire for greater regulation as globalization proceeds, particularly to ameliorate the effects of rapid economic transformation on employment and income patterns and on environmental conditions, certainly resonates well beyond right and left-wing protest movements. For example, as readers will see more fully below, support for globalization by a majority of Europeans is matched by their concern over the consequences of systemic change (European Commission 2003, 34). Global survey data similarly finds that while majorities in most countries support globalization, that support is soft and tempered by the majority view worldwide that globalization erodes prospects for employment, poverty alleviation, and environmental protection (Environics International 2002). All of this suggests, as Ruggie (this volume) puts it, that "efforts to reconstitute the embedded liberalism compromise in the global context would not be lacking in popular legitimacy" (30).

The contributions to this volume run the gamut of possible responses to just such an idea, although none view the new sovereigntist option as attractive or sustainable. On one end of the spectrum, Louis Pauly's chapter, which focuses on the UN's response to recent developments in a globalizing economy, continues to see resiliency in the existing multilateral architecture. Together with the Bretton Woods institutions, he sees the UN struggling to adapt and learn in response to economic and political transformation. For Pauly, international institutions constructed long ago remain central to an ongoing dialogue between leader and follower states. Even as the structure of state power changes, it still largely determines the course of global policies, albeit with multilateral organizations continuing to play an important mediating role.

In the middle are chapters by Ruggie, on the prospects for embedding markets at the global level, and by Steven Bernstein and Maria Ivanova, who address the same problem in environmental governance. While still emphasizing the importance of state authority and the multilateral decision-making form, both chapters note that global governance in the twenty-first century is, and will likely remain, increasingly fragmented. If it is to remain resilient, multilateralism itself then must be adapted to allow deeper and more sustained engagement directly with powerful corporations and increasingly mobilized groups within civil society.

On the other end of the spectrum, Tony Porter, in a chapter on globalized "knowledge networks," argues that the state-centric understanding of multilateralism and embedded liberalism is less relevant today than in the early postwar period, since embedding markets increasingly occurs in decentered, often private, settings rather than inside territorial states. James Rosenau, in his chapter on contradictory tendencies in world order, sees even less opportunity for bargaining and compromise in coherent orderly systems, multilateral or otherwise. Like Porter, however, he sees networks and what he labels "new spheres of authority" emerging at, and across, local and global levels. Rosenau is even more ambivalent than Porter on whether these emerging institutional forms can create order as multilateralism becomes less relevant, seeing rather "continents of desirable order and fragmentation surrounded by oceans of undesirable tyranny and chaos—with neither capable of encroaching on the other" (141).

COMMON THEMES

Legitimacy

For many of the contributing authors, the multilateral form of governance itself is less the issue than the legitimacy it helped ensure for international liberalism. The prospects for responding to challenges to the pillars of embedded liberalism—the extension of US power not perceived as entirely self-interested, multilateralism, and shared social purposes across like-minded states—is the central theme for the volume. Indeed, Ruggie's work highlighted for a generation of scholars the importance of a consequent sense of legitimacy for the creation and proper functioning of international regimes in such fields as trade, finance, and investment. Underneath his linking of power and collective social purpose was the argument that regime content—the values their scope and specific functions promoted—reflected what powerful societal groups believed appropriate. In the case of the Bretton Woods institutions, that meant the promotion of a liberal economic order, but one predicated on domestic intervention.

Looking back, it appears the American postwar planners understood very well that the creation of order involved the politics of legitimation, although they saw the problem very much through the lens of interstate diplomacy. The United States vigorously pursued its economic and political interests, but its leaders acknowledged the necessity of convincing others that the system would also benefit them. The legitimacy of the order itself was essential if American interests were to be met. Multilateralism helped establish the normative basis and the practical decision-making mechanisms for mutually beneficial collaboration. Along this line, John Ikenberry (2003) has argued that the United States pursued its postwar interests through "strategic restraint": rather than relying primarily on its raw power to bargain and coerce, it constructed "a more rule-based, institutionalized order in exchange for the acquiescence and compliant participation of weaker states" (541). Whether one reads the resulting implications of this institutionalized version of American power as relatively benign or as simply masking domination, both Ikenberry's and Ruggie's (1982, 1993a) arguments suggest that the legitimacy of the postwar order was a function of the degree to which multilateral institutions were perceived as mutually binding and as allowing at least some reciprocal influence on actual policies. Shared values and collective intentions, in turn, worked both to shape and to sustain perceptions that the work of such institutions was indeed legitimate (Ruggie 1982). Whether the leading architect of the system eventually came to forget the continuing necessity of attending to the politics of systemic legitimation in a world more globalized in aspiration than in fact is the subject of debate and analysis in the chapters that follow.

A focus on the continuing importance of socially embedding markets even in a globalizing economy is the entry point for contributors' discussions of institutional legitimacy. For the most part their approaches are decidedly sociological. Legitimacy is understood as embedded in social systems that provide a basis of appropriateness, or that make the purposes, goals, and rationale of an institution understandable and justifiable to the *relevant audience in society*.[7] The test of legitimacy therefore, following Max Weber, bears no particular relationship to truth or right, thus ought not to be automatically linked to Western notions of liberal democracy.[8] Rather, the basic question is an interpretive one: What basis of legitimacy holds sway in a particular society or how does a prevailing political order generate an intersubjective *belief* in its legitimacy? Much depends, in this formulation, on the historically contingent values, goals, and practices of the relevant society. This perspective steers a middle course between the sometimes overly optimistic desire for cosmopolitan democracy within much contemporary literature on global governance, and the dour and rigid state-centrism of the neorealist canon.

The contemporary debate on legitimacy has arisen largely in response to pressures exerted by globalization on international institutions. It has focused on the idea of legitimate authority beyond the state, an idea anathema to many international relations scholars during the cold war period.[9] The few works that did focus on legitimacy during that earlier period, including Ruggie's, conceived of legitimacy as largely rooted in domestic politics of leading states or in intergovernmental consensus.[10] The new literature, in contrast, eschews not only the state-centrism of neorealism, but borrows much more heavily from democratic theory in emphasizing procedural legitimacy and accountability to wider audiences. As such, it is susceptible to charges of idealism (e.g., Cederman 2001). Still, a common feature of the old and new literature is the idea that legitimacy lies at the heart of all governance, at whatever level of aggregation. Indeed, given the lack of enforcement capacity beyond the state, legitimacy increases, not diminishes, in importance at the global level just as the mechanisms to produce it are much more difficult to create and sustain. Moreover, such mechanisms are not likely directly substitutable across domestic and global realms.

Whether or not global governance currently faces a serious "legitimacy crisis" is one dispute addressed in this volume. In part, answers depend on where one looks. Wolfe and Mendelsohn, citing public opinion research in Western democracies, suggest that the sense of crisis invoked by public protests against international institutions does not reflect a wider public hostility to trade, trade agreements, or the idea of international collaboration, although citizens in developed countries are more suspicious when confronted directly by the term *globalization*. In contrast, Ruggie, from a more institutional perspective, sees the antiglobalization backlash targeting multilateral economic institutions as directly linked to the erosion of the compromise of embedded liberalism, which provided their underlying rationale. A legitimacy crisis, thus, "result[s] from the perception that they have abandoned their earlier mandates to secure domestic social stability and inclusion in favor of global market expansion and deepening, and that they have failed to embrace quickly and firmly enough such newer concerns as environmental sustainability" (27). From the slightly different perspective of North-South conflict, Jean-Philippe Thérien perceives what is arguably a more fundamental and intractable legitimacy crisis driven by the core community for these institutions—still mainly a community of states—owing to a "lack of consensus on a definition of what constitutes a legitimate distribution of global wealth and power" (72).

Regardless of contributors' positions on the accuracy of the "crisis" label, they treat seriously the contemporary *global* challenge by moving beyond rigidly state-centric conceptions of legitimacy to problematize the composition of the audience to whom questions of authority must be addressed. They recognize that the dynamics of global legitimation may be changing, as the shift from the study of strictly intergovernmental regimes to "global governance" indicates. They also recognize that the audiences granting legitimacy to such governing arrangements increasingly operate transnationally, including an active and diverse set of global civil society actors, as well as corporations and other market players. In the postwar era, international institutions were judged effective if they promoted economic or security cooperation and facilitated domestic political and social stability. Today, these same institutions face rising demands for social regulation as their very success has made more transparent their reach into areas formerly considered internal to the state. Adding to the challenge, contributors note, different audiences of states, global civil society, or market actors may share different criteria or weightings of the values of participation, access, and accountability (procedural or "input" legitimacy), versus achieving values and goals that a governance institution or network pursues (substantive legitimacy).[11] The problem is especially complicated in a globalized world polity, where who counts as a relevant audience member may be contested and the boundaries between members may be highly complex and fluid.

Not surprisingly, our authors differ on the question of where to look for the most relevant audiences. In their respective chapters, Pauly and Thérien, for example, generally accept states as retaining the most important voices. As in Ruggie's initial formulation of embedded liberalism, legitimacy derives from the social purposes or values of societies in major states. To the degree that international institutions reflect these values (and the interests these values inform), they gain political legitimacy. As Thérien puts it, "multilateral institutions represent the most tangible expression of what is referred to as the 'international community'" (74). But all three authors, in their contributions here, also explicitly acknowledge the broadening of that community to include actors previously marginalized, including states in the global South. Any grand bargain is unlikely to be sustainable without due recognition of social purposes within and among those states. If legitimacy is built around the ability of international organizations to reflect consensus within this broader community, the challenge is daunting even if the organizations themselves appear to be moving toward reconciling previously disparate positions. The underlying problem, as Thérien puts it, is that "the notion of 'international community' simply does not mean the same thing to everyone, and in the field of development, the lack of consensus is particularly noticeable" (75).

On this view, the question comes down to whether the basic underlying premises of embedded liberalism still have resonance. If they do, international institutions face a double challenge of promoting adjustments to integrating markets and policy norms promoted by leading states, which incline away from domestic autonomy (Pauly 2002, 81–86), and of encouraging new kinds of regulation and redistribution in countries that, as Ruggie (this volume) puts it, "never enjoyed the privilege of cushioning the adverse domestic effects of international market exposure in the first place" (24).

Wolfe and Mendelsohn's chapter, on citizen support for embedded liberalism, offers one of the first empirical investigations explicitly to test the legitimacy of embedded liberalism within domestic society. It uncovers evidence of its continued resiliency in Canada, and by comparison with other empirical findings, in other Western societies as well (see also Hays, Ehrlich, and Peinhardt 2005). As globalization continues apace, however, pressures on international organizations build. Wolfe and Mendelsohn's study also directly addresses the issue of whether measures to increase their efficiency and effectiveness any longer provide a sufficient basis for their legitimacy. By separating out elements of democracy, they find the cosmopolitan argument for global democracy probably overstates the case that institutional legitimacy requires direct participation by citizens in decision making by international organizations. They also find strong support, however, for greater transparency and accountability in those organizations. Again, these findings point to the importance of rooting understandings of legitimacy to the values of relevant audiences, whose own criteria for legitimacy in global governance may be shifting.

The notion of embedded liberalism as a constitutive norm that defines the legitimate scope of global governance is much more difficult to tap in the developing world, where in most cases it was never institutionalized. The corollary is that both developed and developing countries must now confront the enormous difficulty of promoting such a norm. If embedded liberalism depends, as Wolfe and Mendelsohn (this volume) put it, "on the notion of separable communities able to make their own decisions on the distribution of the costs and benefits of openness" (53), the legitimacy of the global liberal order and the institutions that support it will come under increasing strain in the developing world as economic integration deepens. Under these conditions, legitimacy will increasingly hinge on the ability of institutions of global governance simultaneously to facilitate the delivery of benefits from globalization *and* provide mechanisms, including resources to improve policy capacity and technical knowledge, for developing countries meaningfully to participate in the governance of globalization (Sandbrook 2003).

The continuing debate in the WTO over demands by developing countries for "policy space" to buffer themselves from market forces reflecting the power of early industrializers, or at a minimum to allow sufficient time for adjustment, is one example of an attempt to operationalize embedded liberalism in a more global context. Creating such space in practice, however, has proven difficult, particularly as the scope of trade rules expands to areas including services, intellectual property rights, and investment, which place a significant burden on developing countries to harmonize the structure and regulatory environment of their economies with established practices in more advanced economies (Hoekman 2005). In other words, the burden of adjustment falls most heavily on countries with the least capacity to bear it. The record of operationalizing "special and differential treatment" for developing countries as a way to create policy space has proven double-edged, as it often comes at the expense of market access or other benefits of WTO discipline (Hoekman 2005). Put more directly, globalization, and the pressure it exerts to open economies, reduces policy space. Meanwhile, negotiations within the WTO system on how to operationalize special and differential treatment are, in the words of one long-time observer, "going nowhere" (Ostry, forthcoming).

The dilemma is confronted in Pauly's chapter. It shows that the Bretton Woods institutions have come to realize that they may not by themselves be the best mechanisms even to provide poorer countries with adequate financing for development. Like the WTO, however, they may not be learning about their limits quickly enough (Ostry, forthcoming; Helleiner 2001). In consequence, a rapprochement unimaginable just a few years ago between the UN, the WTO, and the Bretton Woods institutions has recently occurred. Organizations still suspicious of one another for the ideological reasons underlined in Thérien's chapter, and long jealous of their own operational autonomy, are drawn into a search for a new compromise between global economic opportunities and local political and social requirements.

Eric Helleiner's chapter on regional currency blocs documents how the tension between the promise of global markets and resistance to handing over proven domestic adjustment levers has been playing out in some of the more advanced developing economies since even before the time embedded liberalism became institutionalized internationally. Through a highly textured historical analysis of American "dollar diplomacy" in Latin America, he shows that pressure for dollarization in the 1940s was considered incompatible with embedded liberalism and therefore largely abandoned despite earlier enthusiasm. Only by de-dollarizing, it was argued at the time, could Latin American states achieve the kinds of social welfare goals that had become prominent at the national level in the United States in the wake of the Great Depression. Moreover, Helleiner's chapter shows that the basic message of domestic policy autonomy still resonates today and limits the prospects for further integration, even as contemporary neoliberal policies and regional economic integration has created tension in elite policy circles in both the United States and Latin America on the best way forward.

The reemergence of the dollarization debate in Latin America in the 1990s initially seemed to move away from a notion of embedded liberalism with the emergence of a new faith in the ability of markets to force domestic policy adjustments. This thinking largely reflected a shift in US policy circles to embrace neoliberalism and a more limited role for the state. But this shift, Helleiner shows, has been neither deep nor durable. In part, disastrous experiences with dollarization, especially in Argentina in the 1990s, dampened the earlier enthusiasm. Subsequently, dissatisfaction with freer trade and neoliberal policies more broadly swept through many Latin American countries. Populist governments now rode the wave of discontent across much of the region. Prospects for a dollar bloc in Latin America receded. As Helleiner explains, this re-embedded in some countries a confusing mixture of socialism and liberalism. Karl Polanyi may not have been surprised, and there remained a certain resonance with Ruggie's original notion of embedded liberalism, even if the new variant in Latin America looked less than stable.

For Helleiner, the contrasting case of building a successful currency bloc in contemporary Europe provides more evidence of such resonance, but in a policy context that looks more stable. The adoption of the euro is completely consistent with embedded liberalism because member-states have linked it to region-wide adjustment policies, fiscal transfers, and, more broadly, to a belief that Economic and Monetary Union "provides a stable macroeconomic environment [for] progressive supply-side reforms aimed at promoting equity, growth, and employment" (Helleiner, this volume, 56). The prospect for similar regional mechanisms to arise in the Americas is remote. Helleiner's chapter nicely illustrates that embedded liberalism may not determine precise policy outcomes so much as provide an underlying rationale—what Ruggie called a generative grammar—that continues to resonate broadly.

It remains questionable, however, whether the domestic political autonomy defended in the compromise of embedded liberalism is compatible with feasible solutions to new problems wrought by globalization. Bernstein and Ivanova's chapter confronts that issue in the realm of environmental governance, where policy norms have created a situation more akin to "embedded liberalism in reverse," with environmental concerns largely overshadowed by the quest for near-term economic prosperity. A failure to embed markets in sustainable environmental purposes, they argue, not only threatens viable governance institutions but global ecological integrity itself. For them, the solution cannot juxtapose strengthening national capacity with the need for greater and more focused authority at the global level. Rather, it must recognize that effective governance requires an institutional architecture at the global level to enhance local, national, and regional capacity to protect the physical environment at whatever scalar level is appropriate.

Ruggie's response to the requirement to re-embed global markets at various levels is to look beyond the community of states and to conceive of legitimacy in the context of an emerging world society. States and international organizations have a key role to play, but firms and other actors in civil society need to become more directly engaged. His case study of the UN's Global Compact is highly suggestive in this regard.

Similarly, chapters by Porter and Rosenau find that new opportunities for system legitimation are highly dependent on the norms of the communities actually engaged today in providing governance functions: global knowledge networks for Porter, new spheres of authority for Rosenau. Porter argues that the properties of knowledge-based networks make them especially promising locations for the legitimatization of authority, because they share contemporary values that resonate not only within the networks, but with wider society. These values include pragmatic performance criteria relative to shared standards within the network, as well as the capacity to justify the activity of the network with reference to standards of other networks and fields. Moreover, they exhibit openness to new participants. Their evolving authority, according to Porter, hinges especially on whether wider publics also see them producing general benefits. Porter emphasizes transnational networks as a new institutional form, but he, like Ruggie, acknowledges that their legitimacy may ultimately depend on the degree to which they develop the ability to help forge larger compromises between efficiency and social stability, thus shoring up public authority when required for definitive regulation.

Agency

Any discussion of global governance necessarily attributes causal power to agents, be they government officials, nongovernmental groups, international organizations, or transnational business, technical, or knowledge networks. Hence, a central premise of this volume is that agency matters. In other words, our contributors question a tenet of neorealist and some radical theories of international politics, which hold that either global order simply reflects the systemic structure of state power or that a state's position in the international system determines its interests and posture. Ruggie, for example, refutes the argument that attributes the turning away from multilateralism in the early twenty-first century by the United States to its position as the dominant world power. Instead, he suggests that it reflected an ideological turn and domestic political calculations. That these will turn out to be transient is his obvious hope. Such a discretionary move, could be readily reversed by an administration with different preferences and interests (Ruggie, this volume, 35). This contention harkens back to the ontological premise of the original embedded liberalism argument, that international outcomes reflect *both* power *and* social purpose.

Traditional theories of international relations have also long tended to underplay or dismiss the possibility that international organizations themselves may exhibit agency. In their chapters, both Thérien and Pauly, counter such a position in examinations of an emerging ideological rapprochement between the UN and Bretton Woods institutions, especially in the wake of the Asian financial crisis of the late 1990s. They show how change came about as much through the initiatives of international officials and epistemic communities as through the shifting direction of policies in leading states. While changing economic conditions undoubtedly provided a catalyst or impetus for institutional adaptation, Thérien and Pauly convincingly show that they are insufficient to explain specific organizational responses. Retrenchment was (and has been in the past) as likely an outcome as deeper collaboration, with important consequences for economic order and governance. Where the two chapters differ, however, is in Pauly's more sanguine analysis of the leeway available to the economic organizations to foster interagency cooperation, as well as of their ability to help redefine the preferences of states. To the degree they succeed, some modest reconstitution of their own authority may help members respond more effectively to the social challenge of globalizing markets.

Conceptions of agency and bargaining need not be limited to states, governments, or public officials. Porter's chapter, for example, challenges the atomistic view of states and market actors "uncompromisingly" interacting to shape a globalized world. Rather, he argues that compromise is an important dynamic within globalized networks not only among the most powerful actors, but also between them and the less powerful. Rosenau, who has long pointed to neglected sites of agency in global politics (1990; 2003), argues in his chapter that the interactions of individuals at the micro level are as likely as interactions of states and officials at the macro level to shape *both* order and fragmentation in world affairs. Like Porter, he sees some prospect for bargaining and even the development of social contracts within networks or new spheres of authority. He is skeptical, however, that anything resembling a new consensus will prevail at the macro level, precisely because states and international institutions refuse to make sufficient allowances for micro level processes "that are increasingly important drivers of change and sufficiently diverse to inhibit, even prevent, coherence at the macro level" (135).

Our contributors nonetheless eschew explanations of unrestrained agency. The focus on organizations and institutions in many of the chapters highlights not simply their potential agency or mediating role between interests and outcomes, but the way institutional legacies, path dependencies, and ideological orientations may delimit the possibilities of change and channel ideas and actions along some pathways while closing off others. Indeed, the resiliency and deep resonance of the norm of "embedded liberalism" itself highlights the tension between agency and structure, in virtually every chapter. As Porter points out, the essence of the embedded liberalism argument is that institutional arrangements designed to stabilize market interactions and offset their negative effects constrain agency precisely because they render market activity "acceptable to those actors who might otherwise destroy them through political means" (109). This is true even if the institutional setting for embedding liberalism is no longer limited to territorial states, but might occur as well in the global marketplace and public domain (Ruggie), knowledge networks (Porter), or in new institutional forms of non-state authorities alongside innovations in multilateral forms of governance (Bernstein and

Ivanova). The chapters that highlight these diverse potential locations of embedding vary significantly in their assessment of the prospects for doing so, although they agree on the need for significant agency in mobilizing the requisite resources and political will. Indeed, as Porter highlights, the very notion of "embeddedness" captures the middle ground between undersocialized and oversocialized approaches to norms and institutions, viewing them neither as simply efficient outcomes of the interaction of rational actors, nor as imperatives that act with mechanical or socially productive force on behavior and decision making as if human beings were unreflective robots (Giddens 1979, 5). Neither are institutions automatic responses to economic or social needs. The idea of embeddedness suggests institutions are actively constructed, but within an existing normative and institutional environment that enables and constrains the material and ideational resources available for the task.

Thus, whereas no author understands embedded liberalism as an automatic reaction to laissez-faire or "hyper"-liberalism—the equivalent to Polanyi's inevitable double movement following any dis-embedding of the economy from society—nearly every contributor finds the normative resonance of embedded liberalism continuing to delimit the acceptable boundaries of global economic policy. Helleiner's chapter nicely illustrates this to be the case even when strategic interests would dictate otherwise. Despite the shift in strategic interest of the United States from limiting German influence in Latin America during World War II to lowering transaction costs for US exporters and opening foreign markets thereafter, US technical missions to the region continued to promote "de-dollarization" because it fit with its vision of the multilateral Bretton Woods system. This is not simply a story of institutional legacy. As Helleiner points out, the leadership of the Federal Reserve in this period, especially Robert Triffin who headed the Latin American division, actively championed embedded liberal ideas, having learned from the disastrous effects of orthodox "monetary autonomism" during the early 1930s. Again, agency mattered in US international policy making at a time when the idea of embedded liberalism was just becoming institutionalized.

The broader theoretical point is that ideas, institutions, and their legacies—whether or not they are fully consistent with embedded liberalism—constrain and enable agency. Bernstein and Ivanova's chapter, in addressing the prospects for a new compromise in environmental governance, emphasize both the power of the broader normative underpinnings of environmental governance as well as specific organizational legacies that created conditions for the subsequent fragmentation of environmental governance. They argue that for all the desire and creativity of multiple proposals for reform, success likely depends on the ability of specific policies to work within these normative and organizational constraints. Thérien similarly emphasizes how competing development "paradigms" within the UN as opposed to the Bretton Woods institutions make rapprochement between them fragile. Far-reaching institutional change will therefore still require the demonstration of significant political will by member-states.

Given such constraints, many chapters highlight the importance of creativity in finding openings for institutional reform. The chapters by Ruggie and Bernstein and Ivanova, for example, demonstrate the potential of civil society organizations, sometimes by pressuring firms and sometimes in partnership with them, to bypass institutional rigidities or inertia in the system. One irony of globalization is that it enables such opportunities at the same time as it threatens existing compromises by limiting the effectiveness or willingness of public authorities to intervene in the economy. Civil society initiatives have taken a number of forms, including advocacy campaigns, corporate social responsibility codes and principles, and what some have called "certification" institutions or non-state market-driven governance systems (Gereffi, Garcia-Johnson, and Sasser 2001; Cashore 2002; Bernstein and Cashore 2006). In the latter, products are monitored through the supply and production chain as meeting prescribed social, environmental, labor, and/or human rights standards, which are then verified through third-party auditing. Ruggie also highlights the creative agency behind the Global Compact, an initiative of the UN secretary-general that has managed to move ahead of state action by engaging corporations directly to change their transnational behavior. In that case, however, the secretariat has drawn on existing agreements of states in the areas of environment, labor, human rights, and anticorruption, so as not to overstep its formal organizational mandate, which still rests on the power and legitimacy of the sovereign state.

ORGANIZATION OF THE VOLUME

As this introductory discussion has suggested, the chapters in this volume address many common themes, which makes dividing them into discrete sections a matter of judgment. Two primary tensions in Ruggie's original embedded liberalism article served as guides: one between power and authority, the other between order and fragmentation.

First, though, the next chapter launches the discussion with Ruggie's illuminating review of the condition of the embedded liberalism compromise today and the prospects of a new grand compromise that not only "takes embedded liberalism global," but does so in the context of contemporary challenges to the multilateral order. His chapter can be read in part as a synthesis of key strands of his work on embedded liberalism, globalization, institutional change, and multilateralism. In addition, however, it points the way forward toward a reconfiguration of global governance, focusing especially on the challenges in the realm of agency and practice. As he puts it: "[I]n contrast to the state-centric multilateralism of the *international* world that we are moving beyond, reconstituting a *global* version of embedded liberalism requires a multilateralism that actively embraces the potential contributions to global social organization by civil society and corporate actors" (25). The remainder of the chapters carry many of these themes forward, sometimes building upon, and sometimes challenging Ruggie's conclusions on how the basis of order is being reconfigured.

Along the power-authority axis, chapters focus especially on challenges to public authority, both domestically and internationally. Mendelsohn and Wolfe's chapter addresses the question of whether citizens would support a new compromise, through the first empirical analysis of survey data actually to identify the existence of a constitutive norm (embedded liberalism). They focus on the domestic basis of legitimacy upon which international public authority rests. The following two chapters shift the focus to the potential reconfiguration of international public authority in the shape of the major multilateral economic and social institutions.

Thérien's chapter assesses whether changes in international development governance since the 1990s represent the basis of a "new grand compromise," seeing the metaphor of "Left" and "Right" as a useful lens to assess the political struggle over what the elements of such a compromise might entail. His analysis illustrates how underlying ideological divides that play out within many societies have repercussions for the prospects of working out a new compromise in global governance institutions concerned with development. Pauly's chapter concentrates on the interplay between power politics and organizational learning and adaptation in international organizations. Specifically, he assesses their ability to respond to the contemporary challenges to embedded liberalism and international economic stability more broadly. While both chapters see attempts to balance the need for economic prosperity and social embeddedness, and neither sees a "grand" compromise in the making, their analyses lead to different conclusions on the stability of the new rapprochement between "Left" and "Right." Porter's chapter moves from public to private and hybrid authority, focusing on knowledge networks as a possible location for new bargains in global governance.

Along the integration-fragmentation axis, Rosenau's chapter breaks open the dichotomous understanding of these apparent contradictory tendencies with his concept of fragmegration. He uses this concept to assess the possibility of new compromises within various configurations and locations of political order and chaos.

Helleiner's chapter focuses on financial integration as one source of order, specifically whether regional currency blocs are compatible with embedded liberalism. His analysis of US dollar diplomacy not only adds to the comparative understanding of currency blocs, where scholarship has focused primarily on the European Union, but does so in the context of an explicit analysis of how configurations of financial power interact with societal demands within both powerful and weaker, more dependent states.

Bernstein and Ivanova's chapter on environmental governance examines how the combined impact of extant international environmental norms and forces of globalization have reinforced latent tendencies toward fragmentation. This fragmentation can be seen in both the proliferation of organizations and environmental treaties, as well as in the myriad forms of public, private, and hybrid environmental governance. It notes that fragmentation and coherence are not necessarily a contradiction, but that an effective and politically viable institutional architecture that "re-embeds environmental governance in the broader social purposes of world society" (162) will be a formidable challenge under contemporary political, institutional, and normative constraints. That it must be confronted, however, they do not doubt.

CONCLUSION

In the near term, none of the contributors see the emergence of a new grand compromise comparable to the postwar efforts to institutionalize embedded liberalism. Nevertheless, each author finds some evidence of the persistence of that earlier effort and of the existence today of necessary elements at the global level to emulate its achievements as globalization proceeds. These elements are suggested, for example, by the manner in which certain actors, networks, international institutions, and new spheres of authority are responding to the contemporary challenges of industrial and financial development, inequality, human insecurity, and the retrenchment of the United States. Whether those elements can coalesce to create the constitutive basis for a more just and more sustainable global order is for our contributors a pressing and still-open question.

Then again, as Pauly points out in his chapter, the postwar "grand compromise" may only appear grand in hindsight. If the past sixty years reflected less a grand bargain than a series of improvised adjustments in economic and security policies to the imperatives of the cold war, then even early signs of deeper engagement in a dialogue between leading and following states could be a positive indicator for future systemic transformation. Despite much talk about rolling back globalization, either in the wake of a backlash in particular countries or regions or in the presence of a new security landscape, evidence of serious retrenchment remains hard to find. Indeed, the basic institutional architecture and processes that allowed globalization to accelerate and the system to manage the associated crises of the past sixty years could provide the foundation for avoiding disorder in the years ahead. On this view, the challenge of re-embedding liberalism into stable social formations may be met by creatively drawing on experience. On the other extreme, if Rosenau's analysis proves prescient, only a novel and concerted expression of constructive political energy is likely to harness the necessary resources to resolve mounting dilemmas of systemic sustainability and distributive justice.

Ruggie points to a middle path involving wide engagement beyond well-established multilateral institutions and new practices not simply centered on states. Significant experiments along these lines are now underway. As challenges to global order deepen, however, public authority in some form, especially the authority of major powers, will remain necessary to keep that middle path open. If the original compromise of embedded liberalism depended upon imagination and creativity, anything resembling it in the future will require nothing less.

NOTES

The author is deeply indebted to Lou Pauly for detailed comments and suggestions and to Erin Hannah and other contributors for additional helpful comments.

1. Some contributors to this volume (e.g., Wolfe and Mendelsohn, chapter 3) argue that "legitimacy crisis" overstates the problem in the contemporary system of global governance; others find the characterization apt (e.g., Thérien, chapter 4).

2. For a similar reading of Carr, see Jones (1996).

3. Spiro (2000) coined the term *new sovereigntists* to describe them. See also Ruggie (2004; this volume).

4. Rabkin (2000; 2005) and Bolton (2000) are exemplars of this position.

5. For powerful critiques of the logic and accuracy of their claims, see Spiro (2000); Ruggie (2004); Moravcsik (2000).

6. For the argument on the Left, see Wallach and Woodall (2004); Broad (2002); O'Brien et al. (2000).

7. This definition is slightly modified from Suchman (1995, 574), who also presents an extended discussion of sociological understandings of legitimacy.

8. See Connolly (1984, 18).

9. Examples of the new literature include Coicaud and Heiskanen (2001); Porter et al. (2001); Zürn (2000); Steffeck (2003); Bernstein (2004).

10. Other prominent examples include Claude (1966); Kissinger (1964); Franck (1990).

11. Fritz Scharpf (1997) has contrasted "input" to "output" legitimacy, the latter referring to performance and effectiveness. The term *substantive* legitimacy better captures a broader range of values, which might include distributive justice, equity, etc., rather than assuming actors prefer efficiency to these other goals.

TWO

Global Markets and Global Governance

The Prospects for Convergence

JOHN GERARD RUGGIE

THE CONCEPT OF embedded liberalism was intended to convey the manner by which the capitalist countries learned to combine the efficiency of markets with the broader values of community that socially sustainable markets themselves require in order to survive and thrive.[1]

That lesson did not come to them easily. It took the collapse of the Victorian era's variant of globalization—followed by, though not precisely in this order, World War I, extreme left wing revolution in Russia, extreme right wing revolutions in Italy and Germany, militarism in Japan, unprecedented international financial volatility, the shriveling of world trade and the Great Depression. Nor was that the end of it. The social strains produced by *those* upheavals were so powerful that the world descended into yet a second world war in the span of a single generation.[2]

When the lesson finally did take root, the new social understanding was described by different names in different countries: the New Deal state, social democracy, and the social market economy. But the underlying idea was the same: a grand social bargain whereby all sectors of society agreed to open markets, which in some cases had become heavily administered if not autarchic in the 1930s, but *also* to share the social adjustment costs that open markets inevitably produce.

Governments played a key role in enacting and sustaining the embedded liberalism compromise: moderating the volatility of transaction flows across borders and providing social investments, safety nets, and adjustment assistance—but all the while pushing international liberalization within a framework of multilateral principles, norms, and institutions.

In the industrialized world, this grand bargain formed the basis of one of the longest and most equitable periods of economic expansion in human history, from the 1950s into the 1990s.[3] And it provided the institutional foundation for the newest wave of globalization, which is far broader in scope and deeper in reach than its nineteenth-century antecedent.

But today, it seems, the lesson has to be learned all over again, only in far more difficult terrain. Why? Two related transformations have eroded the postwar compromise, one in the domestic political economies of capitalist countries, the other in their global context. On the domestic front, the broadly Keynesian macroeconomic policy tools with which the compromise was associated succumbed long ago to attacks from monetarism, rational expectationism, supply side economics, and other approaches consistent with more orthodox, or neoliberal, economic views and preferences. As Mark Blyth has put it, "attacking embedded liberalism meant attacking Keynesian ideas" (2002, 126)—though there was no inherent reason why technical defects in the policy tools should have undermined underlying preferences. That link, in turn, is best accounted for by the fact that the domestic political coalitions on which the compromise rested, expressing the different ways in which countries accommodated the new relationships among capital, labor, and the state, became increasingly incapable of delivering the goods effectively or, as in the case of the United States, unraveled altogether.

The framework of embedded liberalism was challenged on a second front as well. It was predicated on the existence of an *international* economy: comprised of separate and distinct national markets, engaged in *external* transactions, conducted at *arms length*, which governments could buffer effectively at the *border* by point-of-entry measures such as tariffs, non-tariff barriers, and exchange rates. But markets and firms have gone increasingly global, threatening to leave behind merely national social bargains. Many developing countries are doubly disadvantaged, having never enjoyed the privilege of cushioning the adverse domestic effects of international market exposure in the first place, and lacking the resources, institutional capacity, and, in some cases, the interest on the part of their ruling elites to rise to the new challenges of globalization.

The past is not inevitably prologue. But here is how United Nations Secretary-General Kofi Annan assessed the state of play at the Davos World Economic Forum in January 1999, ten months before antiglobalization protesters and the authorities waged the so-called Battle of Seattle at the ill-fated ministerial meeting of the World Trade Organization:

> Our challenge today is to devise a similar compact [similar to embedded liberalism] on the global scale, to underpin the new global economy.... Until

we do, the global economy will be fragile and vulnerable—vulnerable to backlash from all the "isms" of our post-cold-war world: protectionism, populism, nationalism, ethnic chauvinism, fanaticism and terrorism. (Annan 1999)

The magnitude of this task is monumental. For, while the world economy is becoming increasingly globalized, political authority remains fragmented and anchored in territorial states. International organizations cannot adequately compensate for the resulting governance gaps because they simultaneously lack the global reach of markets, firms, and civil society actors on one side, while being tightly constrained by territorial states on the other—in recent years, especially so by the United States.

In a world comprised of sovereign states a stable economic order requires, I argued in the original embedded liberalism essay, the combination of three factors: shared social purposes, a supportive structure of state power, and a set of institutional means through which the shared purposes can be enacted (Ruggie 1982, 382). Thus, the prospects for a "new grand compromise" today—by which I mean some variant of "taking embedded liberalism global"[4]—hinges significantly on how these factors unfold in the current context.

I can do little more than touch upon a few key dimensions of these very large issues in this chapter. Accordingly, in the first section I address whether the underlying principles of embedded liberalism could still provide the normative basis of a renewed compromise if appropriate means and the political will were found to institute them in the new global context—in light of antiglobalization concerns on the Left, the "new sovereigntist" reaction on the American Right, and the widespread move toward neoliberalism in between. The second section assesses the extent to which the Bush administration's turn against multilateralism is the consequence of a structural change in the distribution of world power, as many have argued, signaling a relatively permanent shift in US foreign policy, or is more volitional and, therefore, subject to modification or reversal. Presumably, if the former were to be the case then prospects for any multilateral reconstitution would be limited. To anticipate, I conclude that neither normative challenges nor the current structure of world power pose insuperable obstacles to reconstituting something like the embedded liberalism framework at the global level.

The truly difficult challenges, therefore, may reside in the realm of agency and practice: who and how? Accordingly, in section three I suggest that, in contrast to the state-centric multilateralism of the *international* world that we are moving beyond, reconstituting a *global* version of embedded liberalism requires a multilateralism that actively embraces the potential contributions to global social organization by civil society and corporate actors; I briefly describe the domain of corporate social responsibility, and specifically Kofi Annan's "Global Compact," as examples of such a multilateral form.

SHARED OBJECTIVES

The legitimacy of an international economic order derives in part from the extent to which its main provisions reflect the shared social objectives of its constituent units. Shared objectives do not imply an identity, merely sufficient overlap and compatibility to provide a coherent platform for international action. The specific domestic institutional forms that embedded liberalism took varied across the capitalist countries, reflecting different national traditions and configurations of interests among leading social sectors. Indeed, securing such a degree of domestic policy autonomy was among its central objectives.

Thus, the International Monetary Fund's original articles of agreement stipulated that the Fund could not oppose any change in exchange rates on the grounds that the full employment policies and social safety nets of the country requesting it had led to the disequilibrium that made the change necessary. Moreover, it not only permitted, but was predicated upon the maintenance of certain forms of capital control. At the same time, however, the pursuit of that policy autonomy was constrained by multilateral principles and practices: no discriminatory exchange rates or competitive exchange rate changes were permitted, liberalization was promoted, and the Fund exercised oversight and conditionality. Finally, the compromise was never intended to be a fixed formula linking greater openness to, say, precisely proportionate increases in domestic public expenditures by each country on a year-to-year basis; it served as a set of constitutive principles structuring social expectations and policy practices in the aggregate and over the longer term.[5]

Although specific instruments of the regime were modified almost from the start, and several jettisoned along the way—the most important being fixed exchange rates and dollar convertibility into gold—in its broad contours it continued to operate for much of the postwar era into the 1980s. For example, Vito Tanzi and Ludker Schuknecht (2000) document levels of public expenditures in the major industrialized countries starting in 1870. They find that the most rapid expansion took place between 1960 and 1980, during the period of the most significant liberalization in trade and monetary relations—much as would be expected from the embedded liberalism compromise.

The 1980s first witnessed the emergence of greater skepticism about the domestic interventionist state, especially in the United States and the United Kingdom. Though public spending continued to rise, it did so at a decreasing pace and it was purchasing fewer social services. This was due in part to increased military expenditures and a growing public sector debt burden, and in part because of the declining cost-effectiveness of traditional social interventions.

More telling, Geoffrey Garrett has found that, whereas greater exposure to trade had been an important contributor to domestic fiscal expansion in the past, by the 1990s marginal increases in trade exposure began to lead to *lower* government spending, reversing the traditional relationship (Garrett 2000b; Garrett and Mitchell 2001). Parallel results hold for marginal increases in financial openness. The magnitudes remain small, but if sustained they may indicate the beginning of a profound shift in the domestic role of the capitalist state: away from a *compensatory* posture vis-à-vis international liberalization under embedded liberalism, to a *competitive* one, allowing the effects of global economic market forces to be imposed more directly on domestic factors of production, especially labor.[6] Indeed, the main resistance to this shift, Garrett (1998) notes, comes from European social democracies where strong left-of-center political parties remain allied with strong and centralized trade unions.[7] The Blair and Clinton administrations sought to chart a "third way" (Giddens 2000), with mixed results, but by and large neoliberalism and the so-called Washington consensus gained broad ascendancy in policy circles by century's end.[8]

But by then so, too, had serious social concerns about globalization. From the Left, the antiglobalization backlash has focused unprecedented popular scrutiny and pressure on multilateral economic institutions. The legitimacy crisis faced by the WTO and ongoing protests aimed at the Bretton Woods institutions result from the perception that they have abandoned their earlier mandates to secure domestic social stability and inclusion in favor of global market expansion and deepening, and that they have failed to embrace quickly and firmly enough such newer concerns as environmental sustainability.[9] By and large, the solutions proposed by the Left consist of a different and more robust system of global economic governance: rebalancing the objectives pursued by the multilateral economic institutions, securing greater public accountability for their decisions and operations, and establishing binding rules governing the behavior of global private sector actors. Rolling back globalization, which is another way of saying greater protectionism, is their default option, should the preferred strategy fail.

The exact mirror image is advocated by American neoconservatives, in this context sometimes described as the "new sovereigntists."[10] Existing forms of global governance, and even more so the European Union, they claim, are already serious threats to American interests and even to the US Constitution, and must be resisted if not dismantled. Writes John Bolton (2000), who went on to become a Bush administration senior State Department official, and then US ambassador to the UN: "In substantive field after field—human rights, labor, health, the environment, political-military affairs, and international organizations—the Globalists have been advancing while Americanists have slept" (206). But now, he states, the great awakening has come. Jeremy Rabkin (2000), one of the originators of the new sovereigntist doctrine, considers the EU to be particularly problematic not only because it has "many practical ramifications for U.S. policy. But it also presents a clear ideological alternative" (273)—by pooling sovereignty, favoring a more active economic role of the state and supporting transnational civil society organizations.

As Andrew Moravcsik (2000) notes, however, it isn't global governance per se that neoconservatives oppose, "just multilateral cooperation around certain emerging policies" (298). They include, as we saw in Bolton's list, environmental sustainability, human rights, and labor standards. Trade treaties arouse no concern as long as they don't touch on "social" issues. The power of transnational corporations is ignored, yet NGOs get a drubbing. Indeed, their political agenda reaches far deeper. Rabkin (1998), for one, doesn't so much want to defend the *current* US constitutional order as to *restore* an earlier one. He writes, nostalgically: "Before the political upheavals wrought by the New Deal in the 1930s, established constitutional doctrine sought to limit the reach of federal power to matters of *genuinely* national concern" (7; emphasis added). And his understanding of what is "genuinely national" does not venture far beyond protecting property rights and national security. Thus, Rabkin desires a rollback not only of certain forms of global governance, but also central elements of the post–New Deal domestic political order onto which the postwar system of global economic governance was built. This position is at least as radical as any on the antiglobalization Left, except that it would push the world in a very different direction.

Where, then, does the public stand in these increasingly bitter debates? For illustrative purposes, I summarize briefly in-depth surveys of public opinion on this subject in two countries, the United States and Canada.

Nowhere has the "disembedding" of the postwar compromise gone farther than in the United States. For example, measured in terms of income distribution the United States may be the most unequal of any advanced capitalist society, while American workers pay a greater share of their own pensions and health insurance—or, in the case of the latter, a larger fraction go without altogether—than is true in other advanced capitalist countries.[11] Yet a University of Maryland survey conducted just prior to the 1999 WTO ministerial meeting in Seattle showed that a solid majority of Americans still expressed views consistent with embedded liberalism. They supported trade liberalization in principle. But they viewed business to be the prime beneficiary: 61 percent of respondents felt that business was better off as a result of lower barriers, compared to only 25 percent who believed workers were. Overwhelming majorities felt that US trade policy makers were giving "too little" consideration to "working Americans" (72 percent), "the general public" (68 percent), or "people like you" (73 percent). Some 60 percent felt that policy makers paid too little attention to trade's "impact on the environment."[12]

However, overall support for trade liberalization soared (to 84 percent) when respondents were offered the option that the government would help workers adapt to changes associated with increased trade. Moreover, 78 percent felt that the WTO should consider issues such as labor standards and the environment in making trade decisions; and respondents were fully prepared to support trade sanctions to advance these (and related) social goals. As for globalization—conceived as the broader process of growing interconnectedness in the world—respondents saw it as having a mixture of positive and negative elements, with the pluses moderately outweighing the minuses.

In a similar survey conducted five years later doubts about free trade had become stronger. But the reasoning continued to reflect the same underlying principles: "People generally do not believe the government is adequately mitigating the effects of free trade. . . . This is a bipartisan consensus; there are only modest differences between the parties" (Kull 2004, 3).

In short, Americans are neither protectionist nor do they favor unfettered global markets. They do view the benefits of free trade to be unequally distributed and safeguards for workers, labor standards, and the environment to be inadequate. Their underlying anxieties resemble some of the antiglobalization concerns, though the broader public is not prepared to adopt the proposed solutions fully. But nor is there any indication that the public supports further rolling back social protections provided by the government in response to the competitive pressures of more extensive globalization; indeed, the evidence is strongly to the contrary. In these survey results one readily sees the political rationale for the Clinton administration's rediscovering the utility of the International Labor Organization and encouraging its closer collaboration with the WTO, and for adding labor and environmental provisions to regional and bilateral trade pacts. The prevalence of such views makes it harder to explain the domestic economic policies of George W. Bush's administration, though it hit the proverbial "third rail" of American politics when it sought partially to privatize the social security system.

Mendelsohn and Wolfe, in their contribution to this volume (chapter 3), examine public attitudes toward these issues in Canada, based on a survey they designed specifically to test whether the principles of embedded liberalism continue to resonate. The Canadian public strongly supports new trade agreements (65 percent positive responses), they find, including a Free Trade Area of the Americas (67 percent positive). Moreover, Canadians favor more international cooperation across a variety of fields, ranging from climate change to promoting democracy and human rights. But when it comes to protecting their own labor and workplace standards, and even more so their social programs, Canadians overwhelmingly want the responsibility to remain in the hands of their own government—by an 83 percent majority in the case of social programs—apparently fearing that they would be less well protected otherwise. The survey questions also permit the authors to differentiate the Canadian public's attitudes toward trade, specifically, and globalization, more generally. Whereas attitudes toward trade reflect individuals' calculations of self-interest as economic agents—their education and skill level, and sense of competitiveness in the marketplace—attitudes toward globalization, about which Canadians are more dubious (46 percent favorable), reflect core values concerning the kind of society in which they wish to live, and their best judgments about how to preserve the essential elements of social community.

To the extent that these findings are broadly representative, the North American public continues to express preferences and attitudes consistent with the underlying principles of embedded liberalism—and less so either with neoliberalism or the protectionist versions of antiglobalization, let alone the neoconservative agenda of rolling back the post–New Deal state and its international complements. There is no reason to believe that European opinion differs significantly in these respects.[13] It is well beyond the scope of this chapter to account for misalignments between public opinion and actual policy practices. My objective has been solely to argue that efforts to reconstitute the embedded liberalism compromise in the global context would not be lacking in popular legitimacy.

THE STRUCTURE OF STATE POWER

The United States exhibited extraordinary leadership and invested considerable resources in the construction of the postwar international order.[14] It entrenched the principles of multilateralism in trade and monetary affairs, de-legitimizing discriminatory and preferential systems. In security relations, the United States grafted a collective security organization onto a concert of power in the form of the United Nations, and when that proved inadequate to deal with the Soviet threat in Europe it implanted indivisible security guarantees in the North Atlantic area—stipulating that an attack on one would constitute an attack on all—and pushed actively for European unification. Even though the United States pursued its own interests vigorously, it did so within a rule-based system that encouraged not only acquiescence but active participation by other and lesser powers. That feature also made it much easier to accommodate the inclusion of new entrants into the system, including, most important, an emerging China and a disintegrating Soviet Union and its East European empire.[15]

In light of that history, the Bush administration's turn against multilateralism—which predates 9/11—jolted transatlantic relations as no other rift before. The divergence came to a head over the Iraq war, but strains had been mounting as a result of the administration's rejection of the Kyoto protocol, the International Criminal Court, and multilateral as well as bilateral arms control treaties, coupled with its attacks on and attempts to marginalize the United Nations.[16] Its new national security strategy expressed the aim of perpetual military predominance, while also proclaiming a highly controversial doctrine of "preventive," in contrast to "preemptive," warfare (White House 2002).[17] Its economic policies on the domestic front further eroded the economic security of the lower half of the American wage distribution, driving an additional wedge into the shared political cultures of the advanced capitalist countries, and internationally they turned the United States into an importer of capital from emerging markets.[18] Its treatment of prisoners from the wars in Afghanistan and Iraq raised serious questions abroad about America's commitment to the rule of law. Reputable polls soon showed favorable attitudes toward the United States in most countries surveyed to have sunk to all-time lows.[19]

Much of this debate has focused on implications for alliance relations between the United States on the one hand, and the European Union and NATO on the other. But multilateral orders contain strong elements of indivisibility that cannot be easily compartmentalized. In good times, this makes it possible to practice diffuse reciprocity among the major players across different issue areas and over time, as opposed to requiring specific quid pro quos on each item and every round.[20] But it also means that questions about any potential new grand compromise in global economic and social organization are unlikely to get resolved in the absence of a more general reinvigoration of the multilateral system itself. And that, in turn, hinges in considerable measure on whether the recent US policy shift represents a permanent or a temporary change. I contend that the shift has been largely discretionary, not structural.

In the run-up to the Iraq war, the opposite was the more popular opinion among American commentators: that we were witnessing the emergence of two genuinely different worldviews based on a deep and growing transatlantic power gap. Americans are from Mars, Europeans from Venus, in Robert Kagan's (2002) evocative and frequently cited phrase. The United States is militarily powerful; Europe, in relative terms, weak. So it is axiomatic that America would use force and project power to pursue its interests, downplaying norms and institutions, while Europe stresses diplomacy and writes checks. America is unilateral because it can be; Europe favors multilateralism because it must. But this reasoning is deeply flawed.

About the power asymmetry there can be no dispute. The United States now spends nearly as much on its military as the rest of the world combined—and yet that still consumes less than 5 percent of its GDP. The gap in technology and combat experience is even greater. Policy differences inevitably will result from an asymmetry of this magnitude. But permissive conditions do not constitute causal factors. Yes, the United States *can* do many of the things Kagan and other neoconservatives ascribe to it, including prosecuting what some among them have happily described as a policy of "democratic imperialism." But it follows neither that it must nor will do those things by virtue of its power differential alone.

Consider the fact that, for all practical purposes, the transatlantic power gap was as great in the 1990s as it is a decade later. When the Soviet Union imploded, the American neoconservative commentator Charles Krauthammer (1990/1991) already heralded the advent of "the unipolar moment" (23–32). Then-Secretary of State Madeleine Albright hectored the allies and the United Nations at every opportunity that the United States was "the world's indispensable nation."[21] And Hubert Védrine (2003), French foreign minister at the time, coined the term *hyperpuissance* to express the unique extent of American hegemony even then. Yet transatlantic grumbling was not appreciably worse than in earlier times. And everyone—including the German Red-Green coalition government—was on board for the US-led Kosovo intervention that arguably had less legal justification going for it than the war against Iraq.

One significant difference between the two decades lies in the politics of legitimation. When the Clinton administration reminded the world of America's indispensability, it invariably did so in the context of values and policy objectives that were broadly shared but which could not be achieved without active US involvement—be they opening global markets, promoting nuclear threat reduction, fielding robust peacekeeping missions, or sustaining the Middle East peace process. Even American triumphalism in the 1990s— and there was plenty of it—celebrated a *shared* achievement: the victory of free markets and democratic governance against an adversary the West, collectively, had combated for much of the twentieth century.

In contrast, in its first term the Bush administration rarely missed a chance to tell others that they were not needed even when they could have been helpful—as in postwar Afghanistan, when it rejected expanding the International Security Assistance Force beyond Kabul, before the regional warlords had a chance to rebuild their power bases; or in the postwar reconstruction of Iraq, when European (and initially Canadian) firms were excluded from bidding on contracts. The new national security strategy assigned no role to multilateralism and, indeed, acknowledged no serious need for international support.[22] The administration's triumphalism was largely self-referential, and it professed as well as practiced the belief that the use of American power was entirely self-legitimating, determined solely by US interests, neither requiring nor welcoming any form of external accountability. And it risked the NATO alliance to fight an elective war on false premises and before other means had been exhausted. This was, in short, a *doctrinal* unilateralism, not simply routine unilateral behavior, of a kind the nation had not seen on a comparable scale perhaps since the time of William McKinley—a president from whom George W. Bush claims to have learned much.

Thus, the extent of American power may be a necessary condition for the Bush administration's turn away from multilateralism, but the sufficient conditions reside elsewhere: in some combination of the political preferences of its electoral base, sectoral interests, and ideological predispositions.[23] But the turn was hardly cost-free, as seen especially in the case of Iraq, an intervention paid for largely by American taxpayers—and the lives of American troops. Indeed, perhaps in recognition of "why the world's only superpower can't go it alone," to borrow Joseph Nye's (2002) poignant phrase, early in its second term the Bush administration exhibited modest signs of changing its posture. The president and his new foreign policy team seemed far more solicitous of the European allies, opposed congressional efforts to begin a new round of withholding UN payments—and even permitted the UN Security Council to refer the Darfur genocide to the International Criminal Court, thereby adding to the court's stature despite having spent the previous four years maligning and undermining it. In broader Republican circles, Newt Gingrich, former House Speaker and an architect of the party's 1994 "Contract with America," one of the original blueprints for doctrinal unilateralism, in 2005 co-chaired a congressionally mandated bipartisan commission that urged serious US engagement with the UN, based on its assessment of American interests (United States Institute of Peace 2005). And the neoconservative commentator of Mars and Venus fame, Robert Kagan (2004), published an article acknowledging, albeit grudgingly, that international legitimacy can be bestowed on a state's actions only by others, not by itself.[24]

The Bush administration is unlikely to take the lead in reconstituting a global grand compromise along embedded liberalism lines, or a new multilateral order more broadly; its domestic and international policy preferences push in very different directions.[25] But my point has been that this fact is not determined by the structure of international power. On the contrary, the recent US move toward unilateralism was highly discretionary and, therefore, in principle it is reversible by an administration with different priorities and interests.

AGENCY AND PRACTICES

Constructing the postwar order was an affair of states, as such matters had been for three centuries. Thus, at Bretton Woods, San Francisco, and later Havana and Geneva, governments created *intergovernmental* means for dealing with *international* problems faced by *national* states. But over the course of the past generation, as an integral part of the globalization process, the role of non-state actors in world politics has grown significantly. They may be animated by universal values or factional greed, by profit and efficiency considerations, or the search for salvation. They include transnational corporations and financial institutions; civil society organizations; faith-based movements; private military contractors that in some respects resemble the mercenaries of yore; and such illicit entities as transnational terrorist and criminal networks. Whatever their other differences, this much they have in common: increasingly they think and act globally; the territorial state is not their cardinal organizing principle; nor is serving national interests their primary driver.

Accordingly, successful efforts to construct a new grand compromise for the global economy can no longer be limited to the interstate realm, as important as it remains. They need also to engage and build upon the global reach and capacities of two sets of non-state actors: civil society organizations (CSOs) and transnational corporations (TNCs).[26] One productive point of intersection between them in responding to the challenge of "taking embedded liberalism global" is the domain of corporate social responsibility.

Non-state Actors

The nonprofit sector, excluding religious organizations, has become a US$1 trillion-plus global industry (Center for Civic Society Studies 1999). US noncommercial private transfers to developing countries, including grants from foundations and private philanthropies, are now twice the size of US official development assistance (Adelman 2003, 9–14). More than thirty thousand nongovernmental organizations (NGOs) operate international programs, and roughly one thousand draw their membership from three or more countries (Smith and Sikkink 2002). There are no reliable numbers for purely national NGOs, many of which have international ties.

The major transnational CSOs, such as Amnesty International, Oxfam, Greenpeace, Human Rights Watch, or the World Wide Fund for Nature, have both global and national presences, much like TNCs. And in their campaign modes, transnational activist networks are capable of acting in near-real time. Perhaps the iconic case remains CSO opposition to the Multilateral Agreement on Investment in the 1990s, when a coalition of more than six hundred organizations in seventy countries sprang into "virtual existence" on the World Wide Web almost overnight (Walter 2001; Kobrin 1998).[27]

The role of CSOs has been fundamental in certain areas of international norm creation and implementation. The global agenda in human rights, the environment, and anticorruption, for example, would not be nearly as advanced were it not for their influence. CSOs exercise that influence through their own global campaigns and operational activities, as well as by direct involvement in official forums such as periodic UN conferences or the ongoing UN human rights machinery—where the documentation provided by Amnesty carries special weight precisely because it is detached from national interests.[28] Moreover, governments increasingly rely on CSOs to deliver humanitarian services and development assistance; fully 75 percent of US Agency for International Development funding for HIV/AIDS in sub-Saharan Africa, for example, is disbursed through such entities (United States Department of State 2003b).

The universe of transnational corporations now comprises more than sixty-five thousand firms, with some eight hundred thousand subsidiaries and millions of suppliers and distributors connected through global value chains.[29]

The foreign sales of TNCs have exceeded worldwide exports of goods and services by a substantial margin for some time. Intrafirm trade accounts for a significant and growing share of overall world trade—approximately 40 percent in the US case (Clausing 2001)—and those figures do not fully capture related party transactions of branded marketers ("manufacturers without factories," such as Nike) and branded retailers (such as the GAP and Wal-Mart) that source overseas but whose ties to suppliers are contractual, not equity, relationships (Gereffi 1999, 2001). Consequently, even as country borders have become more open to the flow of international transactions, in an institutional sense significant aspects of the international division of labor have become internalized at the level of firms or within globally integrated networks in the financial sector.[30]

Improving those companies' social and environmental performance has direct benefits for their employees and the communities in which they operate. But equally important is its potential for generating positive social spillover effects. Three are especially critical for the purposes of the present discussion. First, in the developing world the adoption of good practices by global firms and their local affiliates may exert some upward pull on the performance of other enterprises in the same sector.[31] Second, in the industrialized countries the diffusion of good practices by global companies' social and environmental performance abroad may lessen the fear that a global "race to the bottom" will undermine domestic policy frameworks for achieving social inclusion and economic security at home. Third, successfully involving the private sector in this endeavor would ease the public sector's burdens—political and financial, and within as well as among states—thus potentially helping to narrow the governance gaps that now exist between global markets and state-based authority structures. Broadly speaking, these are the strategic aims behind other social actors' efforts to engage the corporate sector in the rapidly expanding web of corporate social responsibility initiatives.

Corporate Social Responsibility

The rights enjoyed by transnational corporations have increased manifold over the past two decades, as a result of multilateral trade agreements, bilateral investment pacts, and domestic liberalization—often urged by external actors, including the international financial institutions. Moreover, the corporate sector's influence on global rule making is well documented, such as the pharmaceutical and entertainment industries pushing the WTO's intellectual property rights agenda in their favor, or Motorola managing to write many of its own patents into International Telecommunication Union standards.[32]

Along with expanded rights, however, have come demands, initiated by civil society actors, that corporations accept greater obligations. To oversimplify only slightly, while governments and many intergovernmental agencies were creating the space for TNCs to expand and deepen their global operations, other social actors have sought to infuse that space with greater corporate social responsibility (CSR).

For CSOs, the sheer imbalance between global corporate rights and obligations, coupled with their desire to establish some form of countervailing power, has been and remains a key driver.[33] But there are also two more proximate factors behind their strategies of engagement with the corporate sector. First, individual companies have made themselves, and in some instances their entire industries, targets by doing bad things: think of Shell in Nigeria, Nike in Indonesia, the Exxon Valdez spill and others like it, unsafe practices in the chemical industry as symbolized by Union Carbide's Bhopal disaster, upscale apparel retailers purchasing from sweatshop suppliers, unsustainable forestry practices by the timber industry, and so on. Even where companies break no local laws they may stand in violation of their own self-proclaimed standards, or be accused of breaching international community norms in such areas as human rights, labor practices, environmental sustainability, or corruption.

CSOs, in turn, have pushed companies, and in some cases entire industry sectors, to adopt verifiable measures to reduce the incidence of such practices. Firms not directly involved have taken steps to avoid similar problems, or to turn their own good behavior into a brand advantage. A norm of voluntary nonfinancial performance reporting is emerging as a result, in the first instance mainly among large TNCs, which potentially creates the basis for greater corporate accountability.[34]

In practice, this consists of statements of principles and codes of conduct (company-based or sectoral; unilateral or multi-stakeholder); social and environmental performance reports by companies; the growing interest of nonprofits and commercial firms in auditing company codes or providing other forms of third-party assurance; a Global Reporting Initiative, established as a Dutch NGO, which offers standardized social and environmental reporting systems; and so-called certification institutions, which verify that an entire production and distribution cycle—be it of forest products, coffee beans, or diamonds—meets prescribed conditions.

Apart from CSOs, the financial sector has become increasingly involved. Socially responsible investment funds have existed for some time. But mainstream actors—including institutional investors, especially public sector pension funds; some of the world's stock exchanges; and investment banks—have begun to encourage or demand more information from firms on their social and environmental performance, to better account for the risks this may pose.[35]

Nearly three-quarters of the world's largest firms now issue some form of social and/or environmental report (KPMG 2002; ACCA 2004).[36] Nearly fifteen million pages on the World Wide Web address various dimensions of the corporate social responsibility of *Business Week's* Global 1,000; those same firms, in turn, have more than one hundred thousand pages on the same subject on their own corporate websites.[37] And some leading companies, notably Nike, once the "poster child" for bad corporate behavior, have re-engineered how they manage their global value chains as a result of their past experiences and drawing on feedback generated by their CSR programs (Zadek 2004).

In the past few years, yet a third rationale for engaging the corporate sector has emerged: the desire by other actors to take advantage of the fact that it has global reach and capacity, and that it is capable of making and implementing decisions at a pace that neither governments nor intergovernmental agencies can match. Ironic as it may seem, global companies increasingly are being asked to help fill certain global governance gaps and compensate for governance failures, some of which are the results of globalization itself. Few major issue areas have been left entirely untouched; take HIV/AIDS treatment as an example.

AIDS activists picked Coca-Cola for special embarrassment at the 2002 Barcelona AIDS conference, not because Coke causes HIV/AIDS but because the company has a universally recognized brand and one of the largest distribution networks in Africa.[38] "If we can get cold Coca-Cola and beer to every remote corner of Africa," Dr. Joep Lange, president of the International AIDS Society, said to reporters, "it should not be impossible to do the same with drugs" (quoted in Altman 2002, 5). Coke subsequently committed to providing anti-retroviral treatment, in partnership with PharmAccess, the Dutch NGO led by Dr. Lange, not only to its own immediate staff, but also to its independent bottlers throughout Africa (Lindsay 2003).

The motivations of other firms differ. The transnational mining company, Anglo American (2003), offers the most comprehensive workplace coverage in southern Africa and has begun to partner in community-based treatment programs. The fact that some 25 percent of its labor force—heavily male, migrant, and living in dormitories separated from their families—is HIV positive makes its active involvement an economic necessity and also poses a moral dilemma for the company. Merck, the giant pharmaceutical company, faced a public relations debacle over its AIDS drugs pricing and intellectual property policies in poor countries, but also had a long-standing reputation for medical philanthropy to protect; they have partnered with the Gates Foundation and the government of Botswana to provide a comprehensive national HIV/AIDS program in that country (Distlerath 2002).

None of these immediate economic interests played a role in the decisions of Heineken, the Dutch brewery, or DaimlerChrysler, the automotive firm, both of which were also early movers in providing workplace treatment in Africa. Indeed, a net-present-value analysis commissioned by Heineken showed that costs at the margin would exceed direct monetary benefits. Yet the board proceeded to adopt the policy and to accept a broader public role, in light of the inability or unwillingness of governments to act, its own determination to remain in the African market, and on the belief that it was the right thing to do (Barrett and Ballou 2003).[39] Illustrating yet another rationale, Novartis, the Swiss pharmaceutical firm, became the first company to provide anti-retroviral treatment for its employees in China on the grounds that, as a global company, it made strategic sense to move toward greater uniformity in its global human resources policy.[40]

Numerous other companies, driven by varying motivations, have done the same, typically in partnership with CSOs, and often with UNAIDS as well as bilateral and multilateral donors. Similarly, one of the few success stories to emerge from the Johannesburg World Summit on Sustainable Development in 2002 was the number of private-public partnerships undertaken, in areas such as the provision of clean water and sanitation (United Nations Department of Public Information 2002).

The role of companies in third world conflict zones has drawn growing attention. At issue is not only how to reduce the (inadvertent or deliberate) contribution that firms might make to fueling internal conflicts, which are often related to factional competition over the control of natural resource extraction, but also their potential role in conflict prevention (Nelson 2000). The Chad-Cameroon Pipeline may be the most ambitious such partnership yet. It involves several oil companies including ExxonMobil, the World Bank, numerous NGOs, and the respective governments, and is intended to maximize the funds devoted directly to poverty reduction under international safeguards (World Bank 2004).[41]

In other areas, companies are targeted for their political leverage as much as their own inherent contribution to either a problem or its solution. The case of climate change in the United States offers a striking illustration. With federal policy effectively blocked at the moment, the number of shareholder resolutions related to climate change introduced at 2003 annual corporate meetings was double the number in the previous year, and lawsuits have been brought against companies for not assessing and reporting their climate change related risks (Ball 2003; Houlder 2003; Cortese 2002). The hope is, of course, that these firms will become advocates for a more active federal policy, and it is reinforced by the growing involvement of individual American states in this policy domain, which poses the threat of differential standards within the US market (Lee 2003).

Needless to say, some of these actions have generated pushback by firms, and some observers on the Left and Right alike challenge their very legitimacy. Nevertheless, the net result is indisputable: civil society organizations have managed to implant new elements of social responsibility into the global activities of the private sector.[42] That lesson has not been lost on other social actors.

The Global Compact

Recognizing the inherent limits of intergovernmental responses to the challenges of globalization, UN Secretary-General Kofi Annan initiated the UN Global Compact (GC). It engages firms directly in helping to implement ten principles originally intended for states, drawn from the Universal Declaration of Human Rights, the ILO's Fundamental Principles on Rights at Work, the Rio Principles on Environment and Development, and the recent UN anticorruption convention.[43] Beginning with fifty participating firms in July 2000, the Compact now is by far the world's largest voluntary initiative in corporate social responsibility, with more than two thousand firms, over half from developing countries.[44] Other participants include five UN agencies;[45] some two dozen major transnational NGOs; as well as international labor federations representing more than 150 million workers. Voluntary financial contributions from governments fund the effort. Organizationally, the GC is structured as a set of nested networks at global, sectoral, and national levels, in which the center, the Global Compact Office at UN headquarters, is by far the smallest part, serving as network hub and guardian of the brand (Ruggie 2002).[46]

According to an impact assessment conducted by McKinsey (2004), companies value the GC over other CSR initiatives for the universalism of the UN "brand" and the UN's convening power, as well as the personal involvement of the secretary-general. For two-thirds of the developing country companies it is the first such initiative in which they have ever participated, and many do so to enhance their ability to enter into supplier relationships with larger global firms. As of the spring of 2004, nearly half of all companies reported having changed their policies as a result of their participation in the GC, even though a comparable fraction had joined up only within the previous eighteen months and thus had only limited opportunities to do so.

The GC employs three engagement tools to achieve its aims. One is transparency and learning (Ruggie 2002; Kell and Levin 2003). Companies are required to communicate their progress in internalizing the ten principles through an annual submission to the GC Office as well as in their own annual reports or similar public venues. This not only creates a degree of transparency, but is also a means to share experiences and practices. At a "learning forum" held in Brazil in December 2003, for example, some thirty company case studies were presented, vetted by business schools, exploring dilemmas in implementing the GC principles in, among other areas, ensuring noncomplicity in human rights abuses. The UN promotes these good practices, thereby providing a standard of comparison for—and public pressure on—industry laggards.

By means of "policy dialogues" the Compact generates shared understandings: about, for instance, the responsible posture for companies operating in countries afflicted by conflict. The zones of conflict dialogue explored ways for companies to perform impact assessments and reduce the risks that their own behavior may fuel conflicts; achieve greater transparency in their financial transactions with the host government or rebel groups; and devise revenue-sharing regimes that will benefit local populations. The results of these dialogues inform not only companies, but also the UN's own conflict prevention and peacemaking activities, and they play a normative role in the broader public arena.[47]

Lastly, the GC facilitates "private/public partnership projects" in developing countries. Examples include company involvement in micro lending, HIV/AIDS awareness programs for employees in sub-Saharan Africa, piloting sustainable alternatives to child labor, promoting sustainable investment in least developed countries, as well as initiatives in eco-efficiency and other aspects of environmental management.

The Compact has also triggered complementary national, regional, and sectoral initiatives. National networks have been established in nearly forty countries, two-thirds in the developing world—including Britain, France, Germany, and Spain, as well as Brazil, China, Egypt, India, Mexico, and Thailand. Regionally, a Scandinavian network is active, and an African network was recently established. At the sectoral level, Norway's Statoil and the International Federation of Chemical, Energy, Mine and General Workers' Unions (ICEM) have negotiated an agreement within the GC framework whereby Statoil is extending the same labor rights and health and safety standards to all of its overseas operations that it applies in Norway—including Vietnam, Venezuela, Angola, and Azerbaijan (Europe Energy 2001). The same labor federation also negotiated the first ever such agreement with a mining company, Anglo Gold (ICEM 2002).

Other voluntary corporate social responsibility efforts, including Business for Social Responsibility, the Global Reporting Initiative, and the World Business Council on Sustainable Development, have entered into corporate alliance–like relationships with the Global Compact, whereby they develop and operate additional tools and protocols for the implementation of the ten principles. And several initiatives originally intended for entirely different purposes have associated themselves with the Compact. The most unusual is the multi-stakeholder Committee for Melbourne, which incorporated the GC principles into the strategic plan it developed for that Australian city, and is encouraging all firms doing business there to adopt them (Short 2004). Several other cities have also come on board.

The Global Compact is based on universal principles that were originally adopted by and for states. The interests and commitments of participating companies vary considerably, but by virtue of their participation they acknowledge that those universal principles, in some measure, encompass the sphere of transnational corporate activity, not only states. Moreover, the GC also engages civil society, labor, academic institutions, and even local authorities to help bridge the gap between normative aspiration and everyday reality. Those institutional developments, in and of themselves, mark a singular departure for the United Nations—and for the corporate world. But they also have made it easier for governments themselves to play a more active role.

GOVERNMENTS

Governments have acted no less strategically than companies or CSOs. For example, with the support of international business associations the Organization for Economic Cooperation and Development first negotiated voluntary guidelines for multinational enterprises as long ago as 1976—right in the midst of third world–led efforts to devise a binding global legal code. The guidelines remained largely moribund until revised in 2000—shortly after, and no doubt in response to, Seattle (OECD 2000). CSR has played a significant role in "third way" politics. The Clinton administration helped establish the Fair Labor Association, a multi-stakeholder initiative that sets and monitors standards for firms in the textiles and garments industry. And it negotiated an agreement with Cambodia to permit outside inspectors and foster unions in its apparel industry in return for encouraging large international retailers, such as the GAP, to source from Cambodian suppliers.[48] In the United Kingdom, the Blair government promoted the Ethical Trading Initiative, through which British supermarket and garment retailers commit to improving the social and environmental performance in their supply chains. Together, the United States and the United Kingdom issued human rights guidelines for the conduct of private security forces (US Department of State, Bureau of Democracy, Human Rights, and Labor 2001). President Bush, by executive order, brought the United States into compliance with the UN certification scheme prohibiting trade in so-called blood diamonds—which had started as an activist campaign against diamond giant DeBeers ("Bush Bans imports of 'Blood Diamonds'" 2003).

Some developing countries see CSR as a means to promote social development, while international donor agencies, bilateral as well as multilateral, view them as a tool for promoting economic reforms and institutional capacity building. Needless to say, this new dynamic interplay between public and private sectors also offers opportunities for governments to shift or shirk responsibilities.[49]

Responding to antiglobalization pressures, and more generally to governance challenges posed by globalization, several OECD countries—the UK, France, the Netherlands, Sweden, and Belgium among them—have begun to encourage or require companies to engage in social and environmental reporting. A new British draft company statute that will soon take effect may be the most far-reaching of these measures, both in stipulating heightened social expectations about the public role of private enterprise, and in the requirement that companies issue an annual directors' report of social and environmental information relevant to an understanding of the entire business (UK Department of Trade and Industry 2004).

In the domestic politics of climate change in the United States, a group of US state and municipal treasurers, as fiduciaries of public sector pension funds worth nearly $1 trillion, held an Institutional Investors Summit in November 2003. Its aim was to devise a strategy promoting the adoption of climate change policies by firms in their funds' portfolios. As if to demonstrate the blurring of roles between different social sectors, the event was organized by an NGO, co-convened by a Harvard University research center and held in the chamber of the UN Economic and Social Council (ECOSOC).[50]

At the UN, while the Global Compact remains Kofi Annan's flagship initiative in corporate social responsibility, an expert group under the UN Commission on Human Rights drafted and adopted the first-ever set of legal norms in the area of human rights aimed directly at transnational corporations and other business enterprises (Birchall 2003). A divided commission found itself unable either to endorse or reject the proposed norms, but requested the secretary-general to appoint a Special Representative for Business and Human Rights with a mandate to identify and clarify what if any human rights standards may pertain directly to business, and to elaborate on the respective roles of states and the corporate sector in protecting and promoting human rights—with ECOSOC approving that mandate in July 2005.[51]

Let me draw this discussion to a close. I have suggested that the domain of corporate social responsibility illustrates the possibilities of a new multilateralism, involving actors from various social sectors and different levels of government. Putting it purely schematically, nontraditional actors, especially civil society and parts of the corporate sector, experiment with new initiatives; traditional governance institutions, at domestic and international levels, can build on some of those experiences, and in some cases codify certain practices. By directly engaging with actors that are global in reach and capacity the traditional governance system itself is pulled in a more global direction.

At the same time, these developments must not be romanticized. In the entire universe of TNCs, let alone national firms, the uptake of CSR instruments, though increasing, remains relatively limited. And even CSR leaders often undermine or negate, through their lobbying efforts, the positive effects they create by means of their CSR programs. Moreover, new transnational corporate entrants, headquartered in such countries as China and Malaysia, are beginning to operate in often poorly regulated developing countries, and their CSR profiles have yet to be established. Finally, without the effective involvement of public authority it is difficult to bring even the most successful voluntary initiatives to scale, and coordination and free rider problems remain pervasive. Having said all that, CSR initiatives nevertheless have established new sites and new means for social action as well as new political dynamics that can contribute to the challenge of taking embedded liberalism global.

CONCLUSION

In observing what he describes as "millennial capitalism" radiating outward from the United States today, Walter Russell Mead (2004) somberly concludes that the era of embedded liberalism may have been an aberration, a mere interlude between the dominance of more unfettered and socially divisive forms of market organization that are in the ascendancy again. There certainly has been a shift toward neoliberalism, as described briefly earlier in this chapter. And devising new institutional forms for "embedding" global markets in shared social purposes is, as noted at the very outset, truly a historic challenge. Reflecting on how hard it was, and how long it took, for the capitalist countries to institute the original "grand compromise," one can readily conjure up frightful scenarios—and some may well materialize along the way.

But "millennial capitalism" is neither as uniform nor as unmitigated as Mead fears. The corporate world is not a single, unified block, opposed to progressive change. As in any other social domain, there are leaders as well as laggards, and leaders can become allies in meeting global governance challenges. Climate change politics is a case in point. Shell and BP—two major oil companies—lobbied for some type of greenhouse gas emissions limits after President Bush rejected the Kyoto Protocol, having established relatively "green" brands and planning heavy investments in alternative energy technologies. So, too, did Enron, hoping to become a major player in an expanding emissions trading market (Revkin and Banerjee 2001). Exxon, in contrast, remained opposed. Here we have the same (or in Enron's case, a closely related) industry sector; the same market structure; but different individual firm preferences and interests. Now that Kyoto is in force without US adherence, Jeffrey Immelt (2005), CEO of General Electric, an American company whose merger with another US firm was blocked by the European Union and who, therefore, understands well the consequences of operating in conflicting regulatory environments, has called for a consistent transatlantic policy on producing cleaner energy: "For us to remain competitive, we simply cannot navigate a regulatory maze that forces us to tweak and modulate every product and process to suit individual regulatory regimes at their whim." Moreover, he laments the fact that, as a result of policy failure by the United States, "the U.S. has watched Europe and others advance, strengthening their economies and security" (17).

In addition, this chapter has challenged widely held presumptions of inexorability that permeate discussions of globalization on all sides of the debate, and which discount the political possibilities of forging any new compromise, grand or otherwise, intended to better root global markets in broader values of community and social justice. In contrast, I have argued that the principles of embedded liberalism still capture core elements of public aspirations; that the recent doctrinal unilateralist turn by the United States is not structurally determined; and that the new domain of corporate social responsibility provides a laboratory and platform for achieving greater corporate accountability and engaging the corporate sector in other innovative means to build greater global public capacity. Assessing more fully whether or not these possibilities turn into significant probabilities, however, is well beyond the scope of the present discussion.

NOTES

From 1997–2001, the author was assistant secretary-general and chief adviser for strategic planning to United Nations Secretary-General Kofi Annan. Thereafter, he remained the secretary-general's Special Adviser on the Global Compact until his appointment, in July 2005, as Special Representative of the secretary-general for Business and Human Rights. This chapter is based on the author's keynote address at the workshop on "*Global Governance: Towards a New Grand Compromise?*" held at the Canadian Congress of the Social Sciences and Humanities, University of Toronto, May 29, 2002. He is deeply indebted to Steven Bernstein for his help in turning the address into this chapter, and to the Kennedy School Initiative on Corporate Social Responsibility for research support. The views expressed in this chapter are those of the author and do not implicate the United Nations or any other entity.

1. On the concept of embedded liberalism, see Ruggie (1982).

2. Karl Polanyi (1944) magisterially covers this ground and inspired my formulation of the embedded liberalism concept.

3. In a detailed statistical analysis, Salvatore Pitruzzello (2004) shows that postwar embedded liberalism is associated with both better long-term economic performance and greater social protection than nineteenth-century laissez-faire liberalism.

4. In parts, this chapter builds on Ruggie (2003b).

5. Geoffrey Garrett (2000b) tests for the "fixed formula" and doesn't find it. On the difference between constitutive and regulative principles, see Ruggie (1998a).

6. It is difficult to disentangle the impact of globalization and technological changes in accounting for low rates of wage increases or high unemployment in the OECD countries, but Dani Rodrik (1997) offers a plausible account of the former. Globalization makes the services of large numbers of workers more easily substitutable across national boundaries, Rodrik argues, as a result of which the bargaining power of immobile labor vis-à-vis mobile capital erodes. Thus, in the neoliberal countries

labor is obliged to accept greater instability in earnings and hours worked, if not lower wages altogether, to pay a larger share of benefits and improvements in working conditions, as well as more frequent job changes. In the more traditional social democracies and social market economies where employment is more secure, labor is obliged to accept higher rates of chronic unemployment and lack of job creation.

7. I would add Canada to this list, though it exhibits neither of the attributes specified by Garrett, thus suggesting that other factors, too, are at work. Notably, however, rates of private sector unionization in the United States have dropped into the single digits.

8. See, for example, Blyth (2002).

9. For a good sample of views, see Broad (2002).

10. See, for example, Rabkin (1998).

11. Inequality in household income distribution has remained relatively flat over time, due to the increase of multiple-worker households and/or individuals holding multiple jobs.

12. "Americans on Globalization," http://www.pipa.org/OnlineReports/Globalization/global_rep.html.

13. A recent cross-national survey of the United States, Britain, France, and Germany, conducted by the German Marshall Fund of the USA, broadly confirms this conclusion. The only significant deviation was in France, where a majority of respondents opposed globalization, though only 8 percent favored raising tariffs in response. See de Jonquières (2004).

14. For more elaborate discussions of the foundational role of multilateralism in America's postwar strategy of international transformation see Ruggie (1993, chapter 1; 1996). Also see Ikenberry (2003).

15. On the adaptive capacity of multilateral orders, see Ruggie (1992).

16. When, in July 2005, amid difficult nuclear negotiations with North Korea and Iran, the Bush administration proposed selling highly sensitive nuclear technology to India, one of only four countries not to subscribe to the Nuclear Nonproliferation Treaty, the *New York Times* (2005, A20) editorialized that the Bush administration "seems to have almost as much contempt for international treaties as it has for rogue states."

17. Preemptive warfare has a well-established international legal pedigree, but requires "imminence" of threat and "proportionality" of response. After the Iraq war, the administration shifted its rhetoric onto the normatively safer preemptive grounds—but it continued to have a difficult time establishing that the threat the United States faced from Iraq was imminent. On the difference between and respective implications of the two, see Heisbourg (2003); Arend (2003).

18. See, for example, Mead (2004).

19. See, for example The Pew Research Center for The People & The Press (2003); the most recent poll in the Arab world, commissioned by the Arab American Institute and the University of Maryland, is reported in Chung and Halperin (2004).

Also see Kull (2005): "A new poll of nearly 24,000 citizens from 23 countries, conducted by the international polling firm GlobeScan and the program on International Policy Attitudes at the University of Maryland, suggests that the tectonic plates of world opinion are shifting. People around the world are not only turning away from the United States; they are starting to embrace the leadership of other major powers" (36).

20. See Ruggie (1993).

21. As the *Toronto Star* put it shortly after her appointment as secretary of state: "It so happens that the phrase 'indispensable nation,' first minted by the new U.S. Secretary of State Madeleine Albright, is now used constantly by American officials and commentators to describe the overarching role of the United States in the contemporary world. [It] is triumphalist and irritating—which doesn't mean that it isn't apt. From Bosnia to Haiti, only the U.S. has the will and means to address major global problems." See Gwyn (1996).

22. The result of these features, Francois Heisbourg (2003) noted, has been a "hardening of the multilateralist impulse among U.S. allies" (81).

23. Josh Busby and Alexander Ochs (2004) test Kagan's thesis in the area of climate change. Their explanation is that "America's political system permits certain interests—namely climate skeptics and business interests—to exercise veto power over external environmental commitments. European decision makers, by contrast, face environmental movements more capable of exercising influence over electoral politics" (35).

24. As Michael Lind (2004) has said, "Ironically, it was a neoconservative-led war that refuted neoconservative claims about US power" (11).

25. For a slightly more optimistic view, see Louis Pauly's chapter in this volume.

26. For the purposes of this chapter I use the acronym CSOs to encompass transnational social movements, coalitions, and activist campaigns as well as formal nongovernmental organizations.

27. Both authors stress that factors other than activist pressure also contributed to the MAI's demise.

28. On human rights, see Risse (2000); on the environment, see Esty and Ivanova (2002); and on anticorruption, see Galtung (2000).

29. The number of multinationals and their subsidiaries is reported in United Nations Conference on Trade and Development (2001). It is impossible to calculate the actual number of suppliers; Nike, for example, has approximately 1,200 (personal communication from Nike executive).

30. On the latter, see Kobrin (2002).

31. For a careful study in the environmental area, see Garcia-Johnson (2000).

32. See, respectively, Braithwaite and Drahos (2000); Drake (2001).

33. In this respect, CSOs may be playing a role at the global level that is somewhat analogous to organized labor at the national level in the twentieth century, using such market power as they could muster and seeking to turn it into instruments of political change. The notion of countervailing power in this context is due to Galbraith (1956).

34. The most comprehensive survey of company codes is OECD, 2001. On the GRI, consult www.globalreporting.org, and for certification institutions, see Gereffi, Garcia-Johnson, and Sasser (2001); Leipziger (2001).

35. Public sector pension funds, such as CALPERS—the California Public Employees Retirement System—have long been active in promoting such a posture; mainstream institutions are only slowly becoming converts. At the June 2004 Global Compact Leaders Summit, twenty major investment firms, led by Goldman Sachs, presented a report entitled "Who Cares Wins: Connecting Financial Markets to a Changing World," endorsing the idea that social and environmental performance should become a core element in assessing investment risks, and ten stock exchanges, led by Bovespa in Brazil, agreed to explore cooperation with, while another two endorsed, the Global Compact.

36. The first study looked at the top 250 firms, the second at the top 100.

37. Calculations performed in March 2004 by a team from Booz Allen Hamilton as part of a collaborative research project on corporate social responsibility conducted with the Center for Business and Government, Harvard University. Further details are available from the author.

38. A press release entitled "AIDS Activists Protest Coke's Deadly Neglect of Workers with AIDS in Developing Countries," was widely distributed along with a twenty-five-foot inflatable Coke bottle bearing the slogan "Coke's Neglect = Death for Workers in Africa." See Act Up New York (2002).

39. Other brief cases, including DaimlerChrysler, are available online. See World Economic Forum (2003).

40. This policy was announced at a Workshop on HIV/AIDS as a Business Challenge, convened in Beijing by the Center for Business and Government, Harvard University, together with the World Economic Forum and UNAIDS. See Center for Business and Government, Kennedy School of Government, Harvard University (2003). The Novartis workforce in China, admittedly, is relatively small.

41. Revenues from royalties and dividends go into an escrow account in London. After loan service payments, 10 percent is earmarked for a "future generations fund," 5 percent for the producing region, and the remainder is dedicated to priority spending in social sectors, vetted by an oversight group. Also see White (2003).

42. Unfortunately, no systematic impact assessment exists of these diverse developments, so no definitive conclusions can be drawn at this point. For a relatively comprehensive though still impressionistic study, see Vogel (2005).

43. The ten principles are: support and respect for the protection of internationally proclaimed human rights; noncomplicity in human rights abuses; freedom of association and the effective recognition of the right to collective bargaining; the elimination of all forms of forced and compulsory labor; the effective abolition of child labor; the elimination of discrimination in respect of employment and occupation; a precautionary approach to environmental challenges; greater environmental responsibility; encouragement of the development and diffusion of environmentally friendly technologies; and working against all forms of corruption, including extortion and bribery. See www.unglobalcompact.org/Portal/Default.asp for complete texts.

44. The first book-length study of the GC is McIntosh, Waddock, and Kell (2004).

45. The three "guardians of the principles": High Commissioner for Human Rights, ILO, and UNEP; and three operational agencies: UN Development Program, UN Industrial Development Organization, and the UN Office for Crime Prevention. Each provides dedicated staff for the GC agenda, and a small Global Compact Office, in the executive office of the secretary-general, manages the brand and the networks.

46. In this regard, the GC illustrates Tony Porter's point in this volume (chapter 6) that agile global networks, more readily than other institutional forms, can more easily span existing institutions and jurisdictions, and shift or be realigned as circumstances change.

47. The backward linkages to the UN's own policies and activities are quite extensive, and now include weighing the ten principles in such matters as procurement and pension fund management.

48. The United States continues to help underwrite the program, and the ILO arranges for factory monitoring. Thus far, the deal seems to have survived the end of the Multifibre Agreement, with the apparel industry accounting for nearly 90 percent of Cambodia's export earnings (Becker 2005).

49. For example, one plausible rationalist account of South Africa's Mbeki government's slow and erratic approach to providing HIV/AIDS treatment is that it is deliberately trying to off-load as much of the burden as possible onto the private sector—aided by activist pressure on companies.

50. The NGO in question is the Coalition for Environmentally Responsible Economies (Ceres), which was also responsible for the creation of the Global Reporting Initiative. Harvard's Center for Business and Government was a co-convener. The Better World Fund, an offshoot of the Ted Turner's United Nations Foundation, financed the event.

51 See UN Commission on Human Rights (2005). Secretary-General Annan appointed me to this post, which has an initial mandate of two years.

PART II

Power and Authority in Global Governance

THREE

Would Citizens Support a New Grand Compromise?

ROBERT WOLFE AND MATTHEW MENDELSOHN

THE "COMPROMISE OF EMBEDDED LIBERALISM" (Ruggie 1982) is one of the most powerful metaphors in international relations, offering a compelling story about the political foundations of international organization in the second half of the twentieth century.[1] The compromise between free trade abroad and the welfare state at home was one made by states in their own interests, but it was also made by citizens in industrial democracies prepared to accept the constraints of multilateralism in return for a more prosperous and peaceful world. Many scholars worry that the existing compromise as a constitutive rule for global governance is unsustainable in this era of globalization. John Ruggie (this volume) worries, in contrast, that it may not be possible to "take embedded liberalism global" in order to integrate a wider range of countries, institutions, and social actors. In this chapter, we draw on public opinion analysis to make inferences about whether the compromises embedded liberalism requires are still legitimate, and therefore if a new grand compromise for global governance is possible.

The compromise of embedded liberalism was not a grand decision sealed by a treaty, but an ongoing process first evident in the actions of state officials during the 1940s. This postwar international order may have been negotiated at the outset, but its continuing reproduction depends on the social interaction shaped by the compromise itself, which influences the attitudes of citizens toward global governance that are a necessary, if not sufficient, condition for the maintenance of strong international institutions. Democratic governments cannot long sustain commitments that citizens think inappropriate.

Embedded liberalism is not a fixed bargain about levels of social spending or tariff bindings, but a dynamic commitment to allowing countries to be different within a multilateral framework. It is a compromise between the needs for universality on which a strong order must rest, and the needs for particularity that are inevitable in a plural world order. John Ruggie called this constitutive rule part of the generative grammar of the system.[2] If it continues, it should shape how citizens understand their relations with the world, and that understanding should be observable in the responses citizens give in answer to survey questions about free trade, globalization, and the work of international institutions. As described more fully below, we conducted an opinion survey designed to probe how Canadians understand the political compromise between the efficiency of open markets and the security of the welfare state.

Canadian public opinion serves as an excellent plausibility probe into contemporary societal support for embedded liberalism across advanced industrialized countries. As we elaborate below, existing comparative survey data suggest that the same variables that explain individuals' support for trade operate across advanced industrialized countries. Whereas absolute levels of support for trade, globalization, or international institutions differ among countries, their relative support among individuals in each country is remarkably similar. Canadians are not Americans or Europeans, but mass opinion is likely to be structured in similar ways. For example, much of the commentary about the hostility of ordinary Europeans to deeper integration in the summer of 2005 assumed that citizens were concerned about the erosion of the European social model. Our results suggest that many Canadians also worry that the welfare state is threatened by globalization, but that concern is not as tied to trade as one might suspect. It is driven more by values than by an individual's economic interests. We believe, therefore, that our research design and methodology can be used by other researchers in further tests of our causal inferences and conclusions.

The usual narratives about the public's response to globalization are problematic because they focus on individuals' self-interest (Scheve and Slaughter 2001; Gabel 1998). But then, why do privileged people in rich countries seem to protest against the process that has made them wealthy? The dozens of articles that have speculated on the origins and political significance of the antiglobalization protests of the past few years mostly ignore formal research on public opinion. Many observers of the wave of street demonstrations take public protest as an indicator that citizens are hostile to trade, to trade agreements, to multilateral institutions, and to globalization generally, without much evidence. Even the introduction to this volume repeats the standard claim that the antiglobalization protests signal a general crisis of legitimacy for international organizations. Our results show that taking protest as an indicator of public opposition may be misleading because, in many countries, citizens are not hostile to trade or trade agreements or international institutions, although they may be more uncertain about globalization.

The scholarly conceptualization of embedded liberalism depends on the notion of separable communities able to make their own decisions on the distribution of the costs and benefits of openness. Does globalization inherently undermine embedded liberalism? Although most citizens do not think in theoretical abstractions, they may well worry about the concrete manifestations of the process that Ruggie (1993b) has described as the "unbundling of sovereignty." If nothing else, sovereignty implies a community's ability to decide who is in or out, but global interdependence means at minimum that citizens of the advanced economies are not living in isolation. Actions taken elsewhere have implications at home. When a good or a service moves in global commerce, people in different places are brought into contact in new ways. International trade allows people to become more specialized, and the range of that specialization extends in time and space. The creation of global supply chains, part of a global division of labor and increasing market integration, also fragments regulation because the discrete parts of the production process are subject to different authorities. Importing countries, therefore, import not merely goods but the policies under which those goods were produced, policies (for example on workplace safety) that might differ from their own. When environmental regulation or other forms of social regulation in one state intrude on the domain of administrative agencies in another state, the embedded liberalism bargain is under stress (Howse and Nicolaidis 2003, 79). The institutions that govern the trading system now depend on compromise between a great many actors, including domestic regulators, subnational governments, private standards bodies, and economic actors. In such a diffuse and plural system, legitimacy is vital, since no coercive force can create new agreements or enforce existing ones (Wolfe 2005).

Emerging debates around globalization are about more than liberalization, both procedurally and substantively, as trade policy shifts its focus from measures at the border (e.g., tariffs and quotas that affect prices directly) to domestic governance issues such as social regulations (e.g., food safety or environmental standards). These debates engage individuals as citizens, not only as workers, producers, and consumers, and therefore understanding the views of citizens as expressed in mass opinion is important.

The original compromise of embedded liberalism rested on what Ruggie (1982) called, after Weber, "legitimate social purpose." In this argument, if social purposes remain constant, then material change associated with globalization would not be expected to undermine the existing international order. Citizens in industrial democracies accepted the constraints of multilateralism in the 1940s in return for a more prosperous and peaceful world. Are citizens still prepared to make this compromise? In the next section we explain why we think that the continuing legitimacy of the compromise can be assessed using opinion surveys. In subsequent sections we show how Canadians reproduce the underlying values of embedded liberalism when asked questions about trade and globalization, and then we show the strength of their commitment to multilateralism. Canadians have been quite supportive of trade liberalization, and continue to be comfortable with an active role for international institutions, as long as the welfare objectives of the administrative state are maintained, and as long as globalization is not perceived to threaten valued objectives. In the penultimate section we discuss the importance to citizens of what scholars call "input legitimacy." We conclude that citizens would support efforts to craft a new grand compromise.

EMBEDDED LIBERALISM AND PUBLIC OPINION IN CANADA

All normative orders, including global order, emerge in human interaction. The forms of exchange with people far away that we call globalization are one set of such interactions. We assume that such interaction is the basis of global governance and that, therefore, the legitimacy of global governance will ultimately rest on the decisions of individuals. Although we make no claim that individual attitudes are transformed directly into policy at home or abroad, public opinion is relevant for international relations and influences the climate in which policy decisions are made.[3]

We would not dispute an argument that most Canadians would have few well-developed opinions about issues of globalization and international institutions. The issues are complex, they tend to be the purview of experts, they are not the subject of frequent discussion or news stories (except stories about protests), and elections and parties have not mobilized voters around these issues. Responses to survey questions may be random, with contradictory responses given to somewhat similar questions. Many respondents to our survey would not have a great deal of detailed knowledge about international issues, and were likely constructing responses to our questions, rather than recalling and revealing true, preexisting preferences.[4] Nevertheless, people have stable and internally coherent ways of thinking about collective life and their beliefs about foreign policy that do not float freely, with no connection to their wider beliefs. Mass opinion is formed by latent opinion—that is, by widely shared preferences and values—not by the transient response to ephemeral events in the media. The public has policy goals, not preferred instruments. We think that understanding the way citizens use their values and ideologies to construct their response to the greater linkages with the world implied by globalization will be essential to understanding the political basis of global governance. Understanding mass opinion through surveys, therefore, matters for analysts interested in the boundaries of democratic legitimacy and for policy makers who want to understand what we have elsewhere called the "permissive consensus" that Canadian governments enjoy on trade policy (Mendelsohn, Wolfe, and Parkin 2002). To be clear, our argument here is not that the original embedded liberalism compromise rested on public consent, but rather that latent public support enables and constrains the boundaries of acceptable public policy. As demands increase for greater transparency and accountability in global politics, a trend our Canadian survey results also generally support, we would expect public support to be increasingly important for foreign policies as well.

Bear in mind that the compromise of embedded liberalism is an analytic construct. We cannot ask citizens if they still support something of which they have never heard, so we have to ask questions about the components of the compromise that will allow us to draw inferences about its legitimacy. The explicit compromise of embedded liberalism is between liberal trade and the welfare state. The implicit compromise is multilateralism, which requires an acceptance that some decisions will not be made exclusively in the local community. Now as in the 1940s, it also requires that taxes raised from citizens in one country will be expended on behalf of citizens far away in pursuit of global justice: taking embedded liberalism global (for example in increased financial flows to developing countries) requires social solidarity with people far away. We want to know if these two compromises remain legitimate. Our strategy was to ask three sets of questions. First, we contrasted questions about trade and globalization and then analyzed the reasons for the differing responses to see if citizens would reproduce the values associated with embedded liberalism in their answers. Since they do, the next element in our strategy was to probe whether the implicit compromises between policy harmonization abroad and the administrative state at home are legitimate. We show that they are. Finally, we want to probe whether the processes of global governance have sufficient input legitimacy to be sustainable. We executed our strategy in a survey of public opinion in Canada.

The fact that our data come from one country alone can be taken as a caveat, but not a serious shortcoming, given the absence of comparable cross-national surveys. Although national political culture does have an impact on whether a country is supportive of integration, as do political institutions that can either facilitate or thwart integration, the *structure* of opinion does not seem to differ much from one country to another. By this we mean that in advanced industrial democracies, the variables that make individuals more or less likely to support trade are the same from one country to another. For example, Eichenberg and Dalton (1993) find that the basic factors at work affecting changing levels of support for the EU over time are fairly consistent from one country to another: "Although citizens of the United Kingdom, Denmark, and the Netherlands support the EC at far different levels because of differing historical and foreign policy traditions . . . this variation is caused by a similar economic and political dynamic" (530). Even if one accepts that data from a single country can be used for a plausibility probe into contemporary societal support for a continuing global compromise rooted in embedded liberalism, it might still be argued that Canada is an inappropriate test case. We would respond with two observations. First, we see no theoretical reason to think that the structure of Canadian opinion would differ from, for example, that in western Europe. Second, we have found no empirical evidence that suggests any difference. The Program on International Policy Attitudes (PIPA) at the University of Maryland regularly surveys new polls on American attitudes to the world. The picture of the structure of American opinion that emerges from their recent surveys is similar to the one we present about Canadians: citizens support trade, but are less supportive of globalization, and show ambiguous attitudes to international organizations.[5]

We offer one further anecdotal piece of empirical evidence on why Canada is suitable for the probe of mass opinion. The July 2005 G8 Summit at Gleneagles featured new commitments for Africa. In anticipation, some civil society organizations sponsored the series of "Live 8" concerts in all G8 countries. These concerts were attended by hundreds of thousands of people, and watched by millions more on television. The least one can say about the political implications of these concerts is that they are another manifestation of the declining role of traditional political parties in mobilizing young people in the advanced democracies, yet the point was lobbying the leaders of the richest states in the hope that they could solve Africa's problems. We draw two admittedly weak inferences from this anecdote. First, Canadians participated in Live 8 in a way that seems more or less the same as Americans and Europeans, which suggests some similarity in the structure of attitudes. Second, the implicit views of Live 8 participants are consistent with the demands of a new grand compromise.

Our survey instrument was administered by telephone to a random, probabilistic sample of 1,298 Canadians between February 21 and March 13, 2001. The survey was conducted by le Centre de recherche en opinion publique (CROP), a major commercial polling firm. The Centre for Research and Information on Canada, a research think tank, commissioned the survey; we collaborated on the questionnaire design. Up to twelve callbacks were conducted and the response rate was 62 percent. Data were then weighted by region, gender, and age. We subsequently wrote a second wave of the survey using a panel design. The successful re-interview rate was 57 percent, for a sample of 744 for questions in the second wave. It was conducted between June 20 and July 10, 2001.[6]

Deciding which questions to ask is not easy.[7] The issue is, do Canadians still support international openness? The problem is that "trade" is a constructed category, as is "globalization." Its ontological status is ambiguous and its epistemological status is opaque. Traded services, for example, are famously things that you can buy and sell but cannot drop on your foot, which means they exist only as expert abstractions and can be seen only in measurements of transaction flows. To ask about the rules currently governing international trade would be even more ambiguous. We chose, therefore, to ask a question about support for "new trade agreements" generally. Because Canadians have had a highly publicized free trade agreement with the United States since 1989, this question should measure general attitudes toward the expansion of trade and trade liberalization. The concept of "globalization" is more difficult still, because the word can mean different things to activists, business people, and governments (of North and South). Rosamond (2003) observes that so much has been written in so many disciplines that, paradoxically, no single definition of "globalization" is possible. Globalization has become an empty signifier, yet the discourse of globalization is ubiquitous. The term often means either process or condition; it can mean both structure and agency; and, it is used both to denote an exclusively economic condition as well as a social or cultural transformation. We evoke these diverse definitions in our survey questions, but by avoiding undue detail and technical definitions we are then able, through regression analysis, to identify how citizens understand and make sense of emerging debates on "globalization." Table 3.1 reports the results for our core questions (Q1–Q2).

Canadian mass opinion became broadly supportive of free trade agreements during the 1990s (Mendelsohn and Wolfe 2001), and it is therefore

TABLE 3.1
Contrasting Support for Trade Agreements and Globalization

Q1. This next section of the survey is about international trade agreements. By international trade agreements I mean things like the Canada-US free trade agreement, the North American free trade agreement (or NAFTA), and the other international trade agreements that cover Canada and the over 140 other members of the World Trade Organization—the WTO. Do you strongly support, support, oppose, or strongly oppose Canada negotiating new trade agreements with other countries, or do you have no opinion on this question?

Q2. Many people say we are presently experiencing a process of globalization, which means that the economies of all of the countries of the world are becoming more and more linked. Do you strongly support, somewhat support, somewhat oppose, or strongly oppose Canada encouraging more rapid globalization, or do you have no opinion on this?

	Support	*Uncertain*	*Oppose*
New Trade Agreements	65%	23%	11%
Globalization	45%	38%	17%

not surprising that about two-thirds of respondents said they supported the negotiation of new trade agreements, while only about one in ten said they were opposed. Yet fewer than half supported "globalization," and more than one-third were uncertain. For Canadians, support for negotiating new trade agreements is widespread, however the question is asked (see, for example, the tracking question on "negotiating free trade" in EKOS 2003), while support for globalization remains more muted. While this gap is interesting, and suggests that citizens do not see "globalization" as merely the same as trade liberalization, more interesting still is understanding what factors explain why some respondents answer the trade and the globalization questions differently.

When responding to questions about trade or globalization, citizens may be evaluating liberalized trade in general, the actual content of particular agreements, the emerging institutions of global governance, or such attributes of globalization as the Internet, the spread of disease, and increased travel. Some analysts take answers to questions on trade, tariffs, or integration as transparent indicators of citizens' real preferences. We do not use this implicit referendum approach. Rather, consistent with the methodological conventions of research on mass opinion, we assume that questions can mean different things to respondents, and different things than the researcher intended. Comparisons between questions, and a careful examination of the differences in wording and the attendant results, are more important than examining the frequencies with an eye toward identifying "how many Canadians believe x or y." Our primary goal was not to use language that policy experts would agree is "right," but to use language that respondents would understand, that mirrored more complex issues, and from which we could infer values.

Barring follow-up qualitative interviewing with respondents, the only way for a researcher to understand what the question meant to a respondent is to see how they answered other questions, and to see which ones are correlated with answers to the initial question. Accordingly, we conducted a regression analysis on the first wave using a set of theoretically motivated independent variables. The results are reported in detail elsewhere (Wolfe and Mendelsohn 2005), but we do want to highlight five conclusions from that analysis. First, values play an important role in influencing opinion on both globalization and trade, particularly values related to attitudes toward the United States, internationalism, the welfare state, and feelings about multinational corporations. Second, when skills variables are included in our models, the significance of values remains robust, demonstrating that values are not merely surrogates for interests, and they have an independent impact on opinion on globalization across individuals with different skill levels and interests. Third, education and income play an important role with regard to opinion on trade agreements, but do not on globalization, highlighting that attitudes toward globalization are influenced by factors other than one's ability to compete in a more open market, whereas opinion on trade liberalization is more tightly tied to individuals' interests. Fourth, retrospective evaluations of the impact of previous trade agreements are more important influences on individuals' opinions on trade than on globalization, again highlighting that globalization is understood by citizens to be about far more than trade liberalization. Finally, we found that people's assessments of whether human rights or trade was more important had an impact on opinion regarding trade, but respondents who highly value human rights are divided on the question of globalization, in part because they disagree about whether globalization helps or harms human rights. As well, those who support increased immigration and foreign aid are more likely to support globalization. Both findings might be surprising in the context of the large public protests, during which global social justice often appears to be invoked as an important argument against globalization.

Some readers might worry that our data have gone stale, especially since both waves of our survey were conducted before the attacks of September 11, 2001. We are confident, however, that new data would not show a significantly different pattern. First, we probed not ephemeral opinion on daily events, but the structure of underlying attitudes and their relations to each other. Such structures do not change quickly. Second, in an annual tracking question in a poll commissioned by the federal government, Canadian support for "negotiating new free trade agreements" was higher in May 2003 than it had been in May 2001 (EKOS 2003). Third, while it is hard to find questions comparable to our globalization question, a European study is suggestive. The European Commission asked this question in October 2003: "Globalisation is the general opening-up of all economies, which leads to the creation of a truly world-wide market. Are you personally totally in favor, rather in favor, rather opposed or totally opposed to the development of globalization?" The commission reports that 63 percent of respondents were in favor, and 29 percent opposed, with 8 percent not having a view (European Commission 2003, Q2, 15). It is striking that the support is so much higher than on our question, and the uncertainty so much lower. We have no tracking data, so we have no way of knowing if European opinion has shifted since September 11, 2001, but we think it unlikely.[8]

In sum, Canadians are more worried about globalization than trade because they perceive globalization to be more of a threat to a variety of values commonly associated with embedded liberalism, not because of concerns about individuals' inability to compete in a more open market. But even if embedded liberalism is reflected in citizens' values, are the necessary compromises still legitimate?

IS GLOBAL GOVERNANCE LEGITIMATE?

Many scholars have argued that there is an "internationalist" tradition in Canadian foreign policy (Martin and Fortmann 2001), defined as a willingness to engage, in cooperation with other nations, in acts of "good international citizenship" with the aim of "creating, maintaining, and managing a community at a global level" (Nossal 1998–99, 98). We think such attitudes are consistent with the compromises required by embedded liberalism. The data we collected during the first wave of our survey support these arguments, and show that few Canadians believe that Canada should be less active in the world. In the second wave of the survey, we devoted questions to the issue of embedded liberalism and international institutions more directly. Using experimental variations in the wording of the questions, we are better able to understand Canadian attitudes toward domestic autonomy and international collaboration, that is, full policy coordination, even harmonization, abroad but the administrative state at home.

Many discussions of reform of global governance assume that something about the international "architecture" needs fixing. We probed Canadian views by asking whether international institutions should be more empowered, and whether they should act in a more coordinated fashion. We did this in the form whereby respondents were forced to choose between one of two presumably mutually exclusive and rhetorically meaningful options. We found little resistance to more coordination between international institutions, and only about one Canadian in three were worried about the democratic consequences of this kind of coordination. Canadians were somewhat more resistant to coordination when the treatment contained the expression "international institutions like the World Bank and the International Monetary Fund" than when the question referred to "the United Nations and the World Trade Organization." This diffidence to some extent reflects the finding from the first wave of our survey, when we found Canadians were more likely to cede sovereignty to a UN institution than the World Trade Organization (WTO), but in neither question were the differences very large. Nonetheless, they do indicate that Canadians have more positive feelings toward the UN than other international institutions, and are more comfortable with the universalist values with which it is associated. The third treatment presents interesting results. Seventy percent of Canadians say that there are some issues that should never be turned over to an international institution, which is quite high. Nonetheless, 27 percent of Canadians are prepared to agree that if an international institution can do something more effectively, then it should be allowed to do it.

We then wanted to probe whether this support for international institutions has limits. We asked respondents whether the Canadian government or international actors should be making decisions in seven key areas. The seven issue areas remained consistent and were put to all respondents, but the premise of the question was altered experimentally. One-third of our sample were asked: "Do you think that we need *more international cooperation* on each of the following issues?"; one-third were asked: "For each of the following areas of policy, please tell me whether it should be decided by the Canadian government or whether it should be *decided jointly by governments working together at international meetings?*"; and one-third were presented with: "For each of the following areas of policy, please tell me whether it should be decided by the Canadian government or whether it should be *decided by international institutions?*" We could describe these formulations as moving from internationalist, to multilateralist, to globalist. We expected little opposition to "more cooperation" on most issues, but a great deal of opposition to "international institutions making decisions." The results are reported in Table 3.2.

The overwhelming majority of Canadians are willing to say there should be more international cooperation on every issue, so we do not spend much time on these data, other than to note the continued strong internationalism of Canadians (Munton and Keating 2001). On the question of governments deciding things together at international meetings, we find relatively high

TABLE 3.2
Domestic Autonomy and International Collaboration

Questions: "Do you think that we need *more international cooperation* on each of the following issues?"; "For each of the following areas of policy, please tell me whether it should be decided by the Canadian government or whether it should be *decided jointly by governments working together at international meetings?*"; "For each of the following areas of policy, please tell me whether it should be decided by the Canadian government or whether it should be *decided by international institutions?*"

	More international cooperation	*Governments at international meetings*	*International institutions*
Preventing climate change	82	79	68
Curtailing the spread of disease	96	86	59
Protecting democracy and human rights	92	74	56
Regulating the flow of capital, that is, the movement of money across borders	68	56	35
Establishing labor and workplace standards	81	50	27
Ensuring that we have clean water to drink	86	53	22
Establishing standards for social programs	72	42	17

levels of support for these kinds of activities. As long as the democratically elected Canadian government is participating in decisions, Canadians tend not to be too worried about national sovereignty, but there are important differences in Canadians' attitudes toward the various issue areas. We distinguish what could be understood as "international managerial issues" (preventing climate change and curtailing the spread of disease), where Canadians support delegation of these decisions to international meetings, from "domestic political issues" (establishing standards for social programs and standards for the workplace), where there is more support for the retention of national sovereignty. We also highlight the very strong support for collaborative international activity on the issue of promoting human rights, which we interpret to mean that Canadians believe their democratic values should be universally shared. (We do not spend much time on the issue of "regulating the flow of capital" because we suspect that it is the one issue on which there has been the largest movement since September 11, 2001. It was likely the issue that was the most arcane and unfamiliar to citizens prior to September 11, but the media attention since has probably encouraged Canadians to focus on the issue and reconsider their views.)[9]

The results for the third treatment—that is, whether international institutions should actually be making decisions—are especially interesting. On the "international managerial issues," 68 percent and 59 percent of Canadians say that these matters should be decided by international institutions. Similarly, on the "universalist" issue of human rights, 56 percent of Canadians say that the issue should be decided by international institutions. These responses indicate high levels of acceptance for an active role for international institutions, albeit on certain kinds of issues—those that are perceived to be more managerial or "universalist" and less "political": most Canadians believe that democratic principles should be international.

But here is the paradox of "don't touch my welfare state internationalism": Canadians are extremely reluctant to cede sovereignty to international institutions on three issues: standards for social programs, standards for the workplace, and ensuring clean drinking water. The latter is viewed as clearly "local," and the rationale for an international institution being accountable for water safety in Canada is something that Canadians would find far-fetched. The first two, however, can be understood as the two key components of the compromise of embedded liberalism, whereby social security in the form of the welfare state and decent working conditions, have been judged to be the key responsibilities of national governments, and so long as these two pillars were protected, states were free to pursue trade liberalization internationally. On issues of this type, Canadians have little interest in ceding authority to international institutions, and we cannot imagine circumstances under which that would change in the short or medium term.[10]

Given the importance attached to their own autonomy, we were interested in the value Canadians would attach to the autonomy of citizens elsewhere. We asked Canadians about how to engage with countries that do not respect the human rights of their citizens, and how to deal with Canadian companies who may operate abroad in ways that violate Canadian values. We found very strong support for what could be termed "constructive engagement"—only one Canadian in ten believes they should simply keep out of the internal affairs of other countries, but one in four believes Canada should impose trade embargos. Most (61 percent) believe that Canada should maintain economic links and encourage improvements in the country's human rights record. These results confirm our findings from the first wave, when 25 percent of respondents preferred the position: "The government should make the expansion of trade with other countries [like China] a top priority, even if that means taking a softer line on the issue of human rights," while 66 percent opted for: "The government should take a hard line against countries [like China] that violate human rights, even if that means missing out on some opportunities to expand Canadian trade." As we have argued elsewhere (Mendelsohn and Wolfe 2001), most Canadians support engaging with countries that violate the human rights of their people with an eye toward improving that country's behavior.

A final note on the data from the second wave of our survey—it would be appropriate to ask whether we are glossing over significant differences of opinion by writing about "Canadians." Due to the combination of a small number of respondents and the unconstrained and uncrystallized quality of opinions, detailed sociodemographic or other bivariate or multivariate analysis would ask more of the data from the *second* wave than they could actually provide. We did examine all of the second wave questions broken down by educational attainment of the respondent, however, to see whether those with a university degree, who are likely to have the most interest in and influence on the debate and are therefore likely to lead opinion, differed in their views from the rest of the population. It should first be noted that we found few differences between those with a university degree and those without: of the fifty discrete items in the survey, only twelve demonstrated statistically significant differences. We did find three general differences between respondents with more and less education: those with more education are more concerned about the preservation of national sovereignty to set social, labor, and environmental policy; those with more education are more internationalist and interventionist abroad; and, those with more education are less worried about protecting domestic jobs through government action in the face of globalization. From our initial wave, we had also asked our respondents whether they felt attached to Canada, their province, their local community, or the global community. There are no statistically significant educational differences on any of the attachment questions, except that the more educated are significantly more attached to "the international community"—they are more likely to be "citizens of the world." Yet one still needs to keep in mind that the numbers who say they are citizens of the world remains very low: while more than 50 percent in all educational groups say they are "very attached" to country, province, or city/local, only 18 percent say they are very attached to the global community.

THE PROCESSES OF GLOBAL GOVERNANCE

We have argued so far that global governance benefits from a permissive consensus: since most people think that trade deals have worked reasonably well, they are content to leave the details to the government. This positive assessment is retrospective. Citizens may not understand or like trade agreements as such, but the agreements are legitimate because they seem to work. Might this support be shallow? Scharpf (2000) offers an abstract view of democratic legitimation based on what he calls inputs and/or outputs. Inputs are legitimation by the process of decision; outputs are legitimation by showing that policy serves a community's common interests. International cooperation, as it is practiced, limits the possibility for procedural (input) legitimation because domestic processes cannot be determinative of the outcome of multilateral negotiations, making substantive (output) legitimation all the more important. The permissive consensus is clearly a form of output legitimacy. Some opponents of globalization complain, however, about the lack of input legitimation. Part of the public ambivalence about globalization, therefore, may well be due to worries about consequential decisions taken far away by institutions not subject to the domestic political process. In short, are decision processes legitimate?

Debates about how international institutions function are now central to the politics of the WTO, to take one example, in two ways. The first is called external transparency, meaning how well citizens in general and civil society institutions can see into the work of the institution, and the second is called internal transparency, meaning the ability of smaller and developing country members to participate in the institution. The debates are about actor identity and capacity: who is an effective and legitimate participant? Efforts to address one of these two forms of transparency sometimes undermine the other. We used the second wave of our survey to probe Canadian attitudes to both issues.

First, on *external transparency*, we asked Canadians how much role the public should have in decision making in international institutions. When we presented respondents with three different levels of democratization, a strong majority opted for the middle position, very closely mirroring the results from a very similar question asked in the first wave of our survey regarding how much public involvement there should be on trade negotiations. Canadians do not want to leave things to government (or international institutions) alone; about one-third would like the public to be actively involved, but about three in five opt for more transparency and publicity. So long as there is accountability and transparency, Canadians neither believe that one needs to introduce processes for deep forms of public participation, nor believe that international institutions should function according to rules of managerial and corporate governance, whereby the public is shut out. Canadian expectations, therefore, are reasonable: most do not expect to be actively involved in decision making at an international level, but they do expect the kind of transparency that allows them to hold their government accountable.

We also asked about the accountability of international institutions. A slim majority of Canadians reject the argument advanced by many government officials that international institutions are already sufficiently democratic because democratically elected governments send delegates. The argument reflects an older model of guardianship democracy, and does not recognize the evolution in democratic sensibilities. Yet only half of Canadians say that "international institutions are not sufficiently democratic and we should find ways to make them more democratic," while 38 percent say that "international institutions are sufficiently accountable and democratic because the national governments with representation at these institutions are elected and accountable to their own citizens." This finding and the previous one put each other in context: although Canadians do not judge the status quo to be sufficiently democratic, they do not support radical participatory processes at the international level.

We believe one conclusion is unmistakable: Canadians do not expect international institutions to function with as much public access as national governments, but they do expect them to function more democratically than they do today. This observation naturally raised questions about the perceived legitimacy of WTO and NAFTA dispute settlement, a subject of frequent complaint by civil society organizations. These adjudicative procedures are claimed to be too secretive relative to national procedures. Even the Canadian and US governments would prefer to see them more open. We did not have space in our survey to ask a question about Canadian perceptions, but we did try to see if other surveys in Canada or elsewhere had addressed this issue; we found none.

Respondents on the surveys about trade that we found were more likely to be asked whether they think "Free Trade is good for Canada" than "are you confident in the NAFTA trade tribunal?" We found no questions about the WTO dispute settlement system as a "court," about the investor-state provisions of trade agreements (NAFTA Chapter 11), the role of quasi-judicial tribunals, or the status of firms in disputes.[11] This lapse in questions on trade surveys is not surprising—we also found that it is not common on more general surveys to ask questions on attitudes to "access to Justice" or on courts more generally. We do know that Canadians are confident in their courts, as are citizens throughout the Atlantic area (Howe and Northrup 2000). This confidence developed over a period of years; it is not something that can be magically transposed to the international arena. Nevertheless, the fact that decisions are taken by "unelected officials" seems not to be a debilitating problem, although citizens would likely support efforts to make the process more transparent. We have no way of knowing if citizens of countries with a less robust court system would feel the same way about WTO adjudication.

Asking questions about *internal transparency* is harder still, but we wanted to try. Demands to make the WTO more inclusive of all its members now dominate the Doha Development Agenda negotiations. The issue for Canadians is whether there are ways to give citizens of other countries more voice in international institutions. We told respondents that the governments of industrial countries had a lot of power when it came to making decisions about globalization. We then asked half of our respondents which was a bigger priority: giving governments of the South or the general public in industrialized countries such as Canada more power. To the other half, we altered the second choice, replacing "general public" with "civil society organizations" (which had been defined earlier in the survey). The results reveal the hierarchical ordering that Canadians apply to broadening access: the general public in the North is the priority, governments of the South follow, and civil society organizations are least important. This ordering presents a dilemma for policy makers because methods for engaging civil society organizations or governments from the South are clear—even if governments choose not to embrace them—while methods for engaging the general public, particularly on an issue such as global governance, are not necessarily apparent. Nonetheless, as part of Canadians' values and mental maps regarding globalization, they expect more public involvement. We can also infer that they are comfortable offering Canadian support to governments of the South to improve their own ability to meet health and safety standards for products that may be imported into Canada. Helping governments of the South "build capacity" to participate in international institutions in an effective manner appears to be consistent with Canadian values.

A related question concerns relations between governments and firms. Canadians believe that when working in other countries, Canadian companies have a responsibility to act ethically, and when they do not, the Canadian government and individual Canadians have a role to play in holding them accountable. We told our respondents that "sometimes Canadian companies violate the environmental or labor laws of other countries when working abroad." Seventy-eight percent believed that the Canadian government should withhold government contracts from Canadian corporations that violate laws in other countries, while only 18 percent believed that "it is none of the Canadian government's business what Canadian companies do in other countries." We also told our respondents: "sometimes Canadian companies violate Canadian values when working abroad." By a margin of 54 to 40 percent, our respondents were more likely to agree that "Canadian citizens who boycott or protest against these companies are doing the right thing," rather than "we should stay out of the internal affairs of other countries and let local governments decide how to deal with Canadian companies working in their countries." This significantly slimmer majority is probably due to two factors. First, some Canadians do not know what "a boycott" is and this is alien from their experience. Second, many Canadians likely defer to the sovereign government of another country, and the response category highlights that the governments of these countries will be "deciding how to deal with the Canadian company."

CONCLUSION

We think the compromise of embedded liberalism remains a compelling metaphor, one that helps scholars interpret the paradoxes inherent in how citizens use their values to construct their understanding of the relationships between their communities and the world. We stress that the compromise is not a causal factor in world affairs. As a constitutive principle, it can shape how citizens understand the limits of legitimacy without being something that any actor could articulate explicitly. We found that this compromise is reproduced in the values and ideologies of citizens, and it is these beliefs, more than their material interests, that allow them to make sense of what globalization represents. Canadians have been quite supportive of trade liberalization, and continue to be comfortable with an active role for international institutions, as long as the welfare objectives of the administrative state are maintained, and as long as globalization is not perceived to threaten valued objectives. They do not see themselves as citizens of the world, and they do not attach much priority to ensuring that international organizations become more inclusive of civil society organizations.

What we observe in some of the public concerns about globalization is not a new challenge to openness. Karl Polanyi claimed that every economy is socially embedded. When the attempt was made under nineteenth-century laissez-faire to allow the market to be self-regulating, or "disembedded," society protected itself in a "double movement" in which the expansion of the market was countered by society (Polanyi 1944, 131). It is often said that by the end of the nineteenth century, the world was more interdependent than it is now. Polanyi argued that this ever greater pace of commercial exchange, one part of the double movement, provoked an ever more intense social response, and that the institutions of economic management eventually failed. In this failure he found the cause of the catastrophic collapse of nineteenth-century civilization in two world wars. By "embedded liberalism," therefore, Ruggie meant to argue that in the postwar order, the liberalization of the global market was embedded in domestic society, that society controlled the market, with the result that the meaning of the "welfare state" could differ from state to state. He also meant that states had learned from the extreme protectionism of the 1930s: closed markets could be as much a threat to peace as unrestricted commercial exchange. Both, if unchecked by the other, end in disaster.

Today we again see the social arm of the double movement responding to the greater market pressures of globalization: the role and size of the welfare state has increased in response to greater integration, for example in the exponential increase in the extent of economic and social regulations. The world economy must still be organized if it is to be stable, but the ever increasing intrusiveness of such global governance makes it ever harder to maintain national autonomy. We argue that an indicator of the health of embedded liberalism can be found in how citizens perceive this continuing compromise. If citizens are unwilling to accept even the existing compromise, let alone the possibility of tighter strictures, then a new grand compromise will remain elusive. And if Canadians, citizens of a country that has made a national virtue of multilateralism, are unwilling to maintain the compromise, then embedded liberalism is indeed in trouble. Embedded liberalism is a compromise between self and other, or home and away, a precarious balance on which multilateralism and international organization rest. If globalization washes away the capacity of the administrative state that allows countries to be different, then the legitimacy of the international institutions that allow them to work together will also be undermined because governments will no longer be able to act in a way consistent with the compromise.

This erosion of legitimacy has not yet happened in Canada, or so we infer from the fact that a large plurality of Canadians currently support both globalization and further trade agreements. This support is a form of output legitimacy, that is, a conclusion that agreements have been good for the individual and for the national economy, not a support based on the detail of the agreements. As we have argued elsewhere, this "permissive consensus" could erode if the government appears to be losing the ability to act in accordance with Canadian values, but we see no such risks in current trade negotiations. Still, Canadians' higher levels of uncertainty about globalization, as compared to trade, warrants further comparative analysis, especially when read in the context of a majority of Europeans wanting greater monitoring of the development of globalization. Whereas these results do not suggest less legitimacy for embedded liberalism, they may indicate some anxiety that globalization may be eroding it. When read in combination with support for international organizations, it also suggests Canadians will be supportive of the efforts to re-embed (i.e., support increased social regulation) at the global level, although the conundrum exists of whether this is possible in the case of core social policy areas that were part of the original compromise.

Support for the international organization of the postwar era remains strong, especially when multilateralism is framed as a force for enhancing social values. That is, the compromise between domestic autonomy and global collective action described as embedded liberalism remains legitimate. How people understand the world is constructed by embedded liberalism. Letting the market run things, which is what complete liberalization implies, or allowing global governance to displace community governance as implied by increased linkages, would be inconsistent with what Canadians believe to be the legitimate social purposes of their governing institutions. Embedded liberalism as a constitutive rule seems likely to continue shaping attitudes to global governance. As Polanyi showed, however, the continuing social response to the sort of market expansion associated with globalization can as easily lead to war as to enhanced international institutions. Whether the international order of embedded liberalism can be sustained is therefore a separate question. We cannot say whether a new grand compromise is possible, but we do suggest that citizens are willing to try.

NOTES

An earlier version of this chapter was published as Wolfe and Mendelsohn (2004). We are grateful to Andrew Parkin with whom we collaborated on the original survey design and to Steven Bernstein and John Ruggie for helpful comments. Marnie Wallace, Patrick Kennedy, Michael Heal, and Alex van Kralingen were able research assistants at various stages of the project.

1. We understand embedded liberalism as a story about the basis for a multilateral international order rather than the overlapping comparative politics story about domestic institutions aimed at facilitating adjustment to economic change. See Blyth (2002).

2. By calling embedded liberalism a constitutive rule we mean that it offers an explanation of the "what" and "how" of collective life. We do not ask what causes embedded liberalism, nor do we ask whether embedded liberalism causes a particular outcome. See Kratochwil (2000, 78); Ruggie (1998a, 869).

3. Mass opinion is generally thought to bear some relation to policy outputs. See Page and Shapiro (1992). Although this is not always the case—see Monroe (1998)—voter preferences do constrain policy making, even on trade, by placing limits on decision makers. For instance, see Rowe (1995); Verdier (1994).

4. We work within the assumptions of Zaller (1992) and Sniderman and Piazza (1993) regarding the interpretation of survey results on issues on which respondents have not thought a great deal.

5. See their reports on Globalization and Trade at http://www.americans-world.org/digest/global_issues/globalization/general.cfm; and http://www.americans-world.org/digest/global_issues/intertrade/support_trade.cfm.

6. The Law Commission of Canada, through the Social Sciences and Humanities Research Council of Canada, provided funds for a second wave. Frequencies for all questions from both waves are available at http://politics.queensu.ca/~mattmen, and data for replication purposes are available through the Canadian Opinion Research Archive http://queensu.ca/cora.

7. We explain our survey design in more detail in Wolfe and Mendelsohn (2005).

8. One can speculate on the effect of the difference in question wording—the commission asked about support for "the development of globalization" while we asked about "Canada encouraging more rapid globalization." But of greater significance, as the commission probed other answers, they found that Europeans became more critical of the consequences of globalization. For example, they report that more than half of respondents believe that "more regulation is necessary to monitor the development of globalisation" (European Commission 2003, 34).

9. Eric Helleiner suggested to us that the data show support for free trade more than free capital flows, which is consistent with embedded liberalism, since embedded liberalism depends on Keynesian monetary policy. The domestic side of the adjustment bargain does not work if a country is pegged to the American dollar.

10. This result is consistent with the results of an innovative test of the microfoundations of support for embedded liberalism (Hays, Ehrlich, and Peinhardt 2005) that finds that political support for increased imports can be sustained through traditional labor market policies—the welfare state, by providing reassurance to workers at risk from foreign competition, remains a valuable bulwark against protectionism. But note that the question they use from the 1995 International Social Survey Program's survey on national identity is naive in today's trading system since it asks only about "limiting the import of foreign products," yet contemporary trade negotiations deal heavily with domestic policy.

11. EKOS asked if Canadians have heard of any trade disputes in recent months. In May 2003, 56 percent had heard of the softwood lumber dispute with the United States, and 8 percent had heard of some other dispute (EKOS 2003).

FOUR

The Politics of International Development

Approaching a New Grand Compromise?

JEAN-PHILIPPE THÉRIEN

INTERNATIONAL DEVELOPMENT is at the core of any overall analysis of global governance. Already in the late 1960s the Pearson Commission (1969) acknowledged that "[t]he widening gap between the developed and developing countries has become a central issue of our time" (3). Three decades later, in September 2000, the declaration adopted by 147 heads of state and government at the UN Millennium Summit identified the fight against poverty as the international community's highest priority (Ruggie 2000, 1–2). It is easy to understand why so much attention is focused on development: the countries of the North, with 15 percent of the world's population, control 80 percent of global wealth, and nearly three billion people live on less than two dollars a day (World Bank 2003, 1–2).

Sharing Louis Pauly's (this volume) view that the contemporary dialogue around globalization among political actors focuses on a shared desire to "better balance among the objectives of systemic stability, economic efficiency, and distributive justice" (93), I here examine the many transformations in the global governance of development since the mid-1990s. I will show that while it may be appropriate to characterize the recent evolution of international development policies as the expression of a *new* compromise, it is altogether exaggerated to see in it the manifestation of a *grand* compromise. The evidence presented in this chapter supports Pauly's argument that multilateral institutions—which are major players in the development process—have the capacity to learn and to adapt to a changing environment. However, in acknowledging the limitations of that capacity, the analysis converges with a position articulated in Steven Bernstein's introduction to the effect that the contemporary world order faces a deep crisis of legitimacy. In short, the progress of international development is impeded by the lack of consensus on a definition of what constitutes a legitimate distribution of global wealth and power.

The chapter is divided into three parts. The opening section presents a constructivist approach to the development debate. It argues that this debate can be read as a permanent dialogue—or confrontation—between the political Left and UN agencies on one side, and the political Right and the Bretton Woods institutions on the other. Building on this theoretical framework, the second section describes the unprecedented convergence between the UN agencies and the Bretton Woods institutions over the last few years. The third section then explains the limitations of current changes in the global governance of development. Finally, the conclusion summarizes the results of this study and briefly outlines possible scenarios for the future of North-South politics.

THE DEVELOPMENT DEBATE: A CONSTRUCTIVIST APPROACH

This chapter is informed by two sets of theoretical and methodological assumptions. The first set refers to the role of ideas in politics, and the second to the role of multilateral institutions in the field of international relations and development.

As a starting point, I use a constructivist approach that stresses the importance of ideas and ideologies in accounting for social processes. Ideas not only provide conceptual roadmaps and collective images to guide human behavior, they also frame issues. To a large extent, political interests themselves can be viewed as "ideational" (Wendt 1999, 115). One can reasonably conclude that ideas therefore have a major impact on international affairs and North-South relations. Given that ideas are expressed primarily through language and that "naming" structures reality, constructivism has always shown a strong interest in discourse and discourse analysis (Bourdieu 1982, 99). But while constructivists unanimously recognize the importance of political debates, they are far from agreement on the best method of interpreting them. The goal of establishing a general theory of political speech acts will no doubt remain out of reach in the short run. It does seem useful, nevertheless, to ask what a "generative grammar" of political discourse and ideologies might look like.

John Ruggie (1982), in one of his many stimulating insights, borrowed the notion of "generative grammar" from linguistics in order to study international regimes and to emphasize "the underlying principles of order and meaning that shape the manner of their formation and transformation" (380). Ruggie's approach was essentially analogical, in the sense that he considered regimes "akin to language" (380). By extending the scope of his insight, one can hypothesize that the language on which political ideas and norms are grounded is itself constructed from a generative grammar that needs to be investigated. As long as such a generative grammar is viewed as a historical structure in perpetual motion rather than a set of fixed rules, the concept may spawn a seminal research program for constructivists (Cox 2002, 80).

There are, undoubtedly, numerous avenues available for plotting a generative grammar of political discourse, particularly in the field of international relations. While it does not aim for universality—unattainable almost by definition—the method proposed here still has the merit of being parsimonious; it relies on the fact that the vast majority of political speech acts can be located within the Left-Right division. Thus, in what follows, I suggest that the history of ideas about international development can be understood as the history of an ongoing debate between forces of the Left and forces of the Right. At first glance, this interpretation may appear curious, perhaps even simplistic. Yet, while international relations scholars rarely use notions of Left and Right, the Left-Right opposition has long been recognized as a meaningful distinction in comparative politics, political philosophy, and sociology.[1] Indeed, according to one scholar, that distinction is "the most firmly-established method" (Heywood 1992, 9) for categorizing political ideas. It must moreover be underlined that notions of "Left" and "Right" are analytical references commonly used as a political compass by both the general public and the media. As political philosopher Norberto Bobbio (1996) argues, the Left-Right divide has not only survived the end of the cold war, but also continues to be "at the centre of political debate" (89).

Left and Right cannot be easily defined, and it is beyond the scope of this chapter to address all the difficulties involved in formulating such a definition. The present analysis will restrict itself to the widely shared interpretation put forward by Bobbio, whereby the difference between Left and Right rests on "the attitude of real people in society to the ideal of equality" (60). As Bobbio admits, the Left-Right distinction is no more than a metaphor because in the real world it involves a spectrum of attitudes rather than a mere dichotomy. He also emphasizes that Left and Right are context-dependent and that their meaning varies across space and time. In spite of all its limitations, Bobbio's definition has the great advantage of emphasizing that equality remains a central issue of negotiation in modern political life. At any rate, even though the terms *Left* and *Right* point to realities that are far more relative than absolute, those who use them "do not appear to be using words unthinkingly" (29). Anthony Giddens (2000) correctly points out that in the shifting ideological environment of the post–cold war era, Left and Right cannot be considered the "sole and sovereign dividing-line" (38) in political struggles. Yet Giddens also makes clear that Left and Right "still count for a good deal in contemporary politics" (50). There exists no a priori justification for depriving the discipline of International Relations of such enduring analytical categories.

From a different perspective, this chapter is also founded on the conviction that multilateral institutions offer an excellent vantage point to examine political ideas and discourse in the field of development. That conviction is rooted in two complementary observations. First, the production of new ideas constitutes one of the main contributions of international organizations to the dynamics of world politics (Emmerij, Jolly, and Weiss 2001, 3; Bøås and McNeill 2004, 2). Second, the promotion of development and the fight against poverty have long figured among the most fundamental objectives of multilateral institutions (Townsend 1993, 102–103).

Some might argue that analyzing development through the lens of multilateral institutions is uninteresting because international organizations are secondary actors in world politics. After all, as Pauly (this volume) points out, the dialogue on the governance of the global economy is fundamentally shaped by state power. Yet to recognize the special status of the state in no way prevents one from also acknowledging that multilateral institutions provide a unique site for observing the development debate. First, multilateral institutions largely reflect the interests of the states that control their decision-making procedures. They therefore comprise a space where the power relationships between leader states and follower states are crystallized. Furthermore, multilateral institutions wield a political authority, which, though difficult to gauge, is on the increase. While international organizations can never be viewed as wholly autonomous bodies, the thriving literature on global governance amply illustrates the recent expansion of "the nexus of systems of rule-making, political coordination and problem solving which transcend states and societies" (Held and McGrew 2002, 8). A wide range of studies have clearly demonstrated that multilateral institutions function as key agents of global governance because they change the context of government decision making, redefine states' interests, and play a significant role in international development.[2]

Finally, the importance attributed to multilateral institutions can be justified as well by the power stemming from their legitimacy (Coicaud and Heiskanen 2001). It should be recalled that one of the most vital functions performed by international organizations is that of articulating and aggregating their members' interests (Archer 2001, 94–96). Because of this function, multilateral institutions represent the most tangible expression of what is referred to as the "international community." Indeed, the daily work of multilateral institutions consists largely of determining "what is just and what is not" on behalf of the international community (Smouts 1995, 98; author's translation). Multilateral institutions thus enjoy a political legitimacy no single state can attain on its own. This feature certainly warrants the great attention paid to them in the study of international relations and development.

Whereas international organizations have the capacity to legitimize a certain image of the international community, their interests are too disparate for that image to be unified. The notion of international community simply does not mean the same thing to everyone, and in the field of development the lack of consensus is particularly noticeable. For fifty years the "UN paradigm" put forward by UN agencies such as the Secretariat, Economic and Social Council (ECOSOC), United Nations Development Programme (UNDP), United Nations Conference on Trade and Development (UNCTAD), and International Labor Organization (ILO), among others, has opposed the "Bretton Woods paradigm" advocated by the International Monetary Fund (IMF), World Bank, and General Agreement on Tariffs and Trade/World Trade Organization (GATT/WTO) (Jolly, Emmerij, and Weiss 2005; Thérien 1999). As Joseph Stiglitz (2002) suggests, the conflict between these two worldviews has a lot to do with ideology (35). Arguably, it cannot be properly understood without reference to the Left-Right debate alluded to earlier. This approach is, at any rate, very much in line with the conclusion of other students of international cooperation, who have recognized that the "Right-Left axis" could be a useful analytical instrument to map the ideas of multilateral institutions (Bøås and McNeill 2004, 221).

In a nutshell, one could say that the Bretton Woods institutions lean more to the Right, whereas the UN agencies tend toward the Left. This typology, represented in Figure 4.1 below, is a simplification not only because all multilateral organizations have distinct mandates and institutional cultures but also because none is ideologically homogeneous. Still, inasmuch as it focuses on the forest rather than the trees, the proposed typology is useful to synthesize the collective images that fashion the global development debate. Above all, it is supported by the fact that the Bretton Woods institutions champion economic growth and the free functioning of markets, values traditionally associated with the Right, while the UN agencies are inclined to stress social justice and the need for political regulation, ideas generally

FIGURE 4.1
Multilateral Institutions on the Left-Right Spectrum

| UNRISD | ILO | UNCTAD | UNDP | UN | World Bank | WTO | IMF |

Left   Right

associated with the Left. It is sometimes said that the unorthodox vision of the UN is at loggerheads with the economic and financial orthodoxy of the Bretton Woods institutions, or that the neoliberalism of the Bretton Woods institutions stands in opposition to the UN agencies' more Keynesian or social-democratic views.[3] In the final analysis, however, these interpretations of the ideological difference between the UN and the Bretton Woods institutions are no more than reformulations of the Left-Right dichotomy.

The Left-Right framework makes it possible to see in a new light what is often termed the "separation" between the Bretton Woods institutions and the UN (Gwin 1995, 95–116; Mingst and Karns 2000, 130). All observers agree that the Bretton Woods institutions and the UN agencies can be differentiated through their distinct political outputs. Historically, the decisions made by the IMF, the World Bank, and the WTO have generally been congruent with the interests of the minority—the wealthy, leading states; by contrast, the policies advocated by the UN have been far more attuned to the priorities voiced by the majority—the poor, following states. This difference has usually been interpreted as a consequence of the asymmetries of material power that are features of the international system. It is often forgotten that the basis of the distinction between the two mainstays of the multilateral system is also normative, inasmuch as the delineation rests on divergent conceptions of interstate equality. The UN agencies, which have a voting system based on the "one state, one vote" principle, are more egalitarian—and more faithful to left-wing principles—than the Bretton Woods institutions, where decision-making procedures are, de jure or de facto, "weighted . . . in favor of the major developed countries" (Mingst and Karns 2000, 130). In sum, as it involves competing visions of equality, the "separation" between the "economic multilateralism" of the Bretton Woods institutions and the "political multilateralism" of the UN agencies coheres well with the logic of the Left-Right divide.[4]

Based on the preceding considerations, the rest of this chapter offers an analysis of recent trends in multilateral debates on development issues. The analysis demonstrates that the consensus, which for many observers characterizes the global governance of development in these early years of the twenty-first century, remains extremely fragile.

A NEW CONVERGENCE AMONG MULTILATERAL ORGANIZATIONS

The current climate within the multilateral development system is much more harmonious than that which prevailed in the 1980s and 1990s, when "the civil war over structural adjustment" was raging (UNDP 2003a, 2). Alluding to this new environment, UN Secretary-General Kofi Annan recently invited the international community "to take advantage of an unprecedented consensus on how to promote global economic and social development" (UN 2005a, 7). Although the optimism that marked the Millennium Summit has somewhat abated due to the slow progress in meeting the needs of the world's poorest as well as the political tensions generated by the war on terrorism, cooperation and dialogue between the Bretton Woods institutions and the UN agencies are more intensive today than at any other point in the past. One unmistakable effect of this dialogue has been a new ideological convergence among multilaterals. The Bretton Woods institutions now acknowledge that globalization engenders losers, and that "the disparities between the world's richest and poorest nations are wider than ever" (IMF 2002, 2). The UN agencies, for their part, agree more and more that globalization offers "great opportunities" for poor countries (Annan 2000, 6).

In keeping with this change in attitudes, the Bretton Woods institutions attribute greater importance than before to the social dimension of development, while the UN agencies are less hostile to market forces. Among its main achievements, the new multilateral compromise has made it possible to target one critical priority: poverty reduction. Indeed, this theme has become so pervasive in the discourse of international organizations that poverty reduction is, for many, the new name for development. The poverty reduction issue may be destined to quickly fall into oblivion, much like the World Bank's "basic needs" strategy in the 1970s. But at present the level of political support in favor of poverty reduction is without parallel in the history of international cooperation.

The new development consensus was solemnly endorsed with the adoption of the 2000 Millennium Declaration. Recognizing that "the benefits [of globalization] are very unevenly shared," that document commits the international community to reduce world poverty by half by 2015 (UNGA 2000). Other so-called Millennium Development Goals (MDGs) include achieving universal primary education, promoting gender equality, reducing child mortality, improving maternal health, halting the spread of infectious diseases, ensuring environmental sustainability, and developing a global partnership for development. In 2002, the declaration adopted at the Monterrey Conference on financing for development confirmed the importance of the MDGs articulated in the Millennium Declaration and proposed to make the twenty-first century "the century of development for all" (UNGA 2002).

The Monterrey Declaration has the additional distinction of having stated more explicitly than ever before the norms underlying today's development compromise. These norms can be summed up as follows: (1) The global economic system should be more inclusive and equitable; (2) Each country has primary responsibility for its own economic and social development; (3) Development should primarily rely on private flows; (4) Trade is the main engine of growth and development; (5) Aid should be seen as a complement to other sources of development financing; (6) Debtors and creditors must share the responsibility for solving unsustainable debt situations; and (7) The participation of developing countries in global economic decision-making bodies should be strengthened. Kofi Annan has described the Monterrey agreement as a "historic compact" (UN 2005a, 12) and Horst Köhler, the former managing director of the IMF, has elegantly encapsulated why such a description is particularly fitting. The agreement, according to Köhler, succeeded in striking an innovative balance between two principles: "self-responsibility in developing countries" and "solidarity on the part of the international community" (IMF 2003a, 2).

The atmosphere of cooperation that currently characterizes the multilateral development system has been made possible by the rapprochement between the UN agencies and the Bretton Woods institutions that began in the second half of the 1990s. After picking up speed as of 1998, in the wake of a historic meeting of high-level officials from ECOSOC and the Bretton Woods institutions, this rapprochement received an unprecedented boost with the joint signing by the IMF, the World Bank, the UN, and the Organization for Economic Cooperation and Development (OECD) of *A Better World For All* in 2000. In many ways, that groundbreaking document, itself the result of decisions adopted at various UN conferences held throughout the 1990s, laid the foundations for the Millennium Declaration and the Monterrey Declaration. Today, as Pauly also emphasizes elsewhere in this volume, the collaboration and the exchange of views between the UN and the Bretton Woods institutions have been routinized at every level of the bureaucracy. A remarkable example of the higher degree of confidence prevailing in the multilateral system was the appointment of Supachai Panitchpakdi, former head of the WTO, as secretary-general of UNCTAD in 2005. An appointment such as this would have been completely unthinkable only a few years ago.

The recent convergence between the Bretton Woods institutions and the UN agencies marks a turning point in the history of North-South politics. All the Bretton Woods institutions are more sensitive to the problems of poor countries. According to Horst Köhler, poverty has become, "the greatest challenge to peace and stability in the twenty-first century" (IMF 2002, 2). Hence, the IMF has taken a series of measures—the most visible being on the debt issue—to face this new situation. By 2005 the Enhanced Initiative for Highly Indebted Poor Countries (HIPC) that was set up in 1999 had provided a $32 billion (net present value terms) debt reduction to 27 countries (IMF 2005a). In a multilateral environment more open to the needs of the South, it was not at all surprising that the IMF should favorably receive the G8's recent proposal to cancel the debt of the poorest countries. Moreover, the introduction by the IMF of the Poverty Reduction Strategy Papers (PRSPs) has increased "national ownership" in the definition of developing countries' economic policies. In particular, PRSPs have helped to respond more effectively to the needs of the poor by encouraging dialogue with civil society in borrowing countries. Under James Wolfensohn's presidency (1995–2005), the World Bank, too, was much more concerned with poverty reduction (Wolfensohn and Bourguignon 2004, 3–4). This new orientation, quite evident in the Bank's rhetoric and research activities, has had a tangible impact on lending operations and on relationships with NGOs. Finally, taking into account the IMF and World Bank's recent active support of higher levels of foreign aid, most critics acknowledge that international financial institutions pay increasing attention to "making growth 'pro-poor'" (Thomas 2000, 62).

In the field of trade the failure of the 1999 Seattle conference prompted the WTO to engage more closely with developing countries. Using an entirely new language, the WTO now presents poverty reduction and the achievement of the MDGs as a "shared responsibility of the international community" (WTO 2002, 3). More significantly, the trade round initiated at Doha in 2001 is officially referred to as the "Development Round." At that meeting, the developing countries successfully took advantage of more transparent negotiation procedures to make gains on questions including the timetable of future negotiations, the implementation of the Uruguay Round, and technical cooperation (Mutume 2001, 3). Although the Doha trade talks are still under way, it is reasonable to expect the resulting decrease in agricultural export subsidies to benefit the South. Overall, WTO authorities are far more vigorous than before in denouncing the cost of the developed countries' protectionism toward developing countries, estimated to be about $150 billion per year. The WTO certainly does not see itself as a development agency, but it admits that spreading prosperity more widely has become a "moral imperative" (WTO 2005, 6).

In the face of repeated criticisms from the developed countries, the UN paradigm has, for its part, become more "market-friendly." Indeed, the UN has gradually abandoned its longstanding "anti-business prejudice" (Dell 1990, ix), a trend spotlighted by Bill Gates's and Ted Turner's generous support for UN activities. According to one observer, "every UN organization is currently involved in multiform private sector partnerships" (Tesner 2000, 69). Henceforward, it is clear that for the UN in the field of development, markets have to be seen more as part of the solution than of the problem.

The UN's ideological shift has been particularly remarkable within the Secretariat and the UNDP. In *A Better World For All*, for example, by agreeing that third world countries "have to lower their tariffs and other trade barriers and streamline their systems for the flow of imports, exports and finance" (IMF et al. 2000, 22), Kofi Annan has aligned himself with a position traditionally defended by the IMF. At Doha, the secretary-general went still farther, stating that opening markets "is even more important for developing countries and transition economies than for the rest of the world"

(Annan 2001, 1). In 2003, the rapprochement between the UN and the business community was stepped up with the creation of the Commission on the Private Sector and Development (2004) under the co-presidency of then Canadian Prime Minister Paul Martin and Ernesto Zedillo, former president of Mexico. At the operational level, the new willingness of the UN Secretariat to cooperate with "market forces" is no doubt best highlighted by the Global Compact that was launched in 1999. The Global Compact is a multistakeholder network that includes business, labor organizations, NGOs, and the UN. Its objective is to induce the private sector to adopt good practices based on ten internationally approved principles in the areas of human rights, labor standards, the environment, and anticorruption (Thérien and Pouliot 2006). The Global Compact is rooted in the notion that the promotion of corporate social responsibility through voluntary measures is one of the best ways to counteract the "downsides of globalization" (UN 2001a, 32).

The UNDP is another UN agency that has changed considerably in recent years. Basically, it has been won over to a number of ideas long defended by other institutions such as the World Bank and the OECD. The UNDP (2001) has thus embraced the view that since the early 1990s, "development aid has seen a shift away from 'aid-as-entitlement' concepts toward an emphasis on results and performance" (5). In an effort to promote "results-based management," the UNDP is now endeavoring to make its services "more competitive" (12). Another significant evolution is the UNDP's active partnership in the implementation of the PRSPs sponsored by the Bretton Woods institutions. UNDP participation in PRSPs extends to more than sixty countries and covers a wide range of subjects including trade, macroeconomic policy, and poverty monitoring (UNDP 2002a, 3). It is also noteworthy that through programs such as the Growing Sustainable Business Initiative and the United Nations Capital Development Fund, the UNDP has emerged as one of the linchpins in the new strategy of collaboration between the UN and the private sector. Finally, it is striking that the general tone of the UNDP's discourse is less confrontational than in the past. The growing tendency of the UNDP to describe development issues as more technical than political is altogether in line with the "new pragmatism" the UN agencies are striving to foster (Spero and Hart 2003, 284).

A number of factors may explain the emergence of a more widely shared vision of development. The Bretton Woods institutions' shift in attitude can be attributed, in particular, to the lessons drawn from the Asian crisis, the worst economic crisis of the second half of the twentieth century. Many analysts have stressed that the IMF's standard austerity policies had the effect of making the Asian financial crisis of 1997–1998 "deeper, longer and harder" (Stiglitz 2000, 60). With their credibility seriously tarnished, the international financial institutions became less arrogant and more aware of their weaknesses. Another contributing factor in the evolution of the outlook of the Bretton Woods institutions was the simultaneous presence of "Center Left" governments in many countries of Europe and North America during the second half of the 1990s. Leaders such as Bill Clinton in the United States, Tony Blair in Great Britain, Gerhard Schröder in Germany, Lionel Jospin in France, Massimo d'Alema in Italy, and Jean Chrétien in Canada were more favorably disposed toward the Millennium strategy and its development goals than their predecessors. Lastly, the rise of terrorism has no doubt provided an additional incentive for the Bretton Woods institutions to intensify the dialogue with the UN. The World Bank has, for example, recognized that growing income disparities could "lead to popular support for some international terrorist movements" (Wolfensohn and Bourguignon 2004, 31). Although the impact of terrorism on the daily activities of the IMF or the WTO ought not to be overstated, the "terrorist threat" has certainly rendered all the multilateral organizations more sensitive to the importance of the social dimension of development.

On the other hand, the transformations that have occurred within the UN system were due, first, to the demonstration effect generated by developing countries where liberalization has helped achieve higher levels of growth. Noting that "[t]he past 25 years have seen the most dramatic reduction in extreme poverty that the world has ever experienced" (UN 2005a, 7), the UN has come to the conclusion that markets and globalization could be hugely beneficial to global development. This said, one cannot help thinking that the UN's change of attitude results also from a "widespread mood of resignation" (Jordan Valley Declaration 2003, 3). As one UN agency argued, "The ever-present possibility of withdrawal of concessional assistance and debt relief . . . is inhibiting what national authorities feel they can say" (UNCTAD 2002c, x). The subordination of the third world and the UN to the prevailing economic orthodoxy is generally associated with the "global intellectual hegemony" to which the international order has been subjected for what now amounts to a whole generation (Gosovic 2000). But feelings of resignation have probably grown more acute over the recent period. In a lopsided world completely dominated by the hyperpower of the United States, the UN's latitude to stand up to the vision of development strongly advocated by the US government has shrunk significantly. In the final analysis, then, it appears evident that the UN's recent "pro-market shift" has in part been a matter of obligation rather than choice.

The director of UNRISD, Thandika Mkandawire (2000), has accurately noted that, "the ideological climate for rethinking development policy is more favorable than it has been for years" (iii). His colleague Mark Malloch Brown, the former administrator of the UNDP, has offered a persuasive explanation of the conditions that made this evolution possible: "I believe we are at a pivotal moment in global development . . . where the Right has realized that the case for doing something is now too powerful to hide behind past failures and the Left—recognizing these failures—is taking a much tougher approach to performance and results" (UNDP 2002b, 1). Malloch Brown's highly insightful analysis stops short of affirming that the Right is closer to the Bretton Woods institutions and the Left more supportive of the UN, but this is an obvious conclusion for any observer able to read between the lines. In any event, what the former UNDP chief could hardly have foreseen is that the new development "compromise" that emerged in the late 1990s—referred to variously as the post-Washington Consensus, the Copenhagen Consensus, the Santiago Consensus, the Bangkok Consensus, and the Monterrey Consensus—would remain so tenuous.

THE MIRAGE OF A "GRAND" COMPROMISE

For a number of reasons, the recent changes in the relationships between the UN paradigm and the Bretton Woods paradigm do not add up to what could justifiably be referred to as a "grand" compromise. To begin with, the very existence of a new development "consensus" has been met with skepticism within the multilateral system. Not surprisingly, given that this system is characterized by the hegemony of the Bretton Woods institutions and that any form of hegemonic power naturally tends to look to the future with confidence, the skepticism regarding a so-called global deal has been voiced first and foremost by the UN agencies. One of the main cracks in the new development compromise stems from the split between the Bretton Woods' systematic optimism and the UN agencies' more pessimistic penchant. While conceding that, "a radical rethinking of international development cooperation . . . is currently under way," for instance, an UNCTAD report released at the beginning of the millennium vented a widespread sense of frustration by asking, "Why should we expect better results this time around?" (UNCTAD 2000c, i).

In fact, the UN is constantly torn between two attitudes about North-South relations. On one hand, the organization is always ready to believe that the conditions finally exist for "a visionary change of direction in our world" to begin (UN 2005a, 53), and that the rich countries are on the verge of a major revision of their development policies. On the other hand, the UN is ever mistrustful due to the developed countries' reputation for not keeping their promises to third world countries. Today, this mistrust is aggravated by the slow progress made in achieving the MDGs, even though these have been identified as an absolute priority of the international community. Just a few years after their adoption, the MDGs already look unattainable for a great many poor countries. In 2004, the UNDP estimated that, based on prevailing trends, Africa would not succeed in halving poverty until 2147 (UNDP 2004). Of course, the recent announcement of an increase in aid budgets may help to improve the situation. But at the midpoint of the current decade, the mixed results in pursuing the MDGs go a long way to explaining why the UN is still far from ridding itself of its chronic pessimism.

The recent convergence between the UN paradigm and the Bretton Woods paradigm remains superficial because these two worldviews are grounded in distinct mandates, constituencies, and, above all, values (Ruggie 2003a, 305; Thérien 2002, 251). The UN agencies tend to insist on social justice and equality, whereas the Bretton Woods institutions place much more emphasis on economic performance and freedom. In its highly diplomatic summary of these divergent outlooks, the UN (2001b) argues, "[T]he ideal of equitable societies and global equity is little challenged," but admits, "views on what is equitable . . . and how equity can be promoted are subject to interpretation and give rise to acrimonious political controversy" (1). One fundamental aspect of this "political controversy" is that the Bretton Woods institutions speak more in terms of poverty, the UN more in terms of inequality. The former frame the problem of development as one of individuals who are not well adapted to the demands of the market; the latter define it primarily as a structural issue whose solution would require global redistribution measures. Alice Sindzingre helps to understand the gap between the two approaches when she notes that "[t]o speak of poverty is to postpone speaking of development" (Sindzingre 2004, 176). The current consensus on poverty reduction, and the emphasis placed on the need to lift out of "absolute poverty" the 1.3 billion individuals who survive on less than one dollar per day, can be interpreted as a victory of the Bretton Woods perspective. This victory, however, fails to adequately address the concerns of the UN, which denounces as "grotesque" the fact that 1 percent of people receive an income equivalent to that of the poorest 57 percent, or that the income of the world's richest 5 percent is 114 times that of the poorest 5 percent (UNDP 2003b, 39). For the UN such a development pattern is simply unsustainable. Hence its firmness—unparalleled at the IMF or the World Bank—in maintaining that "it is crucial that policies and programmes for poverty reduction include socio-economic strategies to reduce inequality" (UN 2005b, 1).

Because of their differing value systems, the UN paradigm and the Bretton Woods paradigm do not share the same view of globalization. Granted, the UN agencies and the Bretton Woods institutions do currently concur that globalization presents both opportunities and risks. Overall, however, the Bretton Woods institutions underscore the opportunities, while the UN tends to highlight the risks. For years, the development credo of the Bretton Woods institutions has been dominated by the notion that "trade is good for growth" and "growth is good for the poor." Global economic integration is thus seen in a positive light because, by "increasing the size of the cake" (IMF 2005b, 2), it is said to reduce poverty. Ultimately, the Bretton Woods institutions associate globalization with the human desire "for expanded horizons and freedom of choice" (IMF 2002, 1). The UN agencies' analysis of globalization is much more critical. According to the UN *2001 Report on the World Social Situation*, "Globalization is widely perceived as having contributed to uncertainty and setbacks in living standards for many, particularly in less developed countries and for low skilled workers globally" (UN 2001b, 1). Using more metaphoric language, the UNRISD (2000) denounces globalization "with a human mask" because it sees in it a process that is "pushing the world toward unsustainable levels of inequality and deprivation" (13). In a rather similar vein, the World Commission on the Social Dimension of Globalization (2004) established by the ILO categorically concludes that "[t]he current path of globalization must change" because "too few share in its benefits" (2). The UN is apparently far more attentive than are the Bretton Woods institutions to the redistributive impact of globalization.

These opposing ways to evaluate the effects of globalization correspond to the contrasting approaches of the Bretton Woods institutions and the UN toward states and markets. Here again, it is important to acknowledge that the Bretton Woods institutions and the UN agencies are probably closer today than they have ever been in the past. Nevertheless, there remain numerous differences in their agendas and priorities. To cite one example, it is beyond dispute that the Bretton Woods institutions and the UN now agree that developing countries require both growth and foreign aid. But when the IMF suggests that "aid is not enough" (Balls 2005) while the UN declares, "growth is not enough" (UN Daily News Digest 2005), one has to admit that nuances can betray profound political divergences.

UN agencies remain unquestionably more interventionist than the Bretton Woods institutions. The Bretton Woods institutions believe that "[i]n most cases, government intervention distorts and/or rigidifies markets and makes them function less well" (IMF 2005c, 3). In their view, the developing countries that have best succeeded in reducing poverty are the "new globalizers" (Brazil, China, India, Mexico), which have opened their borders to trade and foreign investment (World Bank 2001, 5–7). UN agencies, on the other hand, are more leery of markets. In the words of Kofi Annan, for example, "[T]here is no autopilot, no magic of the marketplace, no rising tide in the global economy that will lift all boats" (UN 2005c). Convinced that markets have little concern for matters of social cohesion, the UNRISD (2000) concludes for its part, "[T]he greater the degree of openness of a market economy ... the more important is the role that must be played by national governments in the field of social policy" (13).

The new development compromise appears fragile also because the reform agenda proposed by the Bretton Woods institutions is quite different from that proposed by the UN. The Bretton Woods institutions place relatively greater emphasis on the domestic conditions of development and on the leeway available to developing countries. "At the end of the day," the managing director of the IMF recently affirmed, "poverty reduction begins at home" (IMF 2005d, 3).

The Bretton Woods institutions thus highlight the "capacity of 'self-help'" (IMF 2002, 5) of poor countries, as well as the need for third world leaders to pay more attention to good governance, corruption, human rights, and property rights. Consistent with this approach, the World Bank tends to direct its resources toward "good-policy countries" as opposed to "poor-policy countries." In the late 1990s, the bank granted the former almost three times the amount of aid allocated to the latter on a per capita basis (World Bank 2002, xix). Moreover, the reforms put forward by the Bretton Woods institutions at the global level are far more superficial than those advocated by the UN. In the area of trade, the WTO's prescriptions consist essentially of accelerating the opening of markets. In the financial sphere, the debate initiated by the IMF concerning the establishment of a "new international financial architecture" tends to be confined to issues such as greater policy transparency, stronger surveillance mechanisms, and improved interorganizational collaboration.[5] The lack of "voice and representation" of Southern countries in the fund's governing bodies has been identified as a problem, but to date there is no serious reform of the body's decision-making process in sight (IMF 2004b).

Though it recognizes that each state is responsible for its own destiny, the UN ascribes much more weight than the Bretton Woods institutions to the systemic constraints on development. In an interdependent world, "no country can put its house in order regardless of the conditions prevailing in its external economic environment" (UNCTAD 2002b, 4). The UN's aspirations for change are also much more ambitious than those of the Bretton Woods institutions. While UN agencies have welcomed as a positive trend the introduction of poverty reduction in the strategic planning of international financial institutions, the PRSPs are far from having met their expectations. According to UNCTAD (2002a), for instance, the PRSPs have meant "no fundamental departure from the kind of policy advice espoused under what has come to be known as the 'Washington Consensus'" (6). In the area of trade the UN has long been calling for a radical overhaul of multilateral rules so as to ensure that "a level playing field" exists for all countries (UN 2005a, 18).

In addition to their goal of placing the UN at the heart of the governance of development, UN agencies have proposed institutional innovations that include the launching of a Marshall Plan for the third world, the introduction of a tax on international financial transactions, the creation of an Economic Security Council, the establishment of a bankruptcy court, and the creation of an international development fund.[6] The United Nations Office of the High Commissioner for Human Rights has made the radical suggestion of defining development assistance as a legal obligation under human rights instruments (UNOHCHR 2001, 5). And, based on the observation that "all countries are consumers of globalization's effects" (Annan 2000, 13), UN agencies regularly stress the need to change voting procedures in major economic forums. So far, all these ideas have been dismissed by the Bretton Woods institutions.

Ultimately, even though the recent convergence between the UN and the Bretton Woods institutions has made possible a certain warming of North-South relations, it has not dispelled the old tensions between rich and poor countries. That the September 2005 Summit devoted to the MDGs was the largest gathering of world leaders in history could be presented as an encouraging sign for development diplomacy. But it is plain to see that governments are far from interpreting the current renewal of multilateralism along the same lines. The countries of the North analyze the situation in a way that draws heavily on the Bretton Woods paradigm. Accordingly, over the past few years, they have come to recognize that they should increase their aid resources, reduce third world debt, and open their markets to the exports of the least developed countries. At the same time the members of the G7 and the OECD remain convinced that globalization represents the only possible road to development, and that the IMF and the WTO are the institutions best able to ensure the smooth operation of the world economic order (G7 2005). The countries of the South, for their part, defend a viewpoint that is demonstrably closer to the norms of the UN paradigm. Consequent to the recent evolution of that outlook, the countries of the G77 are more willing than ever to play by the rules of global capitalism, to liberalize their economies, and to promote the private sector. But they also stress regularly that development cannot depend on markets alone, and that the governance of the international economy lacks legitimacy (G77 2005). Among the many observations that may follow from the differing perspectives of the developed and developing countries, there are two that seem especially pertinent to this study. First, the values of order and justice on which the North and the South base their respective worldviews are pivotal references in the Left-Right debate. Second, the gap between the interpretations of rich and poor countries openly calls for a critical attitude regarding the real nature of recent changes in the politics of development.

The partnership that has taken shape between the UN and the Bretton Woods institutions in the past few years has led some to concur with Voltaire's hero, Pangloss, that "all is well in the best of all possible worlds." But in reality, the extent of the differences remaining between the UN paradigm and the Bretton Woods paradigm suggests that the current development consensus is simply too fragmentary to qualify as a "grand" bargain or a "grand" compromise.

CONCLUSION

This chapter has drawn a portrait of the development debate at the beginning of the twenty-first century. Focusing on the role of multilateral institutions, it has shown how the recent convergence of the UN paradigm and the Bretton Woods paradigm signals a new stage in the evolution of North-South relations, a stage that some have associated with the emergence of a "Global Third Way." As summarized by the UNDP Administrator, "management and staff alike in the UN and the Bretton Woods institutions have never been more aligned" (UNDP 2003a, 3). Yet while it is certainly unprecedented, today's multilateral consensus on development issues remains partial and frail.

The political meaning of the convergence process described here is not easy to unravel. The Left-Right distinction nevertheless offers a powerful analytical framework because it provides a conceptual link between, on the one hand, the global tension that opposes the Bretton Woods institutions and the UN agencies, and, on the other hand, the domestic struggles pitting social groups favorable to neoliberalism against those closer to social democracy. Considering that Left and Right actually refer to an ideological spectrum rather than discrete categories, the new development compromise can be located roughly on the "Center Right." This interpretation suggests that the rapprochement observed since the mid-1990s did not take place at the exact median between the original positions of the UN agencies and the Bretton Woods institutions. The Left (the UN agencies) has in fact conceded more ground than the Right (the Bretton Woods institutions), a conclusion apparently shared by the UN itself. The UN admits that in the great debate of recent years opposing the advocates of equality of opportunity, who prefer market solutions, and the supporters of equality of outcomes, who stress the need for redistributive measures, the former have made gains at the expense of the latter. "A feature of recent years," the UN (2001b) acknowledges, "has been a noticeable shift in the middle ground toward opportunity rather than outcomes" (4).

More important, however, than the precise location of the current development compromise in the Left-Right spectrum, is the crucial question it raises: Can it last? A full answer to this question goes well beyond the scope of this chapter as it would require a detailed analysis of how governments of both developed and developing countries will respond to the challenges of North-South cooperation. After all, states remain the main actors of world politics. Still, following the logic of the Left-Right divide, at least three different scenarios can be envisaged.

According to a first, rosy, scenario, the new consensus will hold and its founding objectives will be achieved. This outcome is obviously the one hoped for by most international institutions involved in the global governance of development and by various groups associated with the political center. The script has the vast majority of third world countries reducing poverty by half and reaching the other MDGs by 2015, the developed countries opening their markets to Southern exports, particularly to agricultural products, and a new financial architecture providing a sustainable solution to the debt problem. In this new world order, a much larger number of countries and individuals would benefit from global capitalism. For now, however, this vision of orderly change seems somewhat utopian. As mentioned earlier, several countries are not on track to achieve the MDGs. Moreover, it is highly unlikely that the MDGs will receive the funding needed for this tendency to be reversed. Finally, sluggish growth has made the countries of the North more reluctant to keep their promises in the area of trade and finance. For all these reasons the first scenario is probably too optimistic to be credible.

A second possibility would involve the breakup of the new compromise and a move farther to the Right. In this scenario, the global governance of development would be increasingly shaped by norms of self-help rather than by norms of solidarity. As a result, the world would become more unequal and polarized, a situation that would add fuel to the clash of civilizations. Unsatisfactory economic performances and growing security concerns would lead the countries of the North to lose interest in development issues. Only those third world countries already well integrated into the global economy could manage to stay afloat. According to this script, the WTO negotiations would get bogged down in a conflict between the major trading powers, the promises of increased aid would be scaled down, and dozens of countries would be incapable of reaching the MDGs. One can easily imagine a variation of this scenario whereby US unilateralism would spread to economic issues and thus worsen the climate of North-South relations. In an environment where global governance is generally "poorly done and poorly understood" (Murphy 2000, 789), this may well be the most plausible forecast.

Less likely than the first two, a third possibility would involve a shift to the Left, entailing a radical transformation of the current development compromise. This "Big Bang" scenario, which brings to mind the "counterhegemonic order" described by Robert Cox (1992, 180), would stress the redistribution of global wealth, the democratization of international politics, and the promotion of environmental sustainability. To foster such changes, the global governance of development would have to give a much more prominent role to third world countries and to civil society groups in both the North and South. This trajectory would also lead to an overall strengthening of the role of UN agencies in the management of world affairs. Admittedly, barring a profound economic crisis, a major war, or a significant escalation of public protest against the international economic system, it is difficult to imagine this as a possible near future scenario. Yet the very fact that it has been put forward by many analysts and activists and includes a number of proposals already articulated within recognized international institutions, requires that, in spite of its idealism, it be regarded as a serious hypothesis.[7]

However fraught with uncertainty the future of the global governance of development may appear, one thing is not in doubt: The ongoing debate will not be restricted to economic issues such as growth rates, interest rates, and market access. It will deal as well with moral questions, in particular, those concerning the distribution of power and wealth on the global level. One can safely predict that the development debate will continue to focus on equality, and that the Left-Right distinction will remain a useful key to understanding events as they unfold.

NOTES

I am grateful to Vincent Pouliot, Frédéric Sirois, and Sylvie Thibeault for their work as research assistants. This research project was supported by a grant from the Social Sciences and Humanities Research Council of Canada.

1. The scholarly literature is replete with references to the notions of Left and Right. See for example, Laponce (1981); Castles and Mair (1984); Bobbio (1996); Baradat (1997); Garrett (1998); Giddens (2000; 2001); Thérien and Noël (2000); Alt (2002); Steger (2002).

2. See, for example, Keohane (1984); Finnemore (1996); Murphy (1994).

3. See Deacon (1997); Jolly, Emmerij, Ghai, and Lapeyre (2004); Murphy (1994); White (2002).

4. The distinction between economic and political multilateralism is formulated by Robert Cox (1992, 164). A final point to consider is that associating the Bretton Woods institutions with the Right and the UN agencies with the Left is also consistent with the facts of domestic political life, for it corresponds to a distinction often found within national governments: the finance department is typically headed by politicians more to the Right, and those in charge of "social" departments such as Health or the Environment are generally closer to the Left.

5. See IMF (2000a, 2000b, 2002).

6. See UN (2002b); UNRISD (2000); ILO (2001).

7. In addition to Cox (1992), variants of this scenario can be found in Thomas (2005); Steger (2002, 145–48); Baudot (2000); Social Movements International Secretariat (2003).

FIVE

The United Nations in a Changing Global Economy

LOUIS W. PAULY

SOME THIRTY YEARS AGO, the central economic organs of the United Nations came to be identified with demands of developing countries for a New International Economic Order. Those demands failed to elicit a positive response from industrial countries, and the potential strategic role of the UN seemed thereafter to shrink dramatically. As Jean-Philippe Thérien clearly points out in his chapter, the now-dominant normative framework for the international economy gives pride of place to market forces, especially to capital market forces, and to the Washington-based international financial institutions that have always jealously guarded their independent status within the broader post-1945 UN system. In an important sense, especially for industrializing countries, that framework seeks sometimes to limit and sometimes to promote what John Ruggie called in his seminal 1982 article, "the resurgent ethos of liberal capitalism" (Ruggie 1982, 413). But none of those countries has resolutely abandoned the effort to contain that ethos within domestic social systems designed to buffer market pressures and maximize national political autonomy. Indeed, between globalizing markets and national systems, there remains room for maneuver for all but the poorest countries in the world. In that policy space lies the continuing rationale for the existence and work of international economic and financial organizations, including key parts of the United Nations.

In recent years, something of a revival, and certainly a significant adaptation, has been occurring in the economic and financial role of the central UN agencies. This phenomenon, which is the subject of this chapter, can be understood as part of a shift within the postwar settlement, a recalibration of the post-1945 "compromise" between the policy autonomy required for states to intervene in their economies and the principles and practices of market liberalism. It is also a key element in a struggle to bring a broadening range of industrializing and developing countries into a system still resting on a recognizable version of that compromise.

OVERVIEW

As Ruggie (2003a) himself has described, the policy language employed by the Office of the UN Secretary-General, the Department of Economic and Social Affairs (DESA), the main headquarters unit supporting the Economic and Social Council (ECOSOC), and the UN Development Program (UNDP) now seems nearly as market-friendly as that language long associated with the International Monetary Fund and the World Bank. More importantly, the Fund and the Bank, as well as the leading industrial states behind them, have lately proved more willing than ever to collaborate openly and directly with UN agencies at the March 2002 Monterrey Conference on Financing for Development and in continuing follow-up work. At the same time, key supporters of the Bretton Woods institutions, the United States and its main industrial partners, supported the articulation of the UN's Millennium Development Goals. They also welcomed the secretary-general's Global Compact initiative to encourage corporate social responsibility in the development process, and they pledged to work with the UN to bridge the "digital divide" between rich and poor nations (Ruggie 2003a). Beyond rhetorical expressions of support, several nearly simultaneous decisions by the US president and the Congress suggested that the UN had recovered a unique role in the field of economic development: the Americans brought their financial accounts in the UN up to date, they rejoined UNESCO, and they structured new types of complementary foreign aid programs in what they called the Millennium Challenge Account and the HIV/AIDS Initiative. In his chapter in this volume, Thérien is surely correct to highlight the tentativeness of the new rapprochement between the UN and the Bretton Woods institutions, just as Ruggie has good reason for skepticism concerning the depth of development policy commitments in Washington. Still, the potential importance, novelty, and coincidence of those phenomena are worth exploring.

To be sure, the UN remained at the center of political storms inside the United States and elsewhere over the future shape of global governance. Investigative reports connected with the Iraqi sanctions mismanaged by UN officials and various UN reform proposals piled up late in Kofi Annan's term as secretary-general. Nevertheless, in the arena of economic and financial policy, the underlying story of the UN has been one of tentative but noteworthy resurgence. It is the story of a sprawling, untidy institution adapting to a turbulent environment.

The obvious question is why an institution marginalized from key economic and financial policy decisions from its inception has not simply been abandoned. After decades characterized by financial crisis in many industrializing countries, by economic backsliding in many of the world's poorest nations, and by unmet promises of aid and development-friendly policy reform within industrial countries, it would be easy to take a cynical position on the revival and adaptation of the UN's economic functions and about parallel reforms in national policies. Indeed, it would be too easy. A determined act of will is required to argue that contemporary changes in the UN's mission, in its relationship with the Bretton Woods institutions, and in industrial-country support for UN-advocated development policies means nothing. Such an argument also relies on a seductive but unrealistic sense of historical continuity and on a conviction that leading states are incapable of discerning their own long-term self-interest.

The postwar "grand compromise" that is the subject of this book was actually a muddle of security and economic policies reshaped by the cold war. After the cold war ended, only the most romantic of liberals—liberals of the nineteenth-century, laissez-faire variety—might have imagined the dawn of a new era of clarity, enlightenment, and broad global agreement on the common good. The subsequent evolution of the economic organs of the UN suggests something less dramatic, or perhaps, as Thérien contends in his chapter, something less grand. What they suggest is the deepening of a mediated policy dialogue between leading and following states in a globalizing economy. That dialogue is fundamentally structured by the continuing realities of state power, but its content increasingly concerns policy changes in market economies that aim to strike a better systemic balance among the objectives of political stability, economic efficiency, and distributive justice. It is this dialogue that has revived and begun to transform the key economic and financial missions of the UN.

THE UNITED NATIONS AND THE POSTWAR INTERNATIONAL ECONOMY

Soon after the end of World War II and just after the United Nations was established, it became obvious that the United States and its key allies had no intention of ceding substantive political authority to any international organizations. Certainly on basic economic and financial questions, they soon proved unwilling even substantially to empower the Bretton Woods institutions, which they arguably could control more intimately than the UN. Very soon, the economic and financial staff of the UN was relegated to working on economic questions of marginal significance to the leading states, questions mainly having to do with decolonization and the future development of poor countries. To the extent that finance ministers and central bank governors thought about international organizations, their attention typically drifted to the International Monetary Fund and the World Bank. For its part, the UN, and especially its Economic and Social Council, became the domain of ministries of marginal significance to economic and financial policy in most member-states, namely foreign and development ministries.

It is also significant that the contemporary system of development finance long ago came to depend on private capital markets and not on national treasuries. For some countries, especially poor countries or those undergoing liquidity or solvency crises, those markets were closed or of limited help. Bilateral aid and resources from specialized multilateral agencies, such as the IMF, the World Bank, and various regional development banks, were often targeted at such countries. During the cold war, such financing from leading states and the agencies they controlled was also regularly made available to strategically important developing countries, such as Mexico, Indonesia, and Turkey. Unlike the Fund and the Bank, the UN was not endowed by its founders with significant financial resources of its own, nor was it given a regulatory role such as the one given the IMF in the arena of exchange restrictions.[1] It is no surprise then that the economic functions of UN headquarters mainly evolved along the line of research and of coordinating for ECOSOC the disparate economic activities of UN agencies. Over time, even its research role had come to be overshadowed by research departments in the Bank and the Fund. It nevertheless maintained an active publication program, not only through DESA but also through the UNDP, and indirectly through the UN Conference on Trade and Development (UNCTAD) and various regional economic commissions.[2] Even before leading states began moving their most prominent multilateral interactions out of classic international organizations altogether, and into more restricted fora such as the G7, it would have been hard to deny that ECOSOC, with its fifty-four member-states and its supportive apparatus, were now of marginal significance (Taylor 2000; Hill 1978).

In the 1970s, the UN's economic machinery came back briefly into public view. With the ultimate failure of an ambitious initiative to shift the terms of international economic development and exchange in favor of developing countries, some observers then saw oblivion just over the horizon (Krasner 1985). During the following two decades, the central economic units within the UN nevertheless persisted, albeit in the shadow of affiliated but "independent" agencies, such as the Bank and the Fund, which possessed their own legal charters, resources, decision-making procedures, and expanding linkages to private capital markets. It could be, as public choice analysts might explain, that bureaucracies once established are intrinsically difficult to disestablish. Clever bureaucrats find ways to keep their salaries coming. But it could also be that such an explanation is too facile. Developments in the early years of the twenty-first century, which occurred in the immediate aftermath of a series of financial crises that shook the post-1945 system to its core, suggested more complicated reasons. They suggested that the very persistence of multilateral political instruments reflected both the continuing necessity and the continuing fragility of public authority underneath a globalizing economy commonly, but incorrectly, depicted as a private market-led juggernaut. Political forums of limited membership did not wither away, but it seemed that the world once again needed the more broadly based conference and policy coordination machinery of the UN (Schechter 2001; Cooper et al. 2002).

As Ruggie does in this volume, students of international relations now widely note the resurgence of unilateralism in the United States, the increasing reliance of the system leader on markets as tools of influence, and its increasing reliance on political "coalitions of the willing" to address security issues and manage environmental, health, financial, and other global challenges. Many also point to the continued overshadowing of broadly based multilateral institutions by regional or "ad hoc" arrangements, such as the G8 and the G20. In such a context, the revival and expansion of the mandate of the United Nations in the broad field of development finance, and the linkage of that mandate not only with other multilateral institutions but also, as we shall see, with innovative national programs for development assistance in the United States, is especially puzzling. The classic intergovernmental organizations established after World War II had once served as focal points for understanding relationships among states as well as between state power and the power of markets. In recent decades, as those organizations came to look marginal or sclerotic, scholars interested in such matters turned their attention to less formal international regimes, informal political clubs, and the hidden structures of global capitalism. Evidence of the revival and adaptation of those established organizations to fit new circumstances, especially in a global system now widely taken to be underpinned by the emergence of "private authority," is worthy of deeper investigation (Rosenau and Czempiel 1992; Cutler, Haufler, and Porter 1999; Hall and Biersteker 2002; Rosenau 2003).

ASSESSING INSTITUTIONAL CHANGE

Inis Claude (1966) famously pioneered the study of contemporary international organizations by emphasizing not their replacement of states but their indispensable role in providing collective legitimation for state-led global projects (Hurd 1999).[3] Consistent with this understanding but intrigued by the subtle changes that can occur even within states as such organizations adapt to changing environments and satisfy new policy demands, Ernst Haas (1990) introduced the disciplined study of international organizational change. Where traditional realists depicted such organizations and their missions as straightforward reflections of the underlying power and interacting interests of states, Haas emphasized the ways in which they could, under certain circumstances, facilitate broad and complex processes of social learning.

On the basis of an analytical frame organized around the concept of "cognitive evolution" and an obviously related normative commitment to the notion of progress in international affairs, one of Haas's seminal studies compared the economic and social agencies of the UN with the Bretton Woods institutions (Haas 1990). The former, he concluded, enjoyed a brief period of "incremental growth" in their early years, but were soon overwhelmed by internal and external pressures. Over time, he depicted the UN agencies as enduring, at best, "turbulent non-growth" in their core authority and institutional legitimacy. Simultaneously, in Haas's view, the IMF, and especially the World Bank, moved beyond incremental growth (and a brief period in the 1970s of turbulent non-growth in the Fund's case) to the successful "management of interdependence" through dynamic processes of organizational learning. Crucial here and in other successful cases was the emergence of respected expert groups outside the organizations, or "epistemic communities," which could form intellectual alliances with innovative, reflective thinkers in official positions. The institutional flowering of the seeds Haas called consensual knowledge also depended on a powerful enough coalition of states with a stake in such an outcome. The results could sometimes be conflicted, but there was no doubting a certain underlying progressive impulse in practical policies (Kahler 1995).

Anticipating the way in which what would come to be called the "Washington Consensus" actually spread, Haas (1990) provided an example of how such results could institutionalize conflict and render organizational adaptation more challenging:

> We thus arrive at a paradoxical picture in which epistemic communities encouraged by the Bank and the Fund—associated with Western thinking even though the individuals are often nationals of Third World countries—dominate policy-making and the administration of loans, while antidependency-minded delegates from the same Third World countries denounce the Bretton Woods twins as "heartless" in the UN General Assembly and in UNCTAD. (149)

By resisting the notion that such conflict would actually cut such organizations out of processes of future policy development, however, Haas in many ways anticipated the recent re-importation of highly suggestive sociological approaches to the study of international organizational adaptation. Certainly the role Ruggie, who was Haas's student, foresaw for international organizations in the working out of the compromise of embedded liberalism fits into such a tradition.

A compatible body of research depicts post–World War II international organizations as embodying a process of global sociocultural structuration. For John Meyer (1997) and his colleagues, who work in this tradition, those organizations constitute a "framework of global organization and legitimation" that both create and assemble "components of an active and influential world society.... The forces working to mobilize and standardize [that society] gain strength through their linkage to and support by the United Nations system and the great panoply of non-governmental organizations around it" (163). However much that system may seem powerless at any given moment, it is in fact an essential part of a macro process through which the nation-state form itself is reconstructed and transmitted, through which state identities are shaped and state behavior transformed by the universalization of an essentially dominant Western culture. World War II ushered in the decisive phase. Afterward, "rationalized definitions of progress and justice (across an ever broadening front) are rooted in universalistic scientific and professional definitions that have reached a level of deep global institutionalization. Conflict is to be expected, but their authority is likely to prove quite durable" (Meyer et al. 1997, 174–75).

Embodying the process through which "world society" is actually rationalized, the adaptation of international organizations would seem necessarily to reflect a politically authorized mechanism for the working out of tensions, for coping with contradictions, and for sustaining the forward movement of societal construction on a global scale. Not by coincidence have such views attracted favorable attention from a new generation of IR scholars seeking to combine the insights of institutionalism and constructivism.

The prominent liberal institutionalist position on the matter of organizational adaptation does not so much contradict this kind of sociological work as attempt to bring to bear models more clearly borrowed from microeconomics. This approach leads us essentially to expect that organizations, once created, can continually work to lower transaction costs and help directly to clarify and resolve problems of collective action. They become useful instruments for encouraging long-term thinking and exploiting new policy ideas. In such a context, they will tend to persist as long as the problems they seek to address remain in existence (Keohane 1984).[4] By their collaborative operation, moreover, they might begin subtly to alter the terrain upon which state interests are recalculated, even in the security arena (Nye 2002). On this view, the process through which they themselves develop is iterative, and it is more likely to be characterized by adaptation than by abrupt change as underlying interests evolve. Scholars advocating a constructivist approach in this field have recently been trying to model this process as either an organic experience of social learning or, when things go awry, of social dysfunction (Adler and Barnett 1998; Adler 2002; Onuf 1989; Barnett and Finnemore 2004). The related work of organizational analysts inspired in part by postmodernism takes this in a more radical direction. While acknowledging the reality of adaptive strategies, they contend that the actual avoidance of festering problems calls for intensive critical examination of the core purposes of agencies such as the UN and for their structural redesign (Knight 2000; 2001). We return to these analytical concepts below, after we look briefly at recent events implicated in the continuing story of the UN's economic and financial mandates.

ADAPTING THE UNITED NATIONS

Some thirty years ago, the UN stood for a kind of solidaristic ideal at a time when capitalist markets were widely believed to be stimulating harsh competition between rich and poor countries, and among poor countries themselves (Emmerij et al. 2001). Perennial calls for UN reform became louder, and the Bank and the Fund, linked to those markets as they were, kept their distance. Since March 2002, however, they have been collaborating ever more intensively with the UN, at both senior management and at staff levels. The UN has become more than a simple forum, its management and staff more than gadflies. Among other things, the UN rationalizes and organizes the participation of a widening array of NGOs and new social actors claiming to speak in the name of "global civil society" in the continuing global dialogue on issues of political economy (O'Brien et al. 2000). It brings newly revived relationships with the IMF and the World Bank into that dialogue. Leading states, moreover, have once again begun to pay attention to its economic work.[5] And in both leading industrial and developing states, that work has forged new linkages between national ministries long accustomed to keeping themselves at arm's length. None of this means that global economic governance of a systematic nature has suddenly arisen. But interesting adaptations are occurring in the original international organizational base for the embedded liberalism compromise.

Late in 1997, the General Assembly of the UN passed yet another in a long series of resolutions relating to the financial challenges of developing countries (Herman 2002). The resolution called for the "convening, inter alia, of a summit, international conference, special session of the General Assembly or other appropriate high-level international intergovernmental forum on financing for development (FfD) to further the global partnership for development, not later than the year 2001" (UNGA 1997). Since analogous resolutions had been passed regularly, at least since 1991, the casual observer may be forgiven for having ignored the resolution. Surely, few would have expected much to come of it, especially since the principal question appeared to be settled in the mid-1970s. The bulk of future financing for development would be delivered by private capital markets, which could in theory be accessed by the straightforward reform of domestic policies within developing countries themselves. Sound macroeconomic fundamentals plus increased openness were expected to deliver development and prosperity.

As it happened, the UN resolution this time coincided with the onset of a downward spiral in international capital markets, a spiral that would eventually threaten prospects for economic development and reawaken memories of global depression. Not only professionally apocalyptic observers, but also normally quite sober participants in those markets, were very soon thereafter to panic, and even to forecast the imminent demise of global capitalism (Soros 1998). In the event, the system did not collapse, but severe payments crises did overwhelm financial policymakers as they spread rapidly from Thailand to Korea, Indonesia, Russia, and Brazil (Blustein 2001). The IMF and the World Bank were quickly swept into the maelstrom; when it ended, their own credibility was hurt. The IMF in particular had been a principal advocate for a world without financial walls. By 1999, the Fund and the Bank were in retreat from crisis-driven efforts to curtail cronyism and statism in indebted developing countries and to open opaque, dysfunctional markets to external competition. They were not alone in marching backward. In the fall of 1998, it seems almost embarrassing to recall, the most open and supposedly transparent exemplar of the world of financial globalization undercut the ideological foundation of the then conventionally accepted development agenda, a foundation often referred to as the Washington Consensus. Efficient markets were asserted, and both winners and losers needed to accept the inevitability of adjustment. But in the United States, during a time of deepening fear, this kind of thinking proved insupportable. In the most spectacular example, instead of then letting a highly leveraged hedge fund named Long Term Capital Management fail after its bets were swamped by a financial panic just then rolling in from East Asia and Russia, the Federal Reserve unofficially organized a bailout (Blustein 2001, chapter 11; Pauly 2004).

It seems implausible to argue for simple coincidence in the fact that desultory discussions just then underway within the UN on the 1997 resolution suddenly attracted new attention. Although it looked as if the 2001 deadline for a high-level meeting might slip, momentum began to build on bringing together debates on a range of new issues spawned by two years of global crisis, issues now graced with the label "new financial architecture." In the background was a refocusing of the World Bank's core mandate on poverty reduction, a continuing erosion in ODA commitments on the part of industrial countries, but a break in their long-standing resistance to providing debt relief to the poorest developing countries under certain conditions. At the same time, international efforts to agree on new OECD guidelines to govern foreign direct investment were defeated, but movement accelerated toward a new round of international trade negotiations that were now meant to take the development challenge seriously (Herman 2002, section 2). An agenda-setting process got underway within the UN, and a preparatory committee now attracted the active participation of the IMF, the World Bank, the ILO, the WTO, the OECD, the European Union, and the Financial Stability Forum.[6] The process engaged UN ambassadors, generally drawn from foreign ministries, but the ultimate goal soon came to complement ongoing interorganizational discussions with innovative ministerial-level discussions among officials drawn not only from foreign ministries but from trade, development, finance ministries, and central banks as well. As it moved in this direction, the preparatory committee also began to receive input from a wide range of nongovernmental organizations. In February 2001, a week-long dialogue opened by the president of the UN General Assembly and the secretary-general attracted a notably wide range of national officials, as well as senior managers from the IMF, the World Bank, and the WTO.[7] This, in itself, was seen by insiders as an accomplishment. As one participant observed,

> If FfD had ever been construed as a way for the UN to instruct or even give advice to other international organizations, the initiative would have died an immediate death. . . . The other [organizations] had to see FfD as a serious initiative that was relatively free of the usual negotiating rigidities of the UN . . . [and] if not an advantage, then at least no danger in drawing closer to the UN. . . . Thus diplomats in New York have succeeded in involving all the major "institutional stakeholders" in the FfD process. Some have come warily and some enthusiastically, but all have been engaged one way or another. (Herman 2002, section 3)

Working in parallel with officials at this level, separate discussions had commenced at the senior governmental level under the chairmanship of Ernesto Zedillo, past president of Mexico.[8] After these discussions, it was still far from certain what the next step might be. Political transition in the United States, among other things, added a new wrinkle; a commonplace view was that the Bush administration was decidedly less receptive to using international organizations as forums for addressing global financial matters. But such a view proved wrong, or at least too simplistic. It likely helped that during the early months of the new administration, Mexico offered to host a high-level summit in Monterrey to follow up on the work of the UN preparatory committee (Herman et al. 2001). But insiders say that more important was lobbying by American business associations in Washington. Most prominently, the Business Council for the UN, an affiliate of UNA-USA, continued a campaign it had begun during the late Clinton years to build support for what would become the International Conference on Financing for Development (Interview, UN, New York, 5 February 2002). One of the assets the UN brings to this and other policy tables is, indeed, its NGO network, which it has officially sanctioned and nourished ever since its founding. Many NGOs have official status at the UN, are formally empowered to address ECOSOC and other bodies, actually deliver certain UN programs, and play a recognized role in many UN activities.

On January 27, 2002, the preparatory committee completed its consultations with national delegations, with the international organizations, and with recognized NGOs. The result was an agreed draft text for the final communiqué to be debated at the Monterrey Conference. Implicitly labeled in such a way as to replace the tattered Washington Consensus, the document spoke of a "Monterrey Consensus." Its main heads were "Mobilizing domestic and international financial resources for development," "International trade as an engine for development," "Increasing international financial and technical cooperation for development," "External debt," and "Addressing systemic issues: enhancing the coherence and consistency of the international monetary, financial, and trading systems in support of development" (UN 2002b). Even the aficionado would be hard-pressed to find much surprising or controversial here. But future historians may well look back and see in the lines that followed a summary of lessons learned during the crises of the late 1990s, and at least an opening for a change in the way international organizations and governments actually confront debt crises.

In March, these careful preparations culminated in the conference itself, which the presence of fifty heads of state or government transformed into a summit meeting. Even more significantly, they were joined by finance, foreign, and development ministers from many more countries, ministers not often happy to meet together in collaborative forums where divergent perspectives and domestic interests were likely to become public and undeniable. Behind the scenes, the conference provided a focal point for unusually intense and unusually open collaboration among officials from the UN Secretariat, the Bank, and the IMF. For their part, IMF officials later explained their interest in going down this path as rooted in three perceptions: (1) that the process would give them a chance to affect the agenda and avoid being blindsided; (2) that it would reinforce concurrent moves to encourage a broad base of member-states to "buy-in" to Fund policies; and (3) that the "legitimacy" associated with a well-prepared UN conference would enhance the possibility that borrowing states would "take ownership" of adjustment programs they negotiated with the Fund.[9] Around the time of the Monterrey meeting, "streamlining" the scope of the Fund's lending conditionality practices had also become the new order of the day. In historical terms, it seems clear as well that by then the UN itself had changed in such a way as to accommodate the views of the Bank as well as the Fund. Gone, or at least much muted, was the rhetoric of radical global redistribution associated with the UN in earlier decades.[10]

In the end, the conferees agreed to the text that had been proposed for their final communiqué (UN 2002a). With a degree of hyperbole, but also with some justification, the text left the distinct impression that both rich industrial countries and poor developing ones were dissatisfied with the conventional wisdom that had dominated the international discourse on development financing during the previous decade. Where the Washington Consensus basically left the challenge of development to the internal economic discipline of poor countries on the understanding that this would enable them to attract adequate capital flows of a mainly private character to meet that challenge, the "Monterrey Consensus" reopened the space for the newly energized post-1945 machinery of intergovernmental cooperation to harness and redirect new kinds of private *and* public capital flows, especially for the poorest countries in the world. In the months following the conference, unusual joint meetings were held between IMF and World Bank executive directors and UN ambassadors, while staff reporting to them sought ways to collaborate more intensively in specific country operations.

THE MONTERREY CONSENSUS AND THE UNITED STATES

Despite its public image as antagonistic to multilateralism, and to the UN in particular, the US administration of George W. Bush welcomed the initiatives coming out of the Monterrey Conference. Indeed, President Bush himself attended the conference and personally endorsed its final report. The fact that his government considered it to have been more than a passing moment was signaled six months later in its much-publicized National Security Strategy. In the relevant chapter, the document best known for its argument in favor of preemptive war in the struggle against global terrorism asserted, "We forged a new consensus at the UN Conference on Financing for Development in Monterrey" (White House 2002). Specifically related to that consensus, President Bush later promised to increase by 50 percent core development assistance provided by the United States.

The detailed proposal finally put to Congress specified a permanent $5 billion increase in US public funding for development assistance, to be distributed through a new government-owned agency called the Millennium Challenge Corporation. The Millennium Challenge "Account" was designed for countries meeting tests of "good governance." It was also to be coordinated with any parallel efforts by USAID, the World Bank, the IMF, and other multilateral and regional agencies (USAID 2003).

In the midst of mounting domestic fiscal problems and difficulties in stabilizing war-torn Iraq, moreover, its actual first-year budget (FY2005) was approved by Congress at a level of US $994 million. To put this number in perspective, total US foreign aid budgets approximated $20 billion in 2004 (in constant dollars), excluding funds for the reconstruction of Iraq. This was up from the post-1945 low of $15 billion budgeted in 1996. Of that total amount, actual funding managed by USAID was $5.7 billion (Tarnoff and

Nowels 2004). President Bush eventually scaled back his target for FY 2006 from $5 billion to $3 billion, and Congress appropriated less than $2 billion.

US officials stoutly defended themselves against accusations that the MCA would not actually contribute much to the achievement of the goals set out in Monterrey.[11] At the same time, they affirmed their continuing support for the signal declaration of the General Assembly of the UN on a broad set of "Millennium Development Goals," thereafter routinely cited by multilateral and national development agencies as more specific expressions of the Monterrey Consensus (UNGA 2002). Ambitious targets for a broad set of objectives related to poverty reduction, improvements in health, and other global economic, environmental, and social conditions were set for achievement by 2015.

Specifically related to these goals, perhaps the most significant institutional achievement of the Monterrey Conference lies buried in its almost impenetrable conclusions, entitled "Staying engaged." They specify a commitment to "make fuller use" of the UN General Assembly and ECOSOC in following up the conference, partly by regularizing "preliminary exchanges" on related matters with the executive boards of the World Bank and the IMF, and with "the appropriate intergovernmental body of the World Trade Organization," by holding a spring meeting among ECOSOC, the Bretton Woods institutions, and the WTO, and by "reconstituting" every two years in the General Assembly, "the current high-level dialogue on strengthening international cooperation for development through partnership" (UNGA 2002, paras. 61 and 63).

THE PERSISTENT COMPROMISE OF EMBEDDED LIBERALISM

Even after memories of the financial crises surrounding the original Monterrey summit had faded, follow-up processes attempted to break some bureaucratic molds and encourage new habits of consultation. Permanent and regular meetings were to occur among national governments and key institutional "stakeholders." On the most important economic and financial challenges confronting developing countries, both directly and through the international civil service, foreign ministries, development ministries, and finance ministries would have to consult with one another and with their counterparts in other countries on a formal and routine basis. Of all the institutional "stakeholders," the UN—where foreign and development ministry officials dominate but are often tested by demands for specialized expertise when dealing with the complicated economic issues—would likely be the one most rejuvenated by this process. Despite continuing concerns about its size and scope of activities, it is significant that other ministries agreed that the UN had to be useful here and would therefore be worth rejuvenating with some expenditure of new resources. In the wake of the financial crises of recent years, and the continuing crisis of underdevelopment in troubled parts of the world, what the UN mainly offered was what it had always represented in principle—a sense of international legitimacy, a good now apparently deemed to be worth putting up with the "inefficiency" of broadly based consultations. Despite all the criticism heaped upon it in recent decades, ECOSOC provided a forum that could engage the broadest range of member-states, collaborative intergovernmental institutions, and, not least, burgeoning nongovernmental organizations.[12]

To be sure, ECOSOC simultaneously found itself yet again at the center of contentious new debates on UN reform. With a financial scandal in the background, various high-level study groups focused on changing the mandates and modes of operation of the secretariat and of most UN agencies. They tended as usual to focus on the UN's core mission in the security arena. Aside from the headlines generated by various plans for expanding membership in the Security Council, serious reports also focused in on the expansive bureaucracy and proliferating expectations surrounding the Office of the Secretary-General. The secretary-general himself convened an expert panel, which weighed in with a study entitled *A More Secure World* (United Nations 2004). In the section dealing with economic and financial matters, the panel acknowledged directly the fact that "decision-making on international economic matters, particularly in the area of finance and trade, had long left the United Nations and no amount of institutional reform will bring it back" (85). ECOSOC had been relegated to the near-impossible task of efficiently coordinating UN funds, programs, and semiautonomous agencies built up over many decades by member-states in response to specific problems of the day. In ECOSOC, however, were co-located three specific UN functions: integrating agreed systemic objectives with country-level programs, allocating limited UN financial and personnel resources, and monitoring the overall performance of UN agencies. Coordinating these functions was always bound to be difficult, but "doing these three things in the same forum had a multiplier effect on pressure towards system-oriented behavior for policy formulators, resource contributors, and program implementers alike" (Taylor 2000, 139). Adapting just such a threefold mission for a new era, the secretary-general's panel advocated three strategies: refocusing ECOSOC on collective security broadly defined through better "normative and analytical leadership" through a new Committee on the Social and Economic Aspects of Security Threats and regular meetings between the presidents of the Security Council and ECOSOC; "measuring key development objectives in an open and transparent manner"; and "transforming ECOSOC into a development cooperation forum" concentrating on the Millennium Development Goals. Executive direction would be provided through a small committee comprised of regional groups and through annual meetings with the Bretton Woods institutions (UN 2004, 85–86).[13]

Among the many other studies and reports that followed, particularly noteworthy is one commissioned by the US Congress and sponsored by the United States Institute of Peace. A bipartisan group led by former Speaker of the House Newt Gingrich and former Senator George Mitchell tackled ECOSOC directly and bluntly. Agreeing that maintaining and strengthening the United Nations continues to serve long-term US national interests, the group advocated "reducing the bloated staffing of the Department of Economic and Social Affairs and ensuring that ECOSOC focuses on useful endeavors rather than, as now, engaging in endless, redundant discourse or pretending that it is the World Trade Organization" (Task Force on the United Nations 2005, 108). The report then went on to endorse verbatim the recommendation of the secretary-general's high-level panel, with the admixture of strong support for enhancing the "key coordinating" role of the United Nations Development Program in such a context (110–11). In the end, with US corporate practice and the idea of "accountability" very much in mind, the panel agreed on recommendations to create a Chief Operating Officer to complement the continuing CEO role of the Secretary General and to strengthen external monitoring, presumably by "contributing member states" (107).

Sometimes vitriolic arguments about the future of the UN continue, and the legacy of the ideological split between the UN and the Bretton Woods institutions analyzed by Thérien in this volume undoubtedly casts a long shadow. But the now-regular meetings among high-level officials from the UN, the IMF, the World Bank, the WTO, and other agencies on new policies consistent with the Monterrey Consensus hold promise.[14] Moreover, despite persistent hand-wringing in continuing debates on UN reform, no serious proposal has emerged to take the UN entirely out of the economic and financial arena. As in the past, debates remain focused instead on institutional adjustment. Complementing new commitments to development financing and debt relief at the national level inside leading states, what else could such debates signify other than a renewed recognition of the need for some kind of collaborative authority underneath an integrating global economy? Certainly they cannot be construed to express a common commitment to nongovernment, or to automatic, depoliticized, market mechanisms. The fact that even a radically nationalist administration in the once and future leader of the post-Monterrey system now signaled a willingness to work routinely not only with the Bank and the Fund but also with central economic organs of the United Nations did certainly emphasize a basic continuity on issues of international monetary and financial governance. That a sense of defensiveness may have been apparent in this regard did not obfuscate the image of states inexorably drawn back into institutional arrangements that still held the promise of promoting a sense of shared global prosperity. Of course, reality continued to diverge from such a goal. But continuing to acknowledge the goal was not a trivial act. At the very least, not walking away from such arrangements itself enhanced the legitimacy of the claim by the United States to continuing systemic leadership.

If Ernst Haas came back today, he would likely still diagnose turbulent non-growth in the economic mission of the UN. He might even decry the cacophony associated with inter-institutional collaboration after the Monterrey summit. Less hopeful analysts might think they hear therein the sound of the post-1945 order entering its last stages. In light of the true global catastrophe Haas and his generation of pioneering scholars actually lived through in the 1930s and 1940s, however, I doubt that he would share in that conclusion. Certainly his students and intellectual heirs, whether they considered themselves institutionalists, contructivists, or structurationists, would find ample reason to discern an emergent global society struggling against the constraints imposed by the still-necessary logic of intergovernmentalism. The continuing absence of authoritative supranational governing institutions testified to the demands of powerful constituencies around the world both for the benefits of deepening economic interdependence and for a meaningful degree of political control over their own lives and fortunes. Such demands were not irreconcilable, but nor were they easily reconciled. International institutions such as the UN and the Bretton Woods institutions stand astride those very demands. Small wonder that their coherence, their decision making, and their bureaucratic pathologies continue to be problematic and in need of reform. At the system level, they remain the embodiment of the persistent and messy compromise underpinning a globalizing economy.

NOTES

Like an earlier draft appearing in Grande and Pauly (2005), this chapter benefited from the able research assistance of Marc Kosciejew and Nisha Shah. Constructive comments from Steven Bernstein, John Ruggie, Emanuel Adler, Erin Hannah, and two anonymous referees prompted significant revisions. Financial support came from the Social Sciences and Humanities Research Council of Canada.

1. On the legal relationship between the UN and the Fund, negotiations initiated by the UN's first secretary-general, Trygve Lie, and the IMF's first managing director, Camille Gutt (IMF 1946), culminated in a formal inter-institutional agreement that came into effect on November 15, 1947. It granted "full autonomy" to the IMF on, for example, the content and form of the Fund's budget, but it also allowed the UN and the Fund to make formal recommendations to one another "after reasonable prior consultations" as long as specific loans were not involved (IMF 1951). On the general topic, see Jolly et al. (1995).

2. Economic research at the UN originally derived directly from prior work in the League of Nations. See Pauly (1997); Hill (1946); McClure (1933); Clavin (2003).

3. The following two sections adapt and update material from my chapter in Grande and Pauly (2005).

4. For a more radical view of economic influences, see Murphy (1994). A narrower institutionalist approach under the public choice label typically emphasizes the critical role played in organizational evolution by self-regarding bureaucratic interests within such organizations themselves. See Vaubel (1986, 39–57).

5. Note also the high-profile announcement by President Bush on September 12, 2002, that the United States was rejoining UNESCO after an eighteen-year boycott; the announcement followed soon after the United States resolved a long-running dispute and began paying outstanding dues to the UN.

6. On the coincident dialogue concerning rules to guide continuing financial liberalization among the EU, the OECD, and the IMF, see Abdelal (2007).

7. Note that the IMF and the World Bank are officially designated as "specialized agencies of the UN." The WTO is not formally affiliated with the UN.

8. Zedillo, with assistance from John Williamson, was commissioned by Kofi Annan to think through the issues that a US congressional initiative, the Meltzer Commission on the International Financial Institutions, had recently examined. The expectation was surely that they would come to a much less anti-institutional conclusion than did the majority of the Meltzer Commission.

9. Interviews, IMF Headquarters, 3 February 2003.

10. That a concession had been made was clear to senior UN officials from that earlier era. "By seeking consensus with the private sector and OECD and close working relations with the international financial institutions, the value added by the UN in developing an alternative paradigm may be threatened." See Emmerij et al. (2001, 144–45).

11. See US Department of State (2003a). Accused by congressional Democrats of "fraud" on both the MCA and HIV/AIDS initiative, the head of the relevant appropriations subcommittee in the House of Representatives responded: "We are constrained by a spending cap that required reductions. . . . We allocated 40 percent more to global AIDS programs than Congress appropriated last year, and the money allocated this year is enough to get the AIDS program and the Millennium Challenge Account started. A plane doesn't take off at 30,000 feet; it takes off slower and it climbs. We do the same thing with programs, which is how you ramp them up" (Stevenson 2003). In June 2005, the same committee allocated an 18 percent increase in the MCA. For a view that balances neatly between skepticism and optimism by someone directly involved in designing the plan within the US Treasury, see Radelet (2003, 104–17). Also see Brainard et al. (2003).

12. See IMF (2003b, 126–27); IMF (2004a, 160); also Scholte (1998, 42–45); Woods (2001, 83–100); Buira (2003). By 2005, more than 2,500 NGOs had received special consultative status from ECOSOC, which allowed them to participate in council deliberations.

13. This section of the report concludes with a tentative endorsement of a Canadian idea for achieving greater "policy coherence." "One way of moving forward may

be to transform into a leaders' group the G20 group of finance ministers, which currently brings together States collectively encompassing 80 percent of the world's population and 90 percent of its economic activity, with regular attendance by the IMF, World Bank, WTO and the European Union. In such meetings, we recommend inclusion of the Secretary General of the United Nations and the President of ECOSOC" (UN 2004, 86; also see UN 2005d).

14. See United Nations (2005e).

SIX

Compromises of Embedded Knowledge

Standards, Codes, and Technical Authority in Global Governance

TONY PORTER

ALMOST TWO DECADES AGO, in a remarkably influential and insightful contribution to a collection of articles on international regimes, John Ruggie (1982) managed to capture key conceptual and practical features of global governance of that period through his development of the concept of "embedded liberalism." The concept was powerful not only in the way it highlighted the complementarity of domestic protections for citizens and international economic liberalization, but also in how it linked this arrangement to an argument regarding the importance of considering *social purpose* together with power in analyzing governance internationally. In doing this, Ruggie enhanced our sensitivity to the constitutive impact of norms in a way that would later make him a founding figure on the constructivist side of the main bifurcation of the field of international relations today (Ruggie 1998a).

This chapter argues that while Ruggie's meta-theoretical arguments remain as relevant today as they were twenty years ago, the practical and empirical correlates of these arguments are very different. Today, as before, market interactions need to be embedded in a set of institutional arrangements that stabilize them and that offset their negative effects to a degree sufficient to render them acceptable to those actors who might otherwise destroy them through political means. In this respect, the constructivist insistence on the way in which institutions and norms constitute and enable rationalistic interactions continues to be crucially important. However, in contrast to the earlier period, this process of "embedding" and of "compromise" increasingly takes place in globalized knowledge networks (Sinclair 2000)[1] rather than territorial states. In this process, standards, codes, and technical authority become more important elements of embedded compromises than they were in the period about which Ruggie was writing.

This argument challenges three prevailing perspectives on the character of contemporary global governance. First, it challenges state-centric perspectives, including Ruggie's 1982 concept of the compromise of embedded liberalism, that see bargains or norms developed among competing territorial states as the primary source of global order. Ruggie's contribution to this book, in highlighting the importance of non-state actors, moves in a similar direction to the present chapter. Second, it challenges liberal economic perspectives that see fluid market forces or atomized rationalistic actors as undermining or bypassing states and independently shaping the development of the global political economy. Third, it challenges perspectives that see powerful states and market actors as uncompromisingly shaping a globalized world without regard for the need to resolve conflicting preferences, not just among powerful actors but between those actors and others with less power as well.

Any effort to assess theoretical claims about something as big as global governance inevitably runs up against methodological difficulties. One difficulty is that if an emerging trend exists, it may be taking place among traditional arrangements. Thus, it is easy for skeptics to point to the persistence of those arrangements as evidence of their greater importance. A second difficulty is that subtle changes in international arrangements, such as increased linkages among national representatives in international discussions, may lead to significant changes in the relationship of states to other institutions even if these are not reflected in the formal and more easily observable features of these arrangements, such as founding treaties or articles of agreement. Nevertheless, some supporting or contrary evidence with respect to the above argument should be possible to find through an examination of particular arrangements that are likely to be emblematic of the relationships in question.

This chapter starts, then, with a conceptual discussion in which I develop and elaborate the reasons behind the assertion that "embedding" and "compromise" increasingly occur in globalized knowledge networks. It then turns to an examination of particular arrangements in finance and trade and how these have changed since the period to which Ruggie applied the label *embedded liberalism*.

CONCEPTUALIZING GLOBALIZATION, EMBEDDEDNESS, AND COMPROMISE TODAY

In this section I discuss the concept of embeddedness. While noting its significance in Ruggie's original formulation, I go beyond this usage to point out how it can be linked conceptually to networks rather than to territorial states. In both cases, embeddedness challenges economic liberal and political realist rationalistic approaches in stressing the role of norms. I then turn to the concept of compromise, indicating the ways in which changes in embeddedness have influenced changes in the character of social compromises.

EMBEDDEDNESS

Social scientists have used embeddedness to refer to the dependence of interactions among individual actors on the institutional context within which they take place. Institutions can be formal, such as legally constituted organizations, or informal, such as sets of tacit business practices. Although this approach to the relationship between individual actors and institutions has a long lineage dating back to Durkheim and beyond, there has been a distinctive and more contemporary set of approaches that, in contrast to the macrosocial character of earlier theorizing, focuses on the rich variation in institutions that shape interactions in particular settings, including specific markets.

In an influential contribution, Granovetter (1992a) distinguishes the notion of embeddedness from both "undersocialized" approaches to norms, which assume that transactions can operate without institutions, and "oversocialized" approaches, which assume that a generalized morality or the imperatives of social norms are mechanical: "a force that insinuates itself into the minds and bodies of individuals (as in the movie *Invasion of the Body Snatchers*), altering their way of making decisions" (57). The notion of embeddedness, in contrast, analyzes "how behaviour is embedded in concrete, ongoing systems of social relations" (Granovetter 1992b, 6).[2] As such, it differs as well from the new institutional economics of North, Williamson, and others, in which institutions are seen as very important but also as efficient outcomes of a market-like process of competition among alternative types of transactions: "[E]conomic institutions do not emerge automatically in response to economic needs. Rather they are constructed by individuals whose action is both facilitated and constrained by the structure and resources available in social networks in which they are embedded" (Granovetter 1992b, 7).

As Granovetter (1992a) notes, often people think of embeddedness as involving a rootedness in territorially defined spaces, especially traditional local communities, and thus vulnerable to contemporary changes:

> It has long been the majority view among sociologists, anthropologists, political scientists and historians that such [embedded] behavior was heavily embedded in social relations in premarket societies but became much more autonomous with modernization. This view sees the economy as an increasingly separate, differentiated sphere in modern society, with

economic transactions defined no longer by the social or kinship obligations of those transacting but by rational calculations of individual gain. It is sometimes further argued that the traditional situation is reversed: instead of economic life being submerged in social relations, these relations become an epiphenomenon of the market. (53)

Similarly, Giddens (1991) writes about globalization as involving processes of "disembedding": the "'lifting out' of social relations from local contexts and their rearticulation across indefinite tracts of time-space" (18).

A number of analyses consistent with the idea of embeddedness have challenged the notion of globalization as a fluid force operating independently of institutions by also stressing the enduring importance of local territorial rootedness. An example is the literature on "glocalization" (which highlights the importance for the global economy of particular districts, such as Silicon Valley, with conglomerations of technical expertise and infrastructure—see Cox 1997). Similarly, scholars such as Thrift and Leyshon (1994) and Sassen (1995) have stressed the importance of financial districts for the governance of global finance. In all these cases, part of the importance of the *place* in question is the physical proximity of parties in interactions involving trust or tacit knowledge that are not well suited to more long-distance means of communication such as e-mail. At the same time, territory is important in the way it stabilizes the community, such as through a built architectural environment or a technical system that would be costly to move.

Ruggie's use of "embedded" in his 1982 article is consistent with this tendency to see action as shaped by territorially grounded norms. Ironically, given the widespread use in the field of international relations of the concept of "embedded liberalism," Ruggie passes quite quickly over the significance of "embedded," instead focusing on the meaning of the two words together:

> My starting point, of course, is the institutional nexus of embedded liberalism. Within this framework, it will be recalled, multilateralism and domestic stability are linked to and conditioned by one another. Thus, movement toward greater openness in the international economy is likely to be coupled with measures designed to cushion the domestic economy from external disruptions. (Ruggie 1982, 405)

Nevertheless, Ruggie's usage is consistent with others in the way in which embedding is counterposed to the more fluid character of orthodox liberalism with its emphasis on unconstrained free trade: from Ruggie's perspective trade takes place within a framework of norms grounded in the territorial state.

Despite the widespread tendency to see embedding as involving local and territorial rootedness, there are a number of reasons to consider the possibility that interactions can be embedded in the shared knowledge and practices of international networks as well. The idea that it is a network rather than a local place that is the locus of contemporary embeddedness is consistent with Granovetter's (1992b) use of the term: actions are "embedded in ongoing networks of personal relations" (4). But can networks that are not primarily rooted in particular places or other territorial locations possess the type of continuity that is needed to make them more than ephemeral ad hoc groupings of individuals? There are a number of reasons to expect that the type of technically oriented knowledge that characterizes these networks can provide a foundation for embedded norms that is comparable to the foundation provided by territorially rooted communities.

One reason to think that embedding can occur in international networks is that well-established routines and practices can themselves often provide a solid foundation for sustaining continuities even without being rooted in particular places. When these are oriented toward a shared pragmatic goal they can have a technical character even if those involved in reproducing them are not themselves technical experts. From the point of view of individual actors, these routines and practices appear as a constraint that cannot be changed if one wants to engage in the activities they govern. Giddens (1991), in discussing "disembedding," stresses the way in which abstract systems, including systems of codified knowledge, provide a "posttraditional" alternative to local communities, sustaining trust and shaping interactions.

In international affairs, considerable work has been done to identify the role of transnational networks concerned with social change. Sikkink (2002), in the conclusion to a collection of empirically oriented chapters on transnational social movements, draws on Ruggie's emphasis on the importance of social purpose to argue that:

> When we see social purpose (or norms and discourses) as a co-determinant of international structure, and if social purpose does not always derive from power, it becomes theoretically and empirically important to consider how these new international norm structures of social purpose are constructed, maintained, and transformed . . . because non-state actors are crucial for the creation of new norms and discourses we can speak of these actors as engaged in a process of *restructuring world politics*. (302)

A similar point also can be made with regard to actors that are more closely entwined with traditional policy-making processes. "Policy networks" is a concept that has been used to refer to the way in which state and non-state actors often work together in institutionalized ways to produce public policies, especially in specialized policy fields. Certain types of policy networks have been identified and these display continuities across time and across jurisdictions, suggesting the type of inertia, either stemming from the functional character of a policy field or from the weight of tradition, in which norms can be embedded. Scholars who have specialized in the comparative study of policy networks in domestic contexts have noted that these networks are becoming globalized (Coleman and Perl 1999).

Work on global commodity and value chains and actor-network theory (Dicken et al. 2001; Gereffi et al. 2005) provide a great deal of insight into the links that sustain the ability of suppliers, buyers, producers, consumers, and other actors to play their respective parts in integrating far-flung transnational production, marketing, and consumption processes. These links can involve, for instance, the dominance of a large retailer over suppliers, but also frequently involve standards. Technical artifacts, such as electronic networks, can also be important in sustaining these links.

Technical systems that are international can play an especially important role in embedding norms. Technology, unlike some other forms of knowledge, is often embedded in machine systems. For instance, technical specifications regarding the character of a production process can be reinforced by the physical configuration of the machines involved or of the operating manuals that are guides to how the machines should be operated. Examples of technical systems that can cross borders include air, sea, road, and rail transport; information processing and communication systems; financial systems; electrical systems; radio systems; chemical and oil pipeline systems—and, more generally, any globalized industry in which cross-border coordination involves mechanisms or objects with a physical dimension. Technical systems also are likely to be able to provide the type of foundation needed for embedding norms because their complexity makes alteration of any particular part difficult. For instance, introducing a light bulb with nonstandard voltage is difficult when electrical grids are configured to deliver a particular voltage.

The technical character of some bodies of knowledge can be an important foundation for embeddedness even where the material dimension of the system is relatively unimportant. For instance, it is difficult for individual actors that do not control the system as a whole to produce new software that is not compatible with existing configurations. While this is especially the case with applied technical knowledge, it is also relevant for more abstract and "pure" scientific paradigms—since philosophers of science such as Kuhn and Lakatos began to stress the embeddedness of particular research projects within larger-scale scientific worldviews or research programs, it has been recognized that there is an element of path dependence in the production of scientific knowledge. In between pure science and knowledge embodied in machines there are a wide variety of systems of technically oriented knowledge that operate simultaneously as a summation of past lessons learned and a guide to future best practices and are therefore well suited to sustaining the continuity of norms over time.

COMPROMISE

Even if it is agreed that norms can be embedded in transnational networks as well as in territorial spaces, in what respect would it be possible to say that these systems of embedded norms can be of any relevance to the type of *compromise* on which Ruggie focused? Ruggie's compromise of embedded liberalism was highly political and the above ways in which norms can be embedded transnationally seem to work against the possibility of political compromise in their distance from the type of state institutions—such as legislatures or diplomatic negotiations—that have traditionally been the places in which such political compromises are developed and in their reliance on technical knowledge, which is often seen as apolitical. This seems especially evident in the case of technical systems, but even for transnational policy networks or social movements it is not obvious that it would be possible to develop or to sustain the scale of compromise that Ruggie identified.

A first point to be made is that the compromise of embedded liberalism was not as robust as it appeared at the time that Ruggie wrote about it. Problems of state fiscal and organizational capacity in general, combined with the inadequacy of solutions reliant on relatively autonomous territorial states managing their own population and borders for dealing with globalized conflicts and hardships, had already begun to undermine the compromise of embedded liberalism. Today the old embedded liberalism is even less viable. Thus, the capacity of transnational networks to sustain compromises should not be compared to the old embedded liberalism as a transhistorical ideal, but rather with respect to the capacities of these two types of arrangements to sustain compromises in response to the distinctive problems of the historical period in which they have been devised.

There are two ways in which transnational networks—or nonterritorial networks that may primarily operate within one jurisdiction but are not tied to it in any specific way—can contribute to the type of compromise that addresses concerns of citizens about the negative consequences of globalization sufficiently to allow economic globalization to proceed—the role played by Ruggie's embedded liberalism. The first, which operates at an individual level, is the way in which transnational networks offer new types of freedom in exchange for acceptance of higher levels of risk. The second, which operates at a more social level, is the acceptance of networks as an alternative form of conflict resolution and compromise to that provided by the territorial state in the period Ruggie examined—a form that is consistent with the higher levels of globalization we are experiencing today. While it is not yet clear that transnational networks will ultimately be able to sustain a compromise equivalent in its viability to embedded liberalism, both the degree to which they are being relied upon and the degree to which they have so far contributed to a sufficient compromise for globalization to proceed are significant. In the remainder of this section I discuss these points in turn.

At the individual level there has been a very dramatic shift away from the idea that governments should use large society-wide measures to protect and compensate citizens with regard to the negative effects of globalization.

There are certainly some important exceptions connected to particular traditional economic policy fields such as agriculture or steel, but even these are more limited in time or scope than the more comprehensive measures in the period considered by Ruggie. Part of the change is a change in values—a shift from an ethic of collective national responsibility to an ethic of individual postnational responsibility—but another part is a practical change in the degree to which individuals can access opportunities with a global dimension through transnational networks that compensate them for the added international risks to which they are subjected.

The way in which this change is manifested simultaneously at the macrosocial and individual level is captured by Beck (2002a):

> We live in an age in which the social order of the national state, class, ethnicity, and the traditional family is in decline. The ethic of individual self-fulfillment and achievement is the most powerful current in modern society. The choosing, deciding, shaping human being who aspires to be the author of his or her own life, the creator of an individual identity, is the central character of our time. (165)

Yet this individualism does not involve atomization, but rather involves a connection and negotiation with a variety of social roles and the nonterritorial networks of specialized bodies of knowledge that sustain them:

> [T]he more tradition loses its hold, and the more daily life is reconstituted in terms of the dialectical interplay of the local and the global, the more individuals are forced to negotiate lifestyle choices among a diversity of options . . . reflexively organized life-planning, which normally presumes consideration of risks as filtered through contact with expert knowledge, becomes a central feature of the structuring of self-identity. (Giddens 1991, 5)

There is an ambiguity in this because it involves both a sense of liberating freedom and a crushing burden of responsibility: "[Y]our own life—your own failure. Consequently, social crisis phenomena such as structural employment can be shifted as a burden of risk on to the shoulders of individuals. Social problems can be directly turned into psychological dispositions: into guilt feelings, anxieties, conflicts, and neuroses" (Beck 2002a, 167).

An example is the way in which some gendered tensions are resolved not by national initiatives such as child-care programs, but by "global care chains" in which women from developing countries, leaving their children in their home country in the care of others, provide care to children in industrialized countries, facilitating the ability of those children's mothers to work (Hochschild 2000). The compromise is apparent in the terribly ambivalent feelings of the migrant caregivers who feel that the opportunity they provide for themselves and their children comes with the almost unbearable sense of loss of missing their children's childhood (ibid.). In this case the trust needed to sustain the networks is fostered by the personal relations of the migrating women. Another example is the shift in personal finances from state pensions to individual financial planning involving an international dimension. In both cases the enormous degree to which experiences of these changes differ depending on one's social class is evident—nevertheless, the sense that there are compensations that come along with increased international risk extend sufficiently across social classes to sustain a significant degree of toleration of these changes, or at least to forestall the emergence of widespread organized opposition to them.

At a more social level, acceptance of networks as a mechanism of conflict resolution and compromise that compensates for the decline of the more traditional state-centric mechanisms associated with embedded liberalism is connected to a number of properties of networks that legitimize them. Two such sets of properties are especially important. The first is the degree to which nonterritorial networks can be seen as an expression of long-range historical tendencies that are accepted because we are used to them. The second and related set of properties are related to characteristics of networks that correspond to widely accepted values that are also present in our acceptance of other types of authoritative practices, including more traditional territorially based democratic ones.

Many theorists have argued that a long-range characteristic of modernity has been the degree to which political authority increasingly operates by coordinating or mobilizing fields of organized activity that have a high degree of autonomy themselves. This is, for instance, the case with Luhmann's (1982) treatment of politics as one among many relatively incommensurable differentiated subsystems, each with its distinctive codes, involving, for instance, truth for science, love for family, or money for the economy (Chernilo 2002, 439). Another example is the literature on "governmentality" inspired by Foucault's work (Foucault et al. 1991), which sees the state as increasingly involved not in directly controlling the conduct of citizens, but instead in coordinating among practices that foster self-regulation. Analyses such as these highlight the degree to which the reduction of the state's role to being a participant in a set of increasingly nonterritorial political networks, which mainly function by coordinating among other relatively autonomous networks, is the culmination of a long historical trend which we accept because we are used to it.

We can also identify a number of properties of most knowledge-based networks that are consistent with contemporary values that legitimize authority. These include performance that is reflexively evaluated relative to standards of conduct shared by (and constitutive of) the network. A pragmatic performance orientation is a key source of legitimacy for contemporary sources of authority. Networks also may include properties of openness to new participants and a capacity to justify the activity of the network with reference to the standards and performance of other networks and fields of practice. This type of openness and linkage of activities to generalized principles is also a key source of legitimacy for contemporary types of authority. Politics and law play an especially important role in providing a medium of communication for this type of justification. Where transnational networks do not possess these properties they are widely considered to be illegitimate, as with terrorist networks. However, those that possess these properties have a significant capacity to legitimize themselves as sources of authority that are an alternative or complement to traditional forms of democratically legitimized territorial states.

Giddens (1991) comments on this process:

> Awareness of the frailties and limits of abstract systems is not confined to technical specialists. Few individuals sustain an unswerving trust in the systems of technical knowledge that impinge on them, and everyone, whether consciously or not, selects among the competing possibilities of action that such systems (or disengagement from them) provide. Trust often merges with pragmatic acceptance: it is a sort of "effort-bargain" that the individual makes with the institutions of modernity. (23)

There is also compromise in the acceptance of difference. As Beck (2002a) puts it somewhat overstatedly:

> Those who live in this post-national global society are constantly engaged in discarding old classifications and formulating new ones. The hybrid identities and cultures that ensue are precisely the individuality which then determines social integration. In this way, identity emerges through intersection and combination, and thus through conflict with other identities . . . the public realm no longer has anything to do with collective decisions. It is a question not of solidarity or obligation but of conflictual coexistence. (169)

In short, citizens accept the role of transnational networks in bringing about embedded compromises because they see these networks on balance as a pragmatic extension of existing political trends, because these networks bring them benefits personally, or because they see the networks as producing the types of benefits for others that they consider to be legitimate. Those transnational networks that they regard with suspicion may be tolerated simply because they know they could oppose them but do not wish to expend the effort to do so.

How adequate are these new mechanisms of compromise likely to be? It is clear that they exhibit bias toward those with knowledge or other resources, but this was the case for embedded liberalism as well. In the period about which Ruggie was writing, not all countries had the resources to protect their citizens from the negative effects of international economic integration, and even in those countries that did, not all citizens were equally protected. It is also clear that remnants of the more traditional mechanisms of compromise and legitimation persist, and thus these new ones do not have to fully substitute for the earlier mechanisms. These new mechanisms allow compromise within transnational networks, as with policy networks involving public sector, private sector, and civil society actors. They also allow compromise through the creation of new transnational networks to address problematic effects produced by the activity of other networks, as with the creation of networks to encourage labor standards in the apparel industry in response to the creation of global apparel production networks. Despite the bias of transnational networks toward those with resources, they can be mechanisms of compromise between those harmed by globalization and those benefiting from it. Embedded compromises, whether Ruggie's embedded liberalism or the compromises embedded in nonterritorial networks, do not mean that political and social conflict and inequality end. Rather, it means that they are managed and systemic crisis is avoided. Indeed, it may be the case that compromise can forestall the type of conflict that would otherwise lead to more just or desirable arrangements.

STANDARDS, CODES, TECHNICAL AUTHORITY, AND THE STATE'S ROLE IN EMBEDDED TRANSNATIONAL COMPROMISES

The above subsections have suggested that the embedding of norms continues to be important and that this is increasingly likely to be carried out in nonterritorial knowledge-based networks, rather than in the traditional territorially rooted communities with which embedded norms are often associated. The previous subsection, drawing on Beck and Giddens, has explored the way in which the networks within which norms are embedded may sustain compromises that foster the social integration of individuals, their acceptance of the character of this integration, and the provision of certain mechanisms that facilitate their management of risk. The key differences with the type of compromise identified by Ruggie (1982) are in the greater decentralization, globalization, and reliance on technical knowledge of these contemporary arrangements.

Sociologists such as Beck and Giddens have a tendency to underestimate the enduring importance of the state, and it is important to recognize that state-led international negotiations have hardly faded away, as is evident with regard to the Doha Round of trade negotiations, the Marrakech agreement on the implementation of the Kyoto Protocol on climate change, and countless other ongoing diplomatic activities. However there are reasons, despite the state's continued prominence, to see its role as having changed significantly, especially with regard to the type of social compromise involving citizens and markets that Ruggie highlighted.

A key difference is the degree to which the state reinforces and stands behind standards, codes, and more formalized laws that are developed and negotiated in networks rather than in conventional diplomatic settings. Sometimes these networks are more oriented toward the public sector, as with the policy areas in which the Organization for Economic Cooperation and Development (OECD) is influential, or in the detailed sectoral negotiations on finance, telecommunications, or intellectual property in the Uruguay Round. In other cases they are primarily nongovernmental, as with the chemical industry's Responsible Care standards for chemical safety or the International Corporation for Assigned Names and Numbers (ICANN) that governs the Internet (Franda 2001).

The role of the state may vary. It may, for instance, include (1) financial and other support for standards research; (2) financing of the negotiation and administration of voluntary standards; (3) coordination across related bodies of nongovernmental voluntary standards; (4) the use of references to voluntary standards in mandatory government standards; (5) licensing (for instance, professional licensing of accountants and others involved in the monitoring of firms or the inclusion of compliance with voluntary standards in the granting of licenses to those firms); and (6) the use of state power as a backup in cases in which voluntary standards fail or to ensure that private standards are followed. Laws can be used by private actors to obtain legal remedies against other private actors. Similarly, uses by firms of private codes, such as human rights codes, can be considered by regulators and courts when assessing their behavior (Government of Canada 1998).[3]

While an increased reliance by the state on standards and codes can be seen in part as resulting from conventional political factors such as regulatory cost-effectiveness or regulatory capture, it also can be seen as related to the features of contemporary embedded compromises as discussed above. In contrast to traditional statutory law or detailed "command and control" regulation, standards and codes are the types of norms that are especially well suited to being embedded in the shared knowledge and practices of transnational networks and also to embodying the type of social compromises that in other times might have been negotiated among states. This is because they allow a wide variety of concerned actors to participate in their development and implementation, because they draw on pragmatic bodies of shared knowledge, and because they permit flexibility in implementation and revision. Standards and codes combine the "ought" and the "is," facticity and validity (Habermas 1998) that are characteristic of traditional law—but without the inflexibility and centralization of the latter.

SOME EXAMPLES

Some evidence for or against the conceptual points made in the preceding sections can be provided by comparing the arrangements that governed citizens' relationship to global markets in the period about which Ruggie was writing, and the corresponding arrangements today. I start with finance and money before moving to production and trade.

Finance and Money Then and Now

It is clear that there has been massive change between the 1960s and 1970s and the present day with regard to international money and finance—but does this involve structural change of the type identified above?

Geoffrey Garrett is perhaps the best-known international relations scholar focusing empirically on the question of whether globalization has eroded the state's capacity to sustain social programs. Along with others, he has pointed out that many of the more extreme fears that social programs would be decimated are overstated. Barriers to global financial integration continue to exist, state spending has often increased with globalization as the needs of citizens for support has increased, and considerable variation in levels of social spending persist across countries, suggesting that there is no inevitable "race to the bottom." In general, he concludes that "there is still a compromise of 'embedded liberalism'—in other words an open international order is accepted since it is combined with domestic policies that cushion short-term market losers" (Garrett 2000a). He goes on to say:

> [T]oday, however, the compromise is increasingly dependent upon the political power of the left and organized labour. In social-democratic-corporatist regimes, governments seek simultaneously to enjoy the benefits of market integration, but also to shield their most vulnerable citizens with extensive public provision of social services and income transfers. In contrast, under more "market liberal" regimes, the insulating effects of the public economy against market-generated risk and inequality are being eroded. (129)

Thus, the social compromise is no longer a generalized one agreed among states as expressive of a commitment that they all share, but is, rather, associated with the strength of certain particular political tendencies. To some degree these political initiatives based on the nation-state can be seen as counterevidence to this chapter's claim that such initiatives are being displaced by compromises embedded in transnational networks. On the other hand, much of the evidence that Garrett presents to counter overstatements about globalization is likely to be attributable to the inertia of previous periods rather than an indication of contemporary social purpose. For instance, enduring barriers to cross-border financial mobility may have more to do with the inadequacy of market institutions to handle such transactions than with the protective intentions of governments. Similarly, increases in social spending may be more related to automatic increases in previously agreed payments as people are thrown out of work or age than to signaling governments' current attitudes to protecting citizens.

Additionally, contemporary social democratic initiatives are themselves more reliant on the mobilization of networks of labor unions and other supporters than was the case in the period in which embedded liberalism was a state policy that was only incrementally affected by mobilized parties.

There are numerous indications of a sea change in attitudes of governments with regard to protecting citizens from the effects of international markets. Even among the types of social democratic governments to which Garrett referred above, initiatives such as the "Third Way" sponsored by Tony Blair and other influential actors are most notable for their desire to shift social democratic politics in the direction of greater enthusiasm for openness toward international markets. A similar shift is evident among developing countries, even those that question the "Washington Consensus" (Gore 2000). More generally, one government after another has removed the types of controls on currencies and capital flows that shielded domestic economies in an earlier period (Goodman and Pauly 1993). Similarly, over the past decade there has been an upsurge in the number of bilateral investment treaties in which governments have legally bound themselves to guaranteeing liberalized access of foreign investors to their national markets—and these currently include a very large number negotiated between developing countries (UNCTAD 2000a). Financial services have been brought into the trade regime at the WTO and the liberalization of cross-border financial transactions is even more advanced among the members of the European Union.

The international financial crises of the past decade provide a useful indicator of contemporary attitudes toward protecting citizens from the negative consequences of global financial markets. The Mexican crisis of 1994, the East Asian and Russian crises of 1997 and 1998, and the Argentine crisis of 2002 all created near-catastrophic hardship for their citizens. While initially there was a tendency to put the full responsibility for the crisis on the emerging market governments and economies that were at the center of the crisis, with complaints about "crony capitalism" or exchange rate mismanagement, this began to be replaced by a recognition that the problem also stemmed from deficiencies at the global level—in the "international financial architecture" (Volcker 2000). Reform of the international financial architecture was a major preoccupation of the G7 and other governments beginning with the Halifax Summit of 1995 and continuing to the present day.

There are two ways in which these developments indicate that the old compromise of embedded liberalism is defunct. The first is the fact that these crises happened. Commentary on the deficiencies of the international architecture varies in the degree to which liberalization is seen as the problem. The G7's emphasis is on the need for stricter international rules that would bring emerging markets into conformity with existing practices in the G7, while others have put more stress on what is seen as an excessively aggressive, self-interested, and irresponsible promotion of rapid international financial liberalization by the US government and US financial firms. However, even in the former case, the G7, the IMF and others have acknowledged that financial liberalization was too rapid, in stressing the need for proper "sequencing"—that is, making sure a viable regulatory structure is in place nationally before opening a country to cross-border financial flows. Thus, it is clear that states permitted or encouraged a degree of liberalization that led to the type of hardship for citizens that the compromise of embedded liberalism was designed to prevent.

Second, in their response to the crises, states generally did not choose to return to the earlier ways of insulating citizens by creating barriers at national borders. There were some exceptions: the Malaysian government's successful use of capital controls and the Chinese government's ability to insulate itself from international financial crises were important for those countries' citizens, but also as evidence for the international community of the continued usefulness of national barriers. As well, Attac and other NGOs enjoyed some success at putting the idea of taxes on cross-border financial flows (such as the Tobin tax) onto the international agenda. Even the official international financial institutions such as the IMF and World Bank began to acknowledge that capital controls could be useful in some circumstances. However, overall the emphasis in official discussions about the international financial architecture was not about the reintroduction of controls at the border, but rather on the establishment of a variety of multilateral standards and codes that would assist in better managing a globalized financial system.

These financial standards and codes fit well with the analytical points made in the conceptual sections of the chapter above. The G7 created a new institution, the Financial Stability Forum, to monitor and promote these standards and codes, but they are a disparate collection of sets of codes that are being developed and implemented in a variety of institutional settings (see Table 6.1). The "issuing body" varies from the centralized and formal organizations of the IMF and World Bank, to the informal committees such as the Committee on Payment and Settlement Systems (CPSS) at the Bank for International Settlements. Two private sector bodies are included, the International Accountings Standards Board and the International Federation of Accountants. The prominence of bodies other than big centralized formal organizations is one indication of the importance of decentralized arrangements in the development and implementation of these standards and codes. As well, in all cases, networks of technical experts that cut across formal organizational boundaries are carrying out the development of these standards. Also, their successful implementation depends on their incorporation into the ongoing practices of the target actors, including firms and states. Considerable effort has been expended in seeking to determine what types of standards and codes would lend themselves to being used in the ongoing routines and risk models of market actors. Since the FSF itself is relatively informal

TABLE 6.1
The FSF's Key Standards for Sound Financial Systems

Subject Area	Key Standard	Issuing Body
Macroeconomic Policy and Data Transparency		
Monetary and financial policy transparency	Code of Good Practices on Transparency in Monetary and Financial Practices	IMF
Fiscal policy transparency	Code of Good Practices in Fiscal Transparency	IMF
Data dissemination	Special Data Dissemination Standard · General Data Dissemination Standard	IMF
Institutional and Market Infrastructure		
Insolvency	Principles and Guidelines on Effective Insolvency Systems	World Bank
Corporate governance	Principles of Corporate Governance	OECD
Accounting	International Accounting Standards	IASB
Auditing	International Standards on Auditing	IFAC
Payment and settlement	Core Principles for Systematically Important Payment Systems	CPSS
Market integrity	The Forty Recommendations of the Financial Action Task Force on Money Laundering	FATF
Financial Regulation and Supervision		
Banking supervision	Core Principles for Effective Banking Supervision	BCBS
Securities regulation	Objectives and Principles of Securities Regulation	IOSCO
Insurance supervision	Insurance Supervisory Principles	IAIS

Source: FSF. For acronyms see hyperlinks at www.fsforum.org.

and primarily functions by bringing together representatives of other regulatory and standard setting bodies along with representatives from G7 states, it too can be seen as a network—indeed, it is a network of networks.

Changes in official discussions about providing finance for development also illustrate the shift from an earlier period of embedded liberalism to the emphasis on networks today. After World War II there was a sense of international responsibility for building up the capacity of developing countries through development assistance. This was a dimension of the compromise of embedded liberalism since it helped developing country governments shield their populations from the effects of a liberalizing economy. The fear on the part of the United States and other wealthy states that developing countries would follow communist or other forms of state-led opting out of the global economy corresponded to the concern about their own citizens' potential opposition to liberal trade. State spending through foreign aid or social welfare programs was seen as the solution.

Beginning in the 1980s a significant shift in official discussions about financing for development began to occur. Through the 1990s a heavy emphasis was put on private capital flows and efforts were made to reorient state policies, at both the national and multilateral levels, toward policies that would facilitate those flows instead of trying to directly intervene in the economy or provide social assistance. However, by the end of the 1990s it had become increasingly clear that the well-being of huge swathes of the world's population was not improving, or declining, and that a backlash against globalization was beginning to build.

There are numerous ways in which wealthy countries have sought to respond to this backlash, including, after September 11, through the use of military force against Islamic extremism, but with regard to financing for development there has been an upswing in interest in reinvigorating efforts to alleviate global inequality, as discussed in the chapters by Thérien and Pauly in this volume. Those chapters emphasize the role of intergovernmental organizations in this process, and in doing so emphasize the continuities with the international dimensions of the earlier grand compromise, with its emphasis on the role of states. It is useful, however, to also note the key differences from the earlier period in the role played in this by standards, codes, and knowledge networks.

A very prominent feature of recent efforts to address the global social problems that have accompanied globalization through financing for development is the degree to which they rely on knowledge networks in their formulation and implementation. In contrast to the earlier period in which one or more states or intergovernmental organizations worked through all the standard stages of the policy process on their own, including agenda setting, formulation, decision, implementation and evaluation, the current process is characterized by a complex web of interactions between formal and informal public sector and nongovernmental actors that is held together as much by shared knowledge as by formal relations of authority.

Two events in 2005 illustrate this point. The first is the G8 summit hosted by the United Kingdom. The G8 is already far more informal than the intergovernmental organizations that Thérien and Pauly highlight, and an examination of the context of their intense focus on Africa and their commitment to double their development assistance at this meeting provides further evidence of the organizational differences from the earlier grand compromise. The G8 actions were an expression of both the legacy of their own summit process and the more formal process of the Millennium Development Goals. As Bayne (2005) notes, "The aim was to review progress under the Africa Action Plan launched at [the G8 Summit in] Kananaskis in 2002 and give it further impetus, looking ahead to the UN summit in September on the Millennium Development Goals (MDGs) and the WTO's Hong Kong ministerial in December 2005." Yet the summit was also interacting with the seven African leaders it had invited, with the New Partnership for Africa's Development (NEPAD), the G8's main interlocutor in Africa, with the Make Poverty History campaign, and with the Live 8 event that took place simultaneously in all G8 countries plus South Africa.

The second event was the presentation of the UN Millennium Project's report to UN Secretary-General Kofi Annan in January. The UN Millennium Project is an independent advisory body headed by Professor Jeffrey Sachs that notes, "[T]he research of the Millennium Project is performed by more than 265 development experts through 10 Task Forces. Each Task Force comprises independent experts drawn from academia, the public and private sectors, civil society organizations, and UN agencies."[4] This report provided a roadmap for the UN secretary-general's own report issued in March, to be considered by the meeting of states at the UN summit on Millennium Development the following September.

These two events display a combination of disaggregation and detail that are characteristic of the technical networks that are the focus of this chapter. Types of knowledge ranged from the basic and emotive awareness of poverty fostered through Live 8 to the highly detailed analysis of the Millennium Project report. The organizational effects of these are evident in the pressure they created on the G8 leaders to increase their aid commitments, but also in the case of the Millennium Project report, in the emphasis on measurable practical standards to foster accountability with governments. This parallels a similar emphasis on peer review in NEPAD, or with the World Bank–IMF Poverty Reduction Strategy Papers process that seeks to hold borrowing countries accountable to local plans created with civil society input.

In certain respects the US role appears to work against this emphasis on networks. UN Ambassador John Bolton, appointed in 2005, has distinguished himself for his hostility to the UN and to international NGOs. Soederberg (2004) has characterized the Millennium Challenge Account (MCA), in which the United States sets out sixteen eligibility criteria as an enhanced form of "preemptive" conditionality that parallels the US commitment to military preemption. Yet the MCA criteria are all based on indicators managed outside the US government, including the World Bank and

IMF, and the nongovernmental Freedom House, Institutional Investor, and the neoconservative Heritage Foundation (295). It therefore seems that it is a particular type of nongovernmental actor that the United States opposes, not nongovernmental actors in general.

The compromises in these arrangements occur at three levels. At one level there are constant negotiations over standards and codes that are specific to particular networks. At another level there is negotiation among governments about the creation of new networks to address problems at the margins that threaten to become serious enough to have implications for the system as a whole. At a third level there are networks of civil society actors (Scholte and Schnabel 2002) that seek to influence other networks or directly involve themselves in practical financial work, as with microfinancing networks that extend small loans in the world's poorest neighborhoods. None of these levels resembles the compromise of embedded liberalism—rather, the emphasis is on compromises involving transnational networks.

Trade and Production

International trade negotiations have taken governments into areas that were previously central to their capacity to shield citizens from international markets, including financial services, stricter disciplines on the use of antidumping measures and countervailing duties, and beginning to bring apparel and textiles and agriculture under the WTO's agreements. There are two ways in which this differs from the earlier period analyzed by Ruggie. First, the emphasis is on restricting governments' ability to take measures to shield their citizens from international market forces. Certainly, the reluctance of governments to include some areas that are most sensitive in this regard, including culture, health care, education, and social services, is a sign of an ongoing commitment of governments to some level of social protection. Nevertheless, the progressive removal of barriers and expansion of trade disciplines into new areas is an indication that the system established in the first four decades after World War II has been substantially altered.

Changes in the character of production that accompany these changes in the trade regime further illustrate the degree to which compromises have shifted from those negotiated among states to those negotiated through transnational networks. During the first four post–World War II decades there was a great emphasis in most countries on building national industries. Governments were involved in this by financing, and in the case of nationalized industries actually managing, key industries, by establishing trade barriers to protect national industries, and by seeking to promote national competence in technologies. During the 1970s and 1980s, when the system began to come under stress for a variety of reasons, including the oil shocks of 1973 and 1979, the rise of the newly industrializing countries, stagflation, and the demise of the Bretton Woods monetary regime, a wide range of trade conflicts emerged in these key industries. The widespread use of voluntary restraint agreements in automobiles, semiconductors, and steel brought these key industries into a similar set of relationships to those already set up in textiles and apparel: government-to-government negotiated market-sharing arrangements in which national industries were preserved and citizens shielded from the effects of global markets.

Today only steel continues to fit this pattern. Each of the other industries has been restructured in a way that integrates production in particular countries into a global network in which current capacity, new investment, and innovation are managed through private knowledge-intensive collaboration.[5] In automobiles there has been a complex set of strategic alliances binding together the already oligopolistic leading manufacturers such as GM, Toyota, Ford, and Honda. Although private actors are prohibited legally, on antitrust grounds, from market-sharing arrangements, these strategic alliances allow firms to manage their capacity and plan their production more effectively. These arrangements in turn are linked to a tendency to contract out an increasing proportion of the manufacturing process to parts firms, which range from the very large to the relatively small. Thus, citizens' participation in the auto industry is dependent not on the ability of their government and national firms to foster a capacity to supply the national market but rather their ability, together with the firms, schools, and governments to which they are connected, to play a part in the global production network.

In semiconductors, the state-led market-sharing arrangements to govern the hotly contested market for memory chips during the 1980s have been replaced by a division of labor in which US firms such as Microsoft and Intel specialize in and dominate the more technically complex microprocessor and software design segments while production facilities in other countries specialize in more commodified components such as memory chips, along with other computer hardware such as flat screens, or disk drives. Large multinational private firms collaborate in consortia such as SEMATECH or Si2 as well as in the World Semiconductor Council. As in the auto industry, market sharing is illegal but production and investment planning is facilitated by the exchange of highly detailed technical information and by joint research and development projects.

In textiles and apparel, most industrialized countries have shifted out of the labor-intensive aspects of the apparel industry and have specialized in the capital and knowledge-intensive segments of the synthetic textile industry, much of which is dominated by large multinational chemical companies such as Dupont, as well as in the design and marketing side of the apparel industry. The industry has been transformed into a globalized set of production networks in which different parts of an international chain of production are carried out in different countries (Dickerson 1999).

Norms embedded in globalized knowledge networks play a key role in the governance of each of these industries. For example, patents and licenses govern the relations among the leading firms that create technologies and the other parts of transnational production networks that need to use or conform to those technologies. In other cases, such as the International Technology Roadmap for Semiconductors developed by leading firms in the semiconductor industry, these are not as connected to the legal system but still structure the industry since all firms must conform to prevailing technical standards if they wish to produce products that are sufficiently compatible with others to be produced or used in conjunction with them. In yet other cases, access or conformity with fashion or marketing knowledge and the associated networks is vital for the viability of participating firms. In the literature on global value chains there has been a great deal of attention devoted to how firms from developing countries can upgrade their roles, for instance by increasing their knowledge of standards and interacting strategically with other actors, including the dominant ones in the value chain for which they produce (Dicken et al. 2001; Gereffi et al. 2005).

These arrangements involve a practical compromise among participants, but one that is very different from the compromise of embedded liberalism. Currently in these industries, access to transnational production networks is granted not primarily through state-to-state negotiations, but rather by negotiations among private actors working in a network arrangement. Governments at all levels seek to improve the prospects of their citizens in these negotiations, by investing in education, infrastructure, R&D, or by negotiating investment treaties to signal their commitment to the preferences of multinational firms engaging in inward direct investment. The compromise, which, in contrast to the earlier period, is not deliberately coordinated, is that sufficient numbers of actors are drawn into these production networks, even if most are in a subordinate position, to assure their acceptance of the system as a whole.

Transnational networks of civil society actors have also shaped compromises in production and trade, as with their role in defeating the negotiation of a multilateral agreement on investment at the OECD, and in bringing about a greater sensitivity to environmental and food safety matters and the public health implications of intellectual property restrictions on pharmaceuticals at the WTO. Transnational actors have increasingly involved themselves in the technical details associated with international production and trade issues. Some of the more promising initiatives of transnational social movements are those that tie into the types of production networks that this chapter has discussed. For instance, corporate codes of conduct with regard to labor or environmental standards are made more effective when they are taken up by leading firms and promoted by them through a chain of production to suppliers in countries around the world. Thus, the types of relatively depoliticized compromises that result in the integration of firms and citizens from different countries into production networks can involve a more politicized normative component as well. The successes of transnational networks in influencing developments in international negotiations and international production networks, while in part explained by the convergence of their interests with those of some states, is nevertheless significant, especially when contrasted to the overall failure of opponents of globalization to bring about a reintroduction at the national level of elements of a compromise of embedded liberalism.

CONCLUSION

The above examples from finance, trade, and production have provided support for this chapter's claim that the compromise of embedded liberalism is being replaced by a set of compromises embedded in knowledge-intensive transnational networks. There are other examples that could be explored. However, in the financial and production networks discussed above more abstract and codified knowledge is crucial, as in standards, codes, established routine practices, technologies, licenses, patents and so on. Transnational knowledge networks involve the distribution of opportunities for participation and reward across a variety of actors in different countries. Unlike arm's length markets, which also distribute resources in this way, knowledge networks involve norms, including standards and codes, which specify and justify more explicitly how those involved in the network should operate. The embedding of these norms in the routine practices of transnational networks institutionalizes relationships and solidifies compromises.

The above case studies have only touched upon the transnational networks that have been created by global social movements although further incorporating these into this analysis would provide additional support for the chapter's claim that transnational networks are a key source of compromise between social needs and international markets. Transnational social movement networks have been heavily involved in trade issues and have had some important successes in bringing about compromises at the global level in connection with the tension between social and economic issues. In the case of financial standards and codes, this type of influence is only beginning, and compromises rely more on negotiations and other discussions in public sector networks. In financing for development issues they have been very active. In these networks, highly technical standards and codes are integrated with rules and norms that reflect more political factors, such as the need to respect local institutions or to shift the costs of crisis away from citizens onto foreign investors.

This chapter's emphasis on the role of transnational networks in social compromise is not intended to suggest that global governance is necessarily heading in the direction of a pluralistic arrangement in which all can participate—an idealistic image, which is present in some of the work of theorists such as Giddens or in some accounts of global civil society. Networks also provide opportunities for leading firms or states to exercise their domination and to exploit weaker parties. Moreover, networks can create new boundaries of inclusion and exclusion, in which nonparticipants are denied access to important resources. These injustices, however, were present in the original compromise of embedded liberalism as well. In both periods, "compromise" signifies an *acceptance* of a set of relationships and not the implementation of an ethical ideal. At the same time, in both periods, compromise also signifies the possibility of negotiating change in a way that more fairly distributes resources, risks, and costs. It is important to identify the differences in the character of international embedded social compromises in the two periods in order to understand both their limitations and their possibilities.

NOTES

1. Sinclair (2000) provides an insightful analysis of "embedded knowledge networks," focusing especially on bond rating. The present chapter differs from his analysis in seeing these networks as present elsewhere than global finance and in considering their relationship to the earlier compromise of embedded liberalism.

2. On the concept of embeddedness, see also Hollingsworth and Boyer (1997).

3. This list is used as well in Porter and Coleman (2002).

4. See www.unmillenniumproject.org/who/index.htm, accessed August 8, 2005.

5. The information on industries in this and the following paragraphs is drawn from Porter (2002).

PART III

Integration and Fragmentation in Global Governance

SEVEN

Big Judgments, Elusive Phenomena, and Nuanced Analysis

Assessing Where the World Is Headed

JAMES N. ROSENAU

ORDER AND FRAGMENTATION have always been integral features of world affairs, but due to technological developments that have shrunk time and distance, today they are considerably more interactive than ever before. The tempo of global life within and among countries has accelerated to the point where it is plausible to assert that each increment of order gives rise to an increment of fragmentation, and vice versa. Such interactions have enormous implications for the prospects for coherent global governance on the basis of a grand compromise. If it is the case, as I have argued at length elsewhere (Rosenau 2003), that increasingly these pervasive interactions are shaped as much by individuals at the micro level as by collectivities at the macro level, and if it is assumed that the compromise would have to occur at the level of macro institutions and states without due allowance being made for microlevel processes that are increasingly important drivers of change and sufficiently diverse to inhibit, even prevent, coherence at the macro level, then it seems highly unlikely that a grand compromise can be forged.

And this low likelihood sinks even farther when it is appreciated that the shrinking of time and distance has also obscured the distinction between local and global circumstances, thereby rendering distant trends ever more proximate for the numerous individuals who once were inclined to regard events abroad as remote and unrelated to their daily routines. Among its many relevant consequences, the local-global overlap has considerably altered and confounded the kinds of bargains required for effective governance in the current era.

So as to stress and capture the extent of the tensions between order and fragmentation, I have long argued that their centrality to the course of events justifies a special label, one that highlights the ways in which the two contrary tendencies are inextricably linked to each other. My label for this linkage is "fragmegration," a term that derives in part from fragmentation and in part from integration and that has the virtue, despite its grating and contrived nature, of capturing in a single word these opposing tendencies and thus serving as a reminder of how closely they are interwoven. Indeed, I would argue that the best way to grasp global life today is to view it through fragmegrative lenses, to treat every circumstance and every process as an instance of fragmegrative dynamics. I submit that the kinds of tensions analyzed in the chapters of this volume, and the very "compromise" discussed in Ruggie's seminal article, are readily accommodated by such a perspective.

To appreciate the links between order and fragmentation it is important to recognize that both concepts are loaded with values, that one person's order is another's disorder, and that what is fragmentation for some is coherence for others. Both order and fragmentation, in other words, can be desirable or undesirable, depending on the value perspective through which they are assessed. Put more specifically, order can suggest group or societal arrangements that process issues peacefully and creatively, allowing diverse groups to participate freely in how the issues are handled; or it can connote a deadly stagnation and tyrannical hierarchy that inhibits free participation by those encompassed by the issues. Likewise, fragmentation can highlight the breakdown of coherence and the onset of chaos; or it can point to a pluralism that affords opportunities for various groups to pursue their goals. Table 7.1 depicts four different societal conditions and political forms that may prevail when the value dimensions of order and fragmentation are taken into consideration.

Once the analytic concepts of order and fragmentation are pondered in the context of value perspectives in this way, and irrespective of whether they

TABLE 7.1
Desirable and Undesirable Order and Fragmentation

	Order	Fragmentation
Desirable	centralized democracy	decentralized pluralism
Undesirable	tyranny	chaos

are approached with the Iraq war and the events of September 11, 2001, in mind, the question arises as to whether any of the four conditions constitute the central tendency at work in the twenty-first century. Quite aside from our preference for either of the two desirable conditions, are they likely to succumb in the long run to either of the two undesirable arrangements? Is the world headed for pervasive tyrannies and endless chaos? Or does humankind have the resources, imagination, and perseverance to sustain and expand some form of democratic order? In short, are fragmegrative dynamics likely to render the future insufferable or manageable?

In good part the answers to these questions must rest on empirical assessments, but they are equally rooted in our temperaments, our inclinations toward optimistic or pessimistic conceptions of the human condition. It is a mistake, I think, to resort to our professional training and treat the questions as simply a matter of gathering data and sifting them for evidence. Inevitably, our responses are rooted in either coherent value schemes or uncoordinated impressions and, as such, they amount to big judgments about elusive phenomena. In an intensely fragmegrative era neither limited judgments nor clear-cut phenomena can yield an adequate understanding of where humankind is headed. Perforce we must engage in nuanced analysis even as we give voice to our underlying impulses and intuitive feelings.

Furthermore, our nuanced analyses have to confront the reality that perforce they have to be developed in what elsewhere I have described as conceptual jails (Rosenau 1990, chapter 2). All of us are ensconced in one or another such jail, in theoretical frameworks that organize our responses to events and that tend to be so thorough as to prevent us from discerning possible responses not encompassed by our frameworks. For example, despite the profound ways in which the 9/11 attacks demonstrated the porosity and weaknesses of states and the high salience of nongovernmental actors, most of us continue to think in terms of national sovereignty and a state-centric world in which the interactions of national governments determine the course of events. It is a powerful jail, so solidly constructed and so lacking in exits that we quickly dismiss as "radical" any ideas that posit transnational institutions as the route to a new and more secure world order. Such institutions are not neglected, but neither are they viewed as alternatives to the state system. In the words of one analyst, we are blissfully unaware of "how mired we all are in the mud of nationalism, unable to devise a genuine transnational policy that will let us begin to function as citizens of the world" (Frankel 2002, 16). Similarly, even as we acknowledge that national sovereignty has undergone diminution and is caught up in profound transformative dynamics, so do we continue to treat it as a constant, as a core concept around which analysis must be organized.

CAN OPTIMISM BE JUSTIFIED?

The question is not easy for me. My temperament is pervasively optimistic, but my analytic antennae tell me that on a global scale the central tendencies may well unfold more toward tyranny and chaos than democracy and pluralism. I can readily construct scenarios in which global governance proves insufficient to cope with the potential for chaos that prevails in most parts of the world. Such a perspective derives not so much from the implications of 9/11 (though that is not a trivial aspect of the possible disarray), but more from the seemingly low, even very low, probability that global governance can effectively reduce the rich-poor gap, control the squalor of ever more crowded urban areas, fashion a modicum of worldwide consensus around a set of core values necessary to the predominance of democracy and pluralism, diminish environmental pollution, replenish the world's supplies of water, raise the income of the more than two billion people who presently earn less than $2 a day, bring a modicum of peace to the Middle East, re-orient the United States in the direction of multilateralism and sharing its wealth more fully, enable the peoples of Africa to lift themselves out of poverty and sickness—to mention only the more obvious problems that seem intractable and enduring.

Yet, an optimistic temperament will not yield readily to a parade of horribles. Further reflection allows for the nuanced possibility that the four conditions set forth in Table 7.1 are not necessarily mutually exclusive. Elsewhere I have argued that a prime characteristic of our fragmegrative circumstances is a widespread and persistent trend toward the disaggregation of authority as people everywhere become more skillful and adaptive with respect to the ways of the world and as the Internet and other microelectronic technologies proliferate organizations and facilitate the formation of horizontal networks that compete with or otherwise circumvent vertical authorities (Rosenau 1997, 61–64, 153–56). Viewed optimistically, at least parts of the disaggregated, networked world can amount as much to an order marked by constructive pluralism as to one mired in deleterious chaos. Indeed, the more disaggregated global governance becomes, the less will be the scope for tyrannies to operate effectively.

Put differently, the more authority is disaggregated, the more will new spheres of authority (SOAs) founded on new social contracts proliferate on the global stage.[1] Some of the emergent SOAs will be fashioned via top-down macro processes, but probably most will spring from bottom-up processes as people at the micro level become more skillful and active. The UN's Global Compact exemplifies the macro processes through which authority at the top initiates a spread of new SOAs. The corporations that signed onto the compact agreed to exercise their authority, each within their own domain, according to the compact's procedures and rules. In effect, each became a new or renewed SOA. An insightful example of the proliferation of bottom-up SOAs is the recent activation of global antiwar and antiglobalization movements, what journalists have called the "world's other superpower." But these movements are far from coherent structures. Rather, they encompass a wide variety of SOAs, each committed to their own set of particular issues that shape the way in which their authority gets exercised even as they converge and merge when circumstances—such as the war in Iraq or meetings of the boards of international financial institutions—evoke their shared concerns. The disorganized nature of their protest marches can be viewed as a measure of the extent to which different SOAs continue to operate on their own terms even as they come together in common cause on the streets.

In sum, the dynamics of fragmegration have led to the evolution of a wide variety of SOAs, as many as there are interests and issues that people feel need to be protected or advanced. Derived as it is from persistent and widespread disaggregation, the global agenda is thus huge and encompasses endlessly varied SOAs. One measure of this variability can be discerned in the fact that in Pakistan today there is an organization of car thieves, the Professional Car Lifters Union, which has officers, dues, a newsletter, and regular meetings (Ko 1998, 34). If a car-thief SOA can evolve, it is not difficult to imagine an ever more crowded global stage on which SOAs from every realm of human endeavor are active.[2]

It follows that it is in the framing and promotion of new social contracts that clues to the governability of fragmegration can be found: for in crucial ways it is the evolution of new SOAs, or the modification of old ones, composed as they are of interacting international and domestic micro actors and macro institutions, that the nature and direction of the new social contracts will be shaped and solidified. Otherwise, in the absence of interactions that help form the contracts for new or renewed SOAs founded on values that enable people to manage their distant proximities and thus make it possible for collectivities to remain intact and move toward their goals, it is reasonable to anticipate that the world is indeed headed for ever greater disarray—for circumstances in which, in effect, chaos prevails in the absence of social contracts.

Yet, a modicum of optimism can be salvaged by viewing the long-run future as likely to consist of pockets of democracy and pluralism managing to function and flourish in the face of widespread and pervasive tyrannies and chaos. Nor can one ignore the democratic and pluralistic institutions committed to overcoming tyranny and minimizing chaos. The power and competence of such institutions, both INGOs and NGOs, is limited, to be sure, but they can draw on deep reservoirs of good will to achieve global governance that is both effective and ennobling. If "effectiveness" is conceived in terms of the ability to generate compliance on the part of those toward whom authority is directed, then the reservoirs of good will can be drawn upon to enable SOAs to move toward their goals. Credit-rating and other standard-setting agencies offer good examples of effective governance on a global scale.

There is, moreover, a dialectic relationship between democratic or pluralistic order and tyrannical or chaotic fragmentation. As instances of fragmentation become more salient they trigger renewed efforts to move in integrative directions. The relationship between Europe and the United States before, during, and after the Iraq war is illustrative of this dialectic. It reminds one of the age-old dilemma of the liberal: ofttimes things need to get worse so as to unleash forces that strive to make them better.

TOWARD EMPIRICAL ASSESSMENTS

Quite apart from the judgmental dimensions of order and fragmentation, empirical analyses of their interactive dynamics present huge methodological problems. Among these, two come immediately to mind. One involves the challenge of tracing the causal paths that link the contradictory forces that sustain fragmegrative dynamics. The central question here is that of assessing when—and to what extent—increments of fragmentation give rise to increments of integration, and vice versa. Conceivably, the two processes can occur sequentially without being causally linked, a possibility that can be rejected if evidence is uncovered that points to individuals and groups being so concerned about the fragmentation that they vow or act to offset the unwanted linkage.

The second challenge focuses on the processes whereby individuals at the micro level shape and are shaped by the macro horizontal networks in which they participate. Micro-macro interactions are elusive phenomena. We know that they operate, that there can be no macro collectivities without micro inputs, but how these links unfold is an underresearched dimension of world affairs. I have sought to probe these interactions at some length, but it proved exceedingly difficult and I have no confidence that I succeeded (Rosenau 2003). In part, success was hampered by the absence of a literature that could provide guidance. One has to feel one's way and there are innumerable obstacles to distinguishing the impact of micro phenomena from the macro actions that would have otherwise occurred.

CONCLUSION

In sum, despite the obstacles, we cannot shy away from assessing where the world is headed. The prospects for order and fragmentation are too crucial to ignore. Collective perspectives voiced from our ivory tower may not always be accurate or informed, but they will be thoughtful and explicit, allowing for reconsideration and revision. Like other contributors to this volume, my present view is that the long-term future is not likely to incorporate a new grand compromise. Rather, I envision continents of desirable order and fragmentation surrounded by oceans of undesirable tyranny and chaos, with neither capable of encroaching on the other—a prolonged stalemate that is unlikely to yield to efforts at alteration in either direction. Too many of the emerging SOAs are products of narrow, self-interested, skillful, and locally oriented populations that are not about to risk their hard-won coherence and contracts for what they perceive as tenuous global bridges across oceans of chaos.

NOTES

1. For a full discussion of SOAs and their contracts, see Rosenau (2003, chapter 13).

2. For analyses of the proliferation and variability of emergent SOAs, see Boli and Thomas (1999); Cutler, Haufler, and Porter (1998); Hall and Biersteker (2002).

EIGHT

Currency Blocs and the Future of Embedded Liberalism

ERIC HELLEINER

INTRODUCTION

AN INTERESTING DEVELOPMENT within the global political economy of the early twenty-first century is the push for large currency blocs. The most dramatic example, of course, is in Europe where a new supranational currency is now being used by most of the existing members of the European Union. But in 1999 US policy makers also began to discuss the creation of a giant currency bloc in the Americas. Instead of proposing a new supranational currency, they began debating whether the United States should be encouraging countries in the region to simply adopt the US dollar. The US discussion about "dollarization diplomacy" has been paralleled by active discussions across Latin America on this question. Indeed, two countries—Ecuador and El Salvador—moved in 2000–2001 beyond discussions and adopted the US dollar as their currency.

What are the implications of this push for currency blocs for the future of embedded liberalism? In one sense, the potential challenge to the embedded liberal values of the postwar world seems clear. One of the central objectives of the Bretton Woods architects was to prevent a return to the currency blocs of the 1930s. They hoped to rebuild a multilateral monetary order with stable exchange rates to replace the prewar situation when relations *between* the giant currency blocs had been characterized by unstable floating exchange rates and the competition for power among leading states. Today, once again, unstable floating exchange rates exist between the major world currencies and many advocates of the euro and the dollar bloc see the creation of these blocs as part of a broader struggle for global influence between the EU and the United States.

In this chapter, however, I am more interested in exploring how the push for giant currency blocs today might challenge embedded liberal values *within* each bloc. The issue is a particularly interesting one to explore in the context of US policy toward Latin America. As I show in the first section of the chapter, the post-1999 US debate on dollarization stands in stark contrast to the 1940s when US policy makers went out of their way to *discourage* the circulation of the US dollar in Latin American countries. In that era, "dollarization" in Latin America was considered incompatible with embedded liberalism. Only by de-dollarizing, it was argued, could Latin American states support the kinds of social welfare goals that had become prominent at the national level in the wake of the Great Depression. In the second section, I show how the post-1999 supporters of dollarization diplomacy reject this earlier "social purpose" of US foreign policy. In its place, they embrace a "neoliberal" ideology which seeks instead to constrain the state's role in the economy. In the third section of the chapter, I show how this neoliberal shift in some US policy-making circles parallels a similar shift in Europe where the Economic and Monetary Union (EMU) project has also been strongly supported by neoliberals.

Does this then mean that the push for currency blocs signals an erosion of embedded liberalism in this second way? Not necessarily. In the US context, key policy makers have not yet been willing to embrace dollarization diplomacy and their caution has partly reflected their continued commitment to embedded liberal ideals. This opposition—as well as broader opposition across the Americas—has to date made the prospects for a dollar bloc unlikely. In the European context, embedded liberals have also continued to play an influential role in debates about the euro. Interestingly, however, many of them have thrown their support behind the EMU project, seeing it as a way to preserve embedded liberal values in a changing international and domestic economic context. Their support has been crucial in enabling the EMU project to succeed.

This chapter thus suggests that the ideology of embedded liberalism clearly remains significant within each region, although it is influencing the prospects for currency union in the two regions in quite opposite ways. In so doing, it reveals two distinct ways in which policy makers are seeking to preserve embedded liberal values in the contemporary world. In the case of the Americas, supporters of embedded liberalism continue to endorse the postwar view that its legitimacy should be grounded at the nation-state level. By contrast, many European policy makers are trying to preserve the compromise of embedded liberalism by shifting it upward to the regional level. In so doing, however, they risk creating a currency bloc whose relations with the outside world could increasingly challenge cooperative multilateral principles at the global level.

DOLLARIZATION AND EMBEDDED LIBERALISM IN US–LATIN AMERICAN RELATIONS

The US debate about dollarization diplomacy in the Americas is an important one for those concerned with the future of embedded liberalism. This is not just because the United States plays such a dominant role in the global political economy. Also important is the fact that US proponents of dollarization diplomacy are turning their backs on this ideology in ways that become particularly clear when we examine the current debate in historical perspective.

The emergence of an embedded liberal ideology in US foreign monetary policy making during the early 1940s is usually discussed only in the context of the Bretton Woods negotiations (Ruggie 1982). But this new ideology also had a profound, although less well-known, impact on US policy toward Latin America in this period. In fact, embedded liberal ideas influenced US foreign policy in this latter context *before* the former. The idea of building an international economic order based on embedded liberal principles was first born in US policy-making circles within this regional context. And it was an ideology that produced a very skeptical view of dollarization diplomacy among US policy makers at the time.

To understand the birth of embedded liberalism in US monetary policy toward Latin America, we must first look back to the pre-1931 era. In that period, US policy makers and private financiers played a lead role in encouraging many Latin American countries to adopt the gold standard and set up independent central banks that could guarantee its maintenance (e.g., Rosenberg 1985, 1999; Drake 1989). Indeed, the American Edwin Kemmerer became the most famous of the foreign "money doctors" promoting monetary reforms along these classical liberal lines across Latin America in the interwar period. He and his colleagues believed that US-led monetary reforms would bring price stability which, in turn, would boost the confidence of foreign investors and encourage the growth of domestic savings and financial markets.

In the early 1940s, US policy makers did an about-face. Explicitly rejecting Kemmerer's approach, they criticized the idea that the principal purpose of monetary policy in Latin America should be to maintain price stability and external equilibrium via the gold standard. Instead, they recommended that Latin American countries pursue activist domestically oriented monetary policies designed to promote rapid economic development. And they set out to promote this goal by developing a new comprehensive approach to regional economic cooperation between the United States and Latin America.

The first significant signs of this new approach came in a set of internal discussions within the US government in late May and early June of 1940. The key catalyst for these discussions was a fear that Germany might try to create formal economic arrangements with Latin American countries, thereby incorporating these countries within its economic bloc. Gardner (1964) notes that US policy makers had been concerned about the growing links between Latin American nationalists and the Axis powers since 1938 (chs. 6, 10). In June 1940, these concerns intensified because of reports that Germany was developing a plan for the postwar international economic order in Europe. At the time, Germany had conquered most of continental Europe, and Hitler had asked his economics minister Walter Funk to publicize how the postwar European economy would be structured. In late July 1940, Funk announced his proposed "New Order" involving the creation of a payments union whose members would maintain fixed exchange rates and free trade amongst themselves, and where trade imbalances would be covered by a central clearing office in Berlin. In trade with the outside world, members of the union would use bilateral clearing arrangements.

It is widely known that Funk's plan provided the prompt for Keynes to first begin thinking about the organization of the postwar international economic order. It is also often noted that Keynes's initial reactions to Funk's proposal were in fact quite positive. The proposal was, he argued, "excellent and just what we ought ourselves to be thinking of doing" (quoted in Skidelsky 2003, 143). Keynes made clear that he saw in Funk's "New Order" the beginnings of a way to build an alternative to the liberal monetary regime of the post–World War I period, an alternative that would endorse the use of such things as capital controls:

> After the last war *laissez-faire* in foreign exchange led to chaos. . . . But in Germany Schacht and Funk were led by force of necessity to evolve something better. In practice they have used their new system to the detriment of their neighbours. But the underlying idea is good and sound. (Skidelsky 2003, 144)

It is interesting to note, however, that Keynes also initially developed his thinking about an international economic order based on these new "embedded liberal" principles in a regional context rather than a global one. When he first put forward a very rough outline of his Clearing Union proposal in April 1941, it covered only the sterling area and did not involve the United States (Skidelsky 2003, 144). Like Funk's proposal, relations between the sterling bloc and the outside world were to be conducted on restrictive terms. Not until later in the fall of 1941—when the US commitment to Britain had become clearer—did he expand his ideas to involve a wider international economic order including the United States.

Prompted by the need to respond to Funk's plans, US officials also first developed their embedded liberal ideology in the regional context of US–Latin American relations. These proposals in fact appeared before those of Keynes. In an important June 10, 1940, memo, Emilio Collado (1940) of the US State Department noted the German planning and argued: "Obviously, we must adopt an inter-American economic program closely linked with our domestic, economic and defense programs, and calculated to permit this Government to resist economic and military aggression if necessary" (361).[1] He proceeded to outline "An Economic Program for the Americas" with proposals that looked quite familiar to some of those that later surfaced as central to the "embedded liberal" ideology of Bretton Woods—although once again only *within* the context of a relatively closed regional bloc.

In the trade realm, he suggested that the United States should offer tariff concessions and promise to buy surplus Latin American commodity exports (and perhaps even reach commodity agreements). He also discussed the possibility of creating a hemispheric trade and production organization. In the monetary and financial realm, he called for the United States to support loans for development purposes from an Inter-American Bank (as well as from the US Export-Import Bank). He also proposed the creation of a fund that could provide short-term "financial assistance to bridge emergency situations" (Collado 1940, 363). Interestingly, he noted that he had already been discussing this latter idea with Harry Dexter White: "I am continuing to explore this point with Dr. Harry White and other officials of the Treasury Department, whose views in general coincide with those expressed in this memorandum and those of officers of the Department" (Collado 1940, 363).

In an address to a meeting of the Inter-American Financial and Economic Advisory Committee on July 11, 1940, US Under Secretary of State Sumner Welles then publicly declared the US goal of promoting this new kind of "comprehensive program of vigorous economic cooperation" (Welles 1940, 371) among the nations of the Western Hemisphere. In explaining the purpose of this new cooperation, he made a special point of highlighting the new US focus on promoting domestic growth in the region:

> Not only must the economic activity of the hemisphere be maintained at the levels already achieved, but the productive capacity of the area and the standard of living of its populations must be increased in order to satisfy the legitimate aspirations of the several nations. It is the opinion of the Government of the United States that, in order to attain these ends, the nations of the Western Hemisphere should join together in a comprehensive program of vigorous economic cooperation, including measures . . . for the development of a healthy orientation and greater diversity of production within the hemisphere. (Welles 1940, 371)

In the monetary and financial realm, Welles (1940) noted that cooperation should include measures "for the avoidance of undue fluctuations in rates of exchange and the strengthening of monetary and exchange systems and institutions" (371). The meaning of the latter phrase soon became clear when the US Federal Reserve began to send technical missions to Latin American governments advising them to reform their domestic monetary systems in ways that would enable more activist policies designed to promote rapid economic development.[2] Where central banks did not yet exist, the United States insisted that they be created. And their charters were written with very different objectives than those of Kemmerer's central banks. To prevent international economic developments from disrupting policy autonomy, new and existing central banks across Latin America were encouraged to loosen the rigid provisions that had linked their note issue and deposit liabilities to gold or foreign exchange reserves. US officials also suggested that countries use capital controls and that they even consider adjusting their country's exchange rate within limits in certain circumstances. In addition, US officials insisted that central banks be equipped with strong powers to promote the development of their national economies, including the ability to control private lending, to lend directly to the public, and even to lend to their own governments.

Of particular significance to this chapter, the US money doctors in this period also encouraged Latin American governments to eliminate the domestic use of foreign currencies, such as dollars. The US dollar circulated widely within a number of Latin American countries at this time. Indeed, this practice had been encouraged by US advisors and businesses earlier in the century within regions where the United States had particular economic and political influence. Soon after it acquired Puerto Rico as a colony, for example, US colonial officials replaced the local currency with the dollar. Elsewhere, US interests encouraged the dollar's use alongside an existing local currency, as in Panama, Cuba, Honduras, and the Dominican Republic. At one point in 1915, Kemmerer even suggested the creation of a Pan-American "monetary union" that would tie all currencies of the region to a common monetary unit equivalent to the US gold dollar and then allow gold coins of each country to circulate freely across the region. In practice, this proposal would have encouraged the wide use of US currency across the Americas because of the confidence the dollar commanded vis-à-vis locally issued currency.

The enthusiasm for promoting the dollar's use within Latin American monetary systems at that earlier time stemmed partly from a belief that this practice would provide a further guarantee—alongside the gold standard—of price stability in those countries. Liberals also applauded how it would foster international commerce by reducing transaction costs associated with currency exchange. It was also linked to broader economic and strategic competition between the United States and European powers in the region. In Rosenberg's (1999) words, US policy makers hoped to "create a gold dollar bloc, centered in New York, to rival the de facto sterling standard" (24) in the region. The use of the dollar in Latin America would provide US businesses with a competitive edge vis-à-vis foreign competition because of their familiarity with the dollar as well as its availability to them. When the United States acquired its first colonies of Puerto Rico and the Philippines, some congressmen also made clear that they saw the introduction of the dollar in those territories as part of the US projection of imperial power; as one politician put it, the dollar would teach the colonized people "the lessons of the flag and impress upon him the power and glory of the Republic" (quoted in Kemmerer 1916, 303).[3]

In the 1940s, the content of US policy in this area changed completely and US officials pressed many of the same countries to remove dollars and all other foreign currencies from the domestic monetary system.[4] They argued forcefully that dollarization was not compatible with the new "embedded liberal" objectives they were promoting. The central bank of a country could not develop a strong and independent monetary policy unless the currency it issued held a monopoly position inside the country. They also noted that dollarization undermined the effectiveness of capital controls and prevented centralized control of a country's foreign exchange resources, a control that was useful in mobilizing these resources for development goals. In addition, they noted how the use of the dollar had meant that countries were "in effect making a loan to the United States" (Wallich 1950, 45).

De-dollarization, then, was promoted by the United States as a central part of its broader efforts to promote "embedded liberal" principles in Latin America. To be sure, one initial motivation for promoting these principles was the fear of German influence, a fear that encouraged US officials to take a more active and positive role in supporting Latin American nationalist goals of economic development and industrialization. But the importance of this strategic motivation should not be overstated since the United States continued to provide this "embedded liberal" advice after World War II in technical missions to the region as well as elsewhere in the South during the late 1940s and 1950s. They did so for "ideational" reasons, not just strategic ones.[5] De-dollarization became a key part of the American vision for the role of Southern countries in the multilateral Bretton Woods system. And those who held this vision were clearly influenced by the Keynesian revolution that was underway.

This was particularly true of the Federal Reserve officials who launched the various "money doctoring" missions. Scholars have generally seen the US treasury as the primary source of support for "embedded liberalism" within US international monetary policy-making circles in this period. But the US Federal Reserve had also been affected by the economic thinking of the New Deal, especially after it became headed by Marriner Eccles, a non–New York banker with quite unorthodox views. Particularly important in developing the new approach to "money doctoring" was Robert Triffin who was head of the Latin American division of the Federal Reserve Board between 1942–1946.

Triffin argued vigorously that the interwar experience in Latin America had highlighted the limitations of the gold standard and passive monetary policies geared externally to respond automatically to changes in the balance of payments. During the 1920s, orthodox central banks in Latin America had reinforced the inflationary impact of sudden capital inflows by expanding the money supply in response to the large balance of payments surpluses these inflows produced. Then, when the balance of payments turned suddenly into deficit in the 1929–1931 period (as capital flows suddenly collapsed and export markets dried up), these banks had reinforced deflationary tendencies by contracting the money supply. In this way, the orthodox "monetary automatism" had magnified—rather than minimized—the impact of international instability on the domestic economy. For this reason, most Latin American governments abandoned the gold standard and introduced exchange controls during the 1930s, and many began to experiment with more activist monetary policies aimed at financing government spending and producing domestic economic growth. During the 1940s, Triffin and other Federal Reserve officials were explicit in acknowledging that Latin American policy innovations had strongly influenced their thinking (Helleiner 2003a, ch.9).

THE CONTEMPORARY DEBATE ON DOLLARIZATION DIPLOMACY

When viewed in this historical perspective, it is surprising to see US policy makers debating the idea of encouraging dollarization in Latin America once again today. Not since the early twentieth century have US officials considered this kind of policy, and by the 1940s the idea had been widely discredited. This recent development is even more striking because US policy makers are debating an even more ambitious idea than the kind of partial dollarization that was promoted in the early twentieth century (outside of Puerto Rico). Now proponents are encouraging Latin American countries to dollarize fully; that is, to abandon their national currencies and adopt the US dollar as their exclusive currency. The most prominent proposal is that the United States could encourage this practice by offering to compensate foreign governments financially for most (85 percent) of the seigniorage revenue they lost from adopting the dollar. In 1999, a bill was submitted to both the US Senate and House of Representatives to empower the treasury secretary to act in this way and hearings on this "International Monetary Stability Act" were held in 1999–2000.

The initial catalyst for placing this issue back on the US policy-making agenda came in fact from abroad. In early 1999, Argentine officials approached the US government to ask what kind of support the United States might be willing to provide if they were to adopt the dollar as Argentina's sole currency. Residents of Argentina already used the US dollar extensively alongside the national currency; particularly since their country had created a currency board tied to the dollar in 1991. The Argentine government was now considering "full dollarization" as a way of reducing the currency-risk premium it was charged when borrowing from abroad.

The Argentine request prompted US government officials and members of Congress to begin to investigate the issue. In Congress, Republican Senator Connie Mack of Florida and his research staff became particularly enthusiastic about promoting dollarization in the Americas and Mack played the lead role in launching the subsequent hearings and the act. His enthusiasm was shared by a number of witnesses called before Congress from the financial sector, various research institutes and the academic realm (US Senate 1999a, 1999b). In the media, too, a number of prominent analysts expressed their support for the idea. And officials within some of the regional Federal Reserve Banks also made clear their interest in the idea (e.g., McTeer 2000).

The arguments for promoting dollarization in the Americas were quite similar to those put forward by US policy makers in the early twentieth century. Some saw the creation of a dollar bloc as a way to respond to the competitive threat of the euro zone. But enthusiasm was particularly strong among those who rejected domestic monetary activism in favor of a "neoliberal" view, which held that price stability should be the primary goal of monetary policy. Dollarization, from this neoliberal standpoint, would bring price stability to countries that had often experienced inflationary monetary conditions during the postwar period. This, in turn, would encourage domestic savings, the development of deeper financial markets, and a more stable macroeconomic environment for capital accumulation. Connie Mack himself was among the strongest supporters of the neoliberal argument for dollarization. He had earlier pushed for legislation that would make price stability the principal goal of the Federal Reserve System itself, and he explained his interest in dollarization abroad as an extension of the monetary principles he promoted at home:

> Those of you who know me know that it's a long-standing aim of mine that the United States ought to seek not only to export our products but to export our principles as well. . . . [I]n terms of global growth, our #1 export right now ought to be our principled approach to price stability. (Mack 2000, 2)

Where Triffin and his colleagues had sought to bolster the policy autonomy of Latin American countries, these neoliberal advocates of dollarization diplomacy hoped to constrain it. Dollarization would make activist national monetary policy impossible, a result that would preclude future inflationary experiences. It would also provide a constraint on state spending by eliminating the possibility of monetary financing of fiscal deficits. In addition, some advocates of dollarization welcomed the fact that the exchange rate could no longer be used as an economic tool of adjustment. Its elimination would impose greater market discipline on domestic workers and firms since they would now be forced to adjust to external economic "shocks" in a more head-on fashion by embracing greater wage and price flexibility.

The political prominence of these neoliberal arguments highlighted the extent to which support had eroded in some US quarters for postwar "embedded liberal" approaches to international monetary policy. As if to reinforce this point, neoliberals sometimes combined the arguments above with an attack on the Bretton Woods institutions themselves. During the widespread currency crises of 1997–1998, many US neoliberal thinkers and politicians—including Mack—became very critical of the large loans that the IMF extended to crisis-stricken countries. Some of these critics began to even call for the abolition of the IMF. In this context, many US neoliberals began to see dollarization as an alternative way of promoting monetary stability abroad. Again, Mack (2000) made the case clearly:

> I see dollarization as an antipoverty, prodevelopment policy. . . . By eliminating the root cause of currency crises, widespread dollarization would eliminate the need for international institutions to make the complex and highly controversial interventions in national economies that have been an integral part of recent currency rescue efforts. (3)

But the influence of these neoliberal views should not be overstated. When Mack's bill was debated in Congress, many within the United States were skeptical of the idea. This included influential members of the US administration at the time. When they appeared before Congress, both Deputy Treasury Secretary Larry Summers and Federal Reserve Chairman Alan Greenspan were not willing to endorse Mack's initiative. They preferred what Cohen (2002) calls a policy of "passive neutrality" in which the United States would neither encourage nor discourage foreign governments from adopting the US dollar. And this view ultimately won the day. Mack's bill was shelved.

Some of the arguments against dollarization were political ones. Like US officials in the 1940s and early 1950s, some policy makers have been wary of stirring nationalist sentiments across the Americas. Given the history of the early twentieth century, critics have noted that dollarization diplomacy might be seen to be simply "reinventing colonialism" (D'Arista 2001, 3). Supporters have been quick to reject this accusation, noting that the International Monetary Stability Act does not pressure any foreign country to dollarize. The fact that the issue was first raised by Argentina has also made it easier for them to deflect criticism that dollarization is a US-led initiative. Indeed, the issue has its prominent supporters across Latin America, particularly in neoliberal circles. But nationalist opposition to dollarization (as well as that of many embedded liberals) has also been quite present in the region, and it could easily grow if the United States was seen to be promoting dollarization very strongly.

The more prominent criticism of Mack's initiative has come from those endorsing an embedded liberal worldview. While usually not endorsing the kind of ambitious Keynesian policies of the midcentury, many US policy makers still share the embedded liberal belief that both exchange rate changes and discretionary domestic monetary policy should remain important economic tools for Latin American governments to optimize social welfare (e.g., Summers 1999, 2). In the absence of an exchange rate, critics of dollarization worry that domestic prices and wages in Latin American countries would be called upon to bear a larger share of the adjustment burden to distinct economic shocks (vis-à-vis the United States). Since wages and prices are usually relatively inflexible in the short term, the result would likely be higher levels of unemployment and lower levels of real output.

As noted above, supporters of dollarization acknowledge this critique, but argue that the inflexibility of domestic prices and wages should not be taken as a given.[6] One of the benefits of dollarization, from their standpoint, is that it would transform the monetary environment in a way that forces business and workers to become more "flexible" and responsive to changing economic conditions. But this argument only reinforces the opposition of those with a more embedded liberal perspective. It makes clear that dollarization is a project that will not only constrain state policy makers but also impose a radical new kind of market discipline on domestic social groups that might lead to severe social dislocation within dollarized countries. Indeed, these predictions have been made more real by Argentina's dramatic financial crisis in 2001–2002, a crisis that has been attributed at least in part to the country's heavily dollarized monetary system.

Some critics of Mack's bill have also pointed out that, in the absence of wage and price flexibility, dollarized countries may turn to alternative adjustment mechanisms which could directly affect the United States. The prominent international economist Fred Bergsten, for example, reminded Congress that if Canada and Mexico adopted the dollar, these countries might require more financial support from the United States, rather than less, in order to compensate for the loss of the exchange rate tool of adjustment. The United States might also find itself receiving more migrants from the countries in response to negative shocks to the Canadian and Mexican economies. These developments might generate opposition within the United States to dollarization diplomacy:

> The United States would . . . have to participate more directly in the adjustment of the dollarized foreign economies to economic dislocation. In essence, we would either have to send more capital to them or accept more workers from them in cases when they ran into recession. This would not be totally different from the current situation, where the United States already takes some of the impact of adjustment vis-à-vis neighbouring countries via the exchange rate and the trade balance. However, the distribution of the effects would be different and the transparency (and hence political awareness) of the impact on the United States could be much greater. (Bergsten 1999, 6)

Critics of dollarization also worry about the implications of removing the possibility of discretionary domestic monetary policy in dollarized countries. When a dollarized country entered a recession, its government would no longer have the option of using a national monetary policy to address the situation. Instead, monetary conditions would now be influenced by the decisions and priorities of the US central bank. If the US Fed was willing to consider the economic conditions of foreign dollarized countries when formulating US monetary policy, this situation might not be so bad. But US officials have made it clear that they have no intention of diluting the focus of US monetary policy in this way. Even Mack's International Monetary Stability Act states that the Federal Reserve is not obligated to consider foreign economic conditions when setting monetary policy.

In this context, critics worry not just about economic conditions in the dollarized countries. They also worry about the impact on the United States. Summers, for example, highlighted his concern that "in difficult times, the loss of domestic monetary sovereignty [in Latin America] would foster resentment and encourage policy makers to deflect blame for problems onto the United States" (Summers 1999, 3). These political pressures might, in fact, then have the impact of forcing the US Fed to consider the preferences of dollarized countries (Christz 2000, 35). US monetary policy autonomy might also be compromised in a second way if the foreign countries dollarizing were large ones. As Bergsten (1999) explains, "Economic developments in those areas would then have a considerably greater impact on overall monetary conditions in the United States itself, requiring greater consideration thereof in the conduct of US monetary policy" (5). In these ways, critics highlight how Latin American dollarization abroad will undermine the ability of not just Latin American governments but also the United States itself to pursue discretionary monetary policy.[7]

Interestingly, some neoliberal supporters of dollarization diplomacy have argued that there is a simple way to guarantee that the Fed is not influenced by foreign pressure: change the Federal Reserve Act to make its purpose much clearer and narrower. Specifically, they suggest that it be given a strict mandate to pursue price stability, following the model of the European Central Bank (ECB) (Schuler 2000, 11). This, in turn, might also have the added benefit of increasing the attractiveness of dollarization to policy makers abroad. But this solution is hardly attractive to those sympathetic to embedded liberal ideals. Such a mandate would, after all, undermine the very thing that critics of dollarization are trying to preserve: a discretionary national monetary policy that is capable of serving a range of domestic economic goals. And again, neoliberals have not been able to win adequate domestic support for this idea within the United States.

In sum, the new interest in dollarization diplomacy signals very clearly that some US policy makers now reject an embedded liberal framework for

US international monetary policy making. Their views are much more similar to those of Kemmerer and his classical liberal colleagues in the early twentieth century than those of Triffin and other embedded liberals of the mid-century era. But the US debate also highlights that these figures are not yet powerful enough to change US policy in this area. Many US policy makers are unwilling to embrace dollarization diplomacy, and one reason is their continuing commitment to embedded liberal principles. To be sure, this commitment is not as strong as in the 1940s when US officials actively encouraged "de-dollarization" in Latin America. But in its more limited form, this commitment has helped to block the US from taking a more active stance in cultivating a dollar-based monetary union in the Americas.

A EUROPEAN COMPARISON

It is interesting to compare this situation to that in Europe where support for regional monetary union is much stronger in most countries. In one respect, the situations look similar. The project of monetary union has, after all, been backed strongly by neoliberals across Europe, and their arguments are similar to those of dollarization supporters in the Americas. EMU is seen as a mechanism that precludes national governments from pursuing discretionary monetary policy. It does this not just by abolishing national currencies, but also by giving control over the euro's management to an independent European Central Bank that is mandated to pursue price stability. EMU also constrains activist national fiscal policy not just because fiscal deficits can no longer be financed by monetary means. Equally important, participants in EMU have agreed under the "Stability and Growth Pact" to limit the maximum size of their budget deficits and public debt. And finally, European neoliberals applaud the fact that EMU should impose greater "market discipline" on firms and workers as exchange rate adjustments can no longer substitute for wage and price flexibility.

Given these implications of EMU, one would anticipate that embedded liberals across Europe would have opposed it. One would also anticipate that this opposition would have been even more influential than in the United States given the much stronger political position of social democrats across Europe. What then explains the fact that the EMU project has proceeded? Part of the explanation is that EMU found support among groups who see it serving broader political goals such as the promotion of European cooperation and the bolstering of European power vis-à-vis the United States. But particularly important from our standpoint is the fact that many embedded liberals across Europe—though by no means all—have been very supportive of EMU. Indeed, Notermans (2001) notes that "social democrats have ranked among the staunchest supporters of EMU" (4), and that their support has in fact been crucial to the success of the initiative.

Given the widespread characterization of EMU as a neoliberal project, why would social democrats endorse it? In the fiscal realm, some of them have argued that the new constraints imposed by EMU are offset by the fact that the euro lowers interest rates by reducing risk premiums that financial markets were imposing, particularly in poorer countries of the EU. Because this often improved governments' budgetary positions considerably and helped prevent cuts to the welfare state, Rhodes (2002) feels justified in describing EMU as more of an "embedded liberal" regime than a neoliberal one (310). In some countries (e.g., Austria), social democrats have also not been very concerned about the elimination of discretionary monetary management at the national level because they have come to see international competitiveness—rather than countercyclical demand management—as the best means to achieve full employment (Veiden 2001).

Indeed, European social democrats have often welcomed the fact that EMU provides a stable macroeconomic environment in which they can pursue progressive supply-side reforms aimed at promoting equity, growth, and employment. In particular, they have applauded the fact that EMU prevents individual countries from being subject to speculative attacks against their national currencies from the increasingly powerful global financial markets. In some countries (e.g., Sweden, Finland, Spain), another source of macroeconomic instability was the fact that social democratic governments lost control over wage demands—often in a context where postwar corporatist wage bargaining structures were breaking down or were already weak—thereby producing situations in which domestic expansionary policies rapidly produced vicious cycles of inflation and depreciation. In these contexts, EMU has often been seen by social democrats—not just neoliberals—as a means to restore a more stable macroeconomic environment by providing an external discipline on wage demands. As Notermans (2001) puts it, "[F]ar from being a threat, EMU has provided European social democracy with a favourable institutional set-up from which to avoid the main problem that brought down its post-war model, namely the inability to prevent inflation in tight labour markets" (270).

But aren't social democrats concerned that the loss of the national exchange rate will increase pressures to make wages and prices more flexible as a way of adjusting to asymmetric external shocks? The importance of this issue is less significant for a core of EMU countries because they experience similar external shocks. Indeed, it is not coincidental that the three countries opting out of EMU—the UK, Sweden, and Denmark—are among the top five countries experiencing the most asymmetric shocks in the EU (the other two are Finland and Ireland) (Aylott 2001, 159). Equally important, however, is the fact that many European social democrats do not see "domestic wage and price flexibility" as incompatible with their goals. In the Latin American context, this phrase is widely seen as code for a neoliberal strategy of labor market deregulation. In some European countries with strong corporatist traditions, however, social democrats have a different perspective. They have seen EMU as an opportunity to reinvigorate corporatist social pacts in which cooperative wage bargaining, employment-friendly taxation schemes, and other social protection measures can assume a key role in the adjustment process (Rhodes 2002; Pekkarinen 2001).

A final reason why some social democrats have embraced EMU is that they have seen it as a necessary step in the construction of a stronger EU in which embedded liberal goals have prominence. For example, many who are less enthusiastic about neoliberal monetary goals have still supported EMU because they have seen it as a mechanism for diluting the monetary influence of the neoliberal Bundesbank across Europe. Although the new European Central Bank has a strict mandate to pursue price stability, they hope that European governments could influence its behavior over time and that EMU would also encourage coordinated EU-wide expansionary fiscal policies.[8] Some social democrats have also supported EMU because they believed it might help strengthen employment rights at the EU-wide level and lead to transnational wage bargaining (as pay structures between countries became more transparent) (Gamble and Kelly 2001; Josselin 2001). In some poorer EU countries, EMU was also seen as an opportunity to press for larger intra-EU fiscal transfers. The Spanish government, for example, withheld its support for EMU until it received a commitment that a new EU "Cohesion Fund" would be created for this purpose.

From these explanations, it is easier to see why embedded liberals in the Americas have generally been less inclined to follow many of their European counterparts in embracing the idea of a regional monetary union. To be sure, some of these arguments could be relevant to the context of the Americas. If dollarization helped the fiscal position of Latin American governments by lowering domestic interest rates, for example, it might be able to win more support from embedded liberals in the region. Dollarization might also be seen as a way to provide a more stable macroeconomic context in which governments in Latin America could focus on progressive supply-side reforms. But in other ways, the context of the Americas is very different. Many Latin American countries lack the kind of strong social corporatist arrangements that exist in many European countries. Even more important is the fact that embedded liberals across the Americas find it difficult to relate to the European notion that monetary union could help construct a stronger regional community in which embedded liberal values have a prominent place. Across Latin America, closer economic integration with the United States has long been seen as a threat to these values. US officials have also made it clear that dollarization will not be accompanied by the construction of regional institutions in which these values could be promoted and in which Latin American countries have a voice. They have not even been willing to discuss seriously the kinds of ideas that Bergsten mentioned: the strengthening of inter-American financial transfers and the easing of migration flows. Unless dollarization is accompanied by these kinds of broader forms of regional cooperation, it is unlikely that it will win the support of embedded liberals in the region. And as we have noted, it is not even clear that embedded liberals in the United States and elsewhere in the region have much interest in promoting this kind of closer regional cooperation.

CONCLUSION

Let us return to the question posed in the introduction: What are the implications of the push for currency blocs in the Americas and Europe for the future of embedded liberalism? If relations *between* these currency blocs are characterized by increasingly competitive and strategic rivalries, then there is no question that their creation threatens the kind of liberal multilateral principles that the Bretton Woods architects endorsed. And as I have noted briefly in this chapter, there are certainly some groups in Europe and the United States who see the creation of regional monetary unions as serving these purposes.

But I have also noted that there is a second way of answering this question, which focuses on the purpose of economic policy *within* each proposed currency bloc. In this respect, the question is more difficult to answer. On the one hand, the push for currency blocs in both regions is clearly coming from neoliberal thinkers who actively reject embedded liberal values. In this sense, this trend looks to be a further signal of the decline of the influence of embedded liberalism in the world monetary system.

On the other hand, however, we have also seen how those who endorse embedded liberal values remain influential in both regions. In the United States, and the Americas more generally, their influence has generally been to oppose the idea of promoting a dollar bloc. In Europe, they have often assumed the opposite role, providing key support for the EMU initiative. The difference reflects the different regional contexts in which embedded liberals find themselves, as well as the different styles of regional monetary union being proposed in each context. Despite their different positions on the question of regional monetary union, they have both had a major impact on policy. Both the successful push for EMU and the lack of momentum behind the proposal for a dollar bloc reflect, in part, the continuing strength of the embedded liberal worldview within each bloc.

NOTES

I am grateful for helpful comments I received from Steven Bernstein, Lou Pauly, and John Ruggie. I also thank the Canada Research Chair Programme and the Social Sciences and Humanities Research Council of Canada for their support.

1. The memo also held open the door for plans for a broader international economic order when it continued, "but to cooperate economically if European policy is directed in more liberal channels" (Collado 1940, 361).

2. The discussion in the rest of this section draws on material from Helleiner (2003a, ch. 9, 2003b).

3. The United States chose not to introduce the dollar into the Philippines after all, in part because of opposition encountered in the earlier Puerto Rico currency reform. See Helleiner (2003b).

4. The advice did not extend to Panama and Puerto Rico.

5. In some cases, however, a strategic rationale reemerged with the onset of the cold war in which US officials found it once more politically useful to adopt an accommodating stance toward the economic goals of Southern nationalists. See Helleiner (2003a, ch. 9).

6. Other defenders of dollarization argue that, because of the volatility and short-term misalignments of exchange rates today, a floating exchange rate is often the source of, rather than the means of adjusting to, external economic shocks.

7. A similar concern is that dollarized countries may encounter difficulties in addressing domestic financial crisis because the national monetary authority no longer has an unlimited capacity to print money for lender-of-last-resort purposes. In these circumstances, the United States might be called upon to bail out troubled financial institutions, and its refusal to do so might trigger resentment abroad. This issue apparently already arose in the context of Argentina's discussions with the United States in early 1999. According to some reports, Argentina's government indicated that it would be more willing to consider adopting the US dollar if the Federal Reserve would agree to assume some lender-of-last-resort functions for the Argentine financial system (Cohen 2002, 73). US officials such as Summers have told Congress that the United States would not consider a lender-of-last-resort role in dollarized countries (Summers 1999). See also Schuler and Stein (2000). Mack's act also specifies clearly that the Federal Reserve is not obligated to serve as a lender of last resort to any dollarized country and is not responsible for bank supervision abroad. A fear of creating unwanted expectations in Latin America concerning these roles also may help to explain why key US policy makers have been so careful not to endorse dollarization abroad in their official statements.

8. Reflecting these goals, Lionel Jospin succeeded in convincing other euro zone governments to establish a common forum of national finance ministers and to establish employment as a new EU priority to accompany EMU at the 1997 Luxembourg EU Council meeting.

NINE

Institutional Fragmentation and Normative Compromise in Global Environmental Governance

What Prospects for Re-Embedding?

STEVEN BERNSTEIN AND MARIA IVANOVA

INTRODUCTION

IN WHAT WAS TO BE the signal global event to mark the dawn of a new post–cold war era, the environment held a principal position in the most ambitious attempt to forge a global compromise since Bretton Woods. The 1992 Earth Summit in Rio de Janeiro aimed at nothing less than building a grand compromise to shape global governance into the twenty-first century. The United Nations Conference on Environment and Development centered on the concept of "sustainable development," promising to link the environment, development, and social agendas in a way that captured the world's imagination and provided an ideological basis to build a new vision of global governance.

The Earth Summit capitalized on the new optimism in international cooperation to solve global problems. The combination of environment, development, human rights, and engagement of civil society at local and global levels captured the alternative international agenda so long buried under the cold war preoccupation with superpower conflict. The Earth Summit's organizers—mostly veterans of the UN system and North-South diplomacy—also saw a chance to promote the new face of multilateralism. Rio, they hoped, would be a catalyst for a post–cold war order characterized by an open, market-friendly international economic system and a peaceful, multilateral political system, tempered by a global management regime to steer economic development in a more sustainable and equitable direction. In effect, the Earth Summit could be characterized as an attempt to internationalize embedded liberalism by expanding the bargain to the developing world and deepening its normative and institutional underpinning. By design, the Rio process would not deliver hard bargains among the great powers on the post–cold war architecture. Rather, its uniqueness relative to other contemporary efforts to reform or redesign international institutions lay in its wide engagement of the world community, its focus on a North-South bargain, and its wide-ranging vision for the future of global governance.

In some ways, this volume as a whole can be viewed as an assessment of whether the Rio vision of global compromise still has legs in a world where multilateralism appears under threat, the world's democracies are at odds over economic, environmental, and social agendas, North-South conflicts threaten to undermine the stability of the trading system, and the Western alliance on which much of the post–World War II institutional order was built is at its most tenuous in the last forty years. This chapter looks at the environmental piece of that puzzle, but does so in the context of these general strains on the entire governance architecture.

The Earth Summit occurred precisely when underlying economic, social, and political forces associated with globalization began to threaten to unravel embedded liberalism (Ruggie, this volume). The result for global environmental governance was a weak compromise that showed signs of strain and contradiction almost upon inception. Some fifteen years later, the promise of sustainable development remains largely unfulfilled and environmental governance has evolved in conformity with the changing demands of a hyper-liberal global political economy, rather than vice versa (Bernstein 2001). If this outcome had resulted in the institutional capacity and resources necessary to respond to the world's most serious environmental problems, such a shift would have been welcome. By almost any measure, however, that has not been the case. Indeed, the overwhelming sense among official and nongovernmental delegates alike at the 2002 World Summit on Sustainable Development (WSSD)—the global conference meant to reinvigorate the implementation of the Rio agreements—was that for all the rhetoric, agreements, and promises of action over the previous thirty years, actual institutions, processes, and resources have fallen woefully short of addressing the problems for which they were established (Speth 2003).

Our goal in this chapter is both to explain why the current compromise in environmental governance has led to a fragmented institutional architecture under increasing stress and to argue for the need for institutional reform that re-embeds environmental governance in the broader social purposes of world society. In our analysis, we show how forces of globalization have reinforced fragmentation by further undermining the capacity of intergovernmental management, elevating the authority of international economic institutions, and directing environmental governance toward increasing engagement with the global marketplace. In developing prescriptions, we pay close attention to the prospects and limits of reform in the context of the social forces limiting the effectiveness of current arrangements. Underlying this argument are two analytic themes addressed in this volume. First, we address the legitimacy requirements of world order. This focus highlights how the shifting basis of legitimacy created a tension that pushed the importance of the marketplace, but also put strain on the underlying social purpose of achieving environmental goals, creating a need for some rebalancing. Second, we address the tension of order and fragmentation, and assess whether a fragmented system of governance can be adapted to serve the social purposes for which it was constructed.

The argument proceeds in three parts. First, we outline how global environmental governance evolved to the current compromise, and the contemporary challenges to its legitimacy and effectiveness. Second, we explain the tendency toward fragmentation in the institutional architecture and analyze the implications of fragmentation for responding to the contemporary governance challenge. Third, we assess proposals for a new institutional architecture in light of the normative and institutional requirements of a new compromise, but also in light of governance failures and institutional trajectories that militate against major structural reform.

HOW WE GOT HERE: THE CRISIS OF LIBERAL ENVIRONMENTALISM

The Legitimation of Liberal Environmentalism

The integrity of the world's environment was noticeably absent from the agenda of the post–World War II planners of the embedded liberalism compromise. To the degree it was addressed at all in the Bretton Woods agreements, the environment—or more precisely natural resources conservation and animal and plant health—was hived off in GATT article XX (which identifies "general exceptions" or policy areas not subject to GATT rules). In other words, the environment was considered strictly in the realm of discretionary domestic policy. The immediate post–cold war world—which saw an explicit attempt to forge a new global compromise that *included* the environment—was a vastly different place.

In many ways, the legacy of embedded liberalism helped to reintroduce the environment to the global agenda. It established multilateralism as the ideal of global governance and institutionalized the need to embed the liberal international economy in domestic social purposes. Thus, when Western societies began to recognize environmentalism as an additional social purpose, embedded liberalism provided fertile ground for a new multilateral global bargain that incorporated this concern. Environmental movements in the 1960s and 1970s also played a role by helping to push the issue from the margins to the mainstream of public policy. Subsequent environmental disasters, from massive oil spills to the 1986 Chernobyl nuclear incident, combined with increased scientific knowledge of human-induced damage to planetary life support systems, reinforced the place of the natural environment in the embedded liberalism equation. They also reinforced an idea of planetary interdependence and the need for international rather than only domestic responses—although how to incorporate environmental concerns into national and international policy was the subject of much debate. The ideal of "sustainable development," which promised to integrate the environment, the economy, and societal needs under a single grand rubric, became the dominant response of the international community, and gradually emerged as a central component of the new post–cold war vision.

The 1987 Brundtland Commission report (WCED 1987) articulated sustainable development as the underpinning of global environmental governance in its idealized form. This was not a negotiated document, but a visionary statement meant to mobilize domestic and international action on the twin themes of environment and development. Its articulation of the sustainable development concept captured world opinion, but also addressed competing social purposes and priorities of developed and developing countries. In particular, it responded to worries that environmental concerns would trump economic growth, poverty reduction, and access to the markets of wealthy countries. This tension between environmental goals and the fear they provoked among Southern elites had plagued attempts to forge an international consensus since the 1972 Stockholm Conference on the Human Environment, the first major UN-sponsored world environmental conference. In response, the Brundtland Commission's report promised to integrate environment and development. The intergenerational equity and focus on human needs in its definition of sustainable development—"development that meets the needs of the present without compromising the ability of future generations to meet their own needs" (WCED 1987, 43)—was, in hindsight, less significant than its integrative proposition that action on the global environment rested on a foundation of liberal economic growth.

Indeed, the Brundtland report made accelerated economic growth its top strategic priority (WCED 1987, 50–51, 89). Although the report supported some global redistribution, it did so through a loosely interpreted Keynesian liberalism in the international economic order: liberal interdependence, management of the global economy by industrialized powers, and free trade tempered by managed interventions (such as increased foreign aid or compensatory financing to offset commodity price instability) to cushion and facilitate adjustment in the South and direct development on a path less likely to harm the environment (WCED 1987, 67–91). Unlike the Bretton Woods bargain among Western industrialized countries, Brundtland's proposition for a global bargain that included the South recognized that forty years of development policy had exposed the inadequacy of simply leaving room for domestic interventions. Instead, global liberalism itself needed to be more tightly managed in order to provide the necessary resources, expertise, and economic environment to enable national governments in the South to fully benefit from a liberal order while, like the North, maintaining domestic stability and broader social goals.

But Brundtland's formulation did not merely reflect a North-South compromise. Policy makers in the North had increasingly examined their own environmental policies through economic lenses and sought ways to address environmental problems without disrupting economic priorities. For example, elsewhere Bernstein (2001) has shown the direct influence on the evolution of the sustainable development concept adopted by the Brundtland Commission of policy work in the Organization of Economic Cooperation and Development (OECD). That work focused primarily on ways to internalize environmental costs through principles such as Polluter and User Pays and to develop market mechanisms to address environmental problems. This work helped catalyze changes in environmental policies and policy instruments in many industrialized countries. The Brundtland commissioners and staff were also conscious of previous failures to move the environment and development agendas forward, including the cool reception of concepts such as eco-development, which were perceived as too environmentally focused.

At a time when the forces of globalization were less visible, the Brundtland report also reflected what today might seem like naive confidence in the state-centric, multilateral institutional form to take embedded liberalism global. It reframed poverty and environment as global problems requiring global solutions, even if the effects were local and local action would be needed. Liberalization would still provide the necessary engine of growth, but a system of multilateral management and redistribution would provide political will and resources where local technical and material capacity was lacking.

By managing to place these goals under a single rubric, as well as taking advantage of its high-profile status as a UN General Assembly mandated initiative, the Brundtland Commission significantly increased the legitimacy of the concept of sustainable development and environmental governance more broadly. Following Brundtland, it would no longer be possible to discuss global environmental governance absent consideration of development goals. Nonetheless, questions remained as to how these lofty goals would be institutionalized in actual mechanisms of governance.

Charged with that task, the global negotiations of the Rio Summit process, to the surprise of many environmentalists, produced a compromise that might be likened to embedded liberalism in reverse. Instead of recognizing the need to embed the economy in society, the political compromise that emerged premised environmental governance on embedding the environment in liberal markets. The result has been crisis, fragmentation (institutionally, in the location of authority, and in the mix of public and private governance), and the subordination of environmental goals to market principles. What the architects of sustainable development failed to anticipate was the way in which forces of global economic integration, the hegemony of neoliberal economic orthodoxy, and the failures of aid-driven development policy would push policy in a direction that would militate against global multilateral management and interventionist policies. Their failure is understandable in light of underlying structural changes that were poorly understood, which, as Ruggie describes in this volume, assumed an *international* bargain among states that would reinforce something like embedded liberalism. But in a more *global* world, the strength of norms that reinforce the global market have become a powerful legitimating force in their own right, even if their sustainability is questionable.

The immediate effects on environmental governance were to promote market mechanisms, the privatization of global commons as opposed to centralized or collective management, and the idea, most notably stated in Principle 12 of the Rio Declaration on Environment and Development, that free trade and environmental protection were perfectly compatible. That principle states, in part, that, "[s]tates should cooperate to promote a supportive and open international economic system that would lead to economic growth and sustainable development in all countries, to better address the problems of environmental degradation" (UN 1992).

Globalization and Disembedded Global Environmental Governance

The 2002 World Summit on Sustainable Development in Johannesburg—sometimes referred to as Rio + 10—further reinforced global liberalism, the importance of the private sector, and the declining hope for multilateral management. It thereby reflected underlying structural conditions of freer and accelerated transaction flows, globalizing markets, and the fragmentation of political authority. Rio provided the normative foundations for environmental governance to adapt to such conditions. Thus, environmentalists should not have been surprised that a number of Northern delegations went to great lengths to ensure that the Johannesburg Declaration and Plan of Implementation, the two negotiated texts produced by the conference, did not contradict or undermine existing trade agreements (Wapner 2003, 6;

Speth 2003, 27). Such arguments simply reinforced Rio Principle 12, which, following the Earth Summit, began to serve a legitimating function for major trade agreements. For example, trade ministers negotiating the World Trade Organization (WTO) agreed, citing Principle 12, "that there should not be, nor need be, any policy contradiction between upholding and safeguarding an open, non-discriminatory and equitable multilateral trading system on the one hand, and acting for the protection of the environment, and the promotion of sustainable development on the other."[1]

The WSSD also heralded the legitimation of another trend consistent with the pattern of working with the market and private sector: public-private partnerships for sustainable development. Most analyses identify the endorsement of partnerships as one of two things most notable about the summit, the other being its recognition of the dismal progress since 1992 on implementing the Rio agreements combined with its failure to generate any significant new commitments or financing. The combination of the move to the marketplace to solve environmental problems and the lack of progress within multilateral environmental agreements contributed to the further fragmentation of environmental governance. It broadened the location of environmental activity, but without deepening core commitments by states or improving multilateral coordination efforts.

Partnerships work under the assumption that combining the resources, skills, and commitment of non-state actors with the authority of states will succeed where state action has not. Almost three hundred such partnerships were identified before or at the Johannesburg Summit (Doran 2002). They range from links between medical schools in the North with physicians and social programs in the South to establish public health programs, to a partnership between Shell and the Philippine government for the multi–billion dollar Malampaya Deep Water Gas to Power Project.[2] While such partnerships appear to be the poster children of sustainable development—combining economic, environmental, and social goals and usually involving community stakeholders and NGO input—skeptics worry that their success depends on the good will and voluntary participation of the private sector.

The ultimate aim of partnerships is to embed the marketplace in broader social and environmental goals. Ideally, they also ought to put in practice demands for greater corporate responsibility and accountability. Yet, the summit made much less progress in these areas. Moreover, as Paul Wapner (2003) has pointed out, "so far the number and magnitude of the partnerships proposed seem minuscule to the tasks at hand. . . . Indeed, the WSSD's embrace of the private sector to spearhead partnerships has led many critics to refer to the Summit as 'Rio-minus-10'" (4).

The engagement of the corporate sector at WSSD is part of the larger response to globalization within the UN system, particularly in development policy.[3] Another example of this trend is the Global Compact, which enlists the corporate sector to endorse a statement of environmental principles derived from the Rio Declaration, along with labor, human rights, and anti-corruption principles.[4]

Not content with leaving corporate engagement to governments or international institutions, some nongovernmental groups have similarly opted to directly target firms in the global marketplace through the creation of non-state governance systems. The most common are "certification" systems, where products, processes, or services get "certified" as meeting specific standards of sustainability established by the system, and sometimes get a label so buyers can identify products or services that meet those standards. Such governance systems arose partly in response to the lack of progress in multilateral negotiations, but also because NGOs worried about the limitations of voluntary codes of conduct, self-regulation, or learning networks, even when backed by the United Nations.[5] A small but accelerating number of such systems have started to operate at the transnational level over the last ten to fifteen years as demands for governance of the global marketplace have increased. They currently cover aspects of forestry, food safety and production, labor standards, tourism, fisheries, and human rights. Others are in development in the energy/electricity and mining sectors. Most include specific performance criteria and employ systems of third-party verification and regular auditing and monitoring of compliance in which firms must participate to maintain "certified" status. They also frequently have governance structures that include representation from corporations, broader civil society, and affected local communities. To the degree they exhibit the above characteristics, they can be considered "governance" systems with significant authority as opposed to strictly voluntary or self-regulatory schemes (Bernstein and Cashore 2006).

Such governance systems take advantage not only of globalizing markets, but also the spread and influence of global consciousness and civil society organizations to create pressures on companies to participate. Whereas these non-state governance systems engage the marketplace, environmental concerns also drive the more critical and broader anticorporate globalization backlash, precisely owing to globalization's perceived failure to deliver on its promise of sustainable development for all. Put another way, the globalization backlash stems in large part from its threat to social purposes—now including environment protection—at the heart of the embedded liberalism compromise.

Taken together, these trends suggest that environmental governance has settled in a similar place to global development policy as described by Jean-Philippe Thérien (this volume): teetering on a "thin" re-balancing between Right and Left. This precarious balance is showing signs of strain. While it may be too strong a characterization to call the current situation in environmental governance a full-blown legitimacy crisis, early warning signs point in that direction.

The legitimacy of a governance system rests on relevant communities viewing it as appropriate and justified within some broadly accepted system of norms. If the premise of this volume is correct, that embedded liberalism is a key constitutive component of that broader system of norms upon which contemporary global governance rests, then one of two things would need to occur to avert a full-blown crisis in environmental governance. One possibility would be to deepen the original liberal environmental compromise. That would require market liberalism to somehow further buttress its own legitimacy dynamics. The globalization backlash, however, belies any trend toward greater legitimacy for deepening market liberalism. Similarly, the collective findings of contributors to this volume suggest that the norm of embedded liberalism still has resonance, even if embedding increasingly must occur globally or through networked forms of governance, not only nationally. A second, and more promising, response to avert a legitimacy crisis, therefore, is for contemporary liberal environmental governance to more deeply re-embed itself in broader societal purposes rather than vice-versa.

The poor performance record of contemporary governing institutions has reinforced a sense of crisis. Liberal environmentalism, though it succeeded in bringing environmental concerns from the margins to the mainstream of the international agenda, has proven limited in its ability to provide a normative foundation for effective environmental governance. Just as the experience of globalization has revealed the limitations of the hyperliberalism and "Washington consensus" policies of the 1990s, so too has it shifted the terrain of what is considered acceptable or appropriate environmental governance.

Before taking up the possibility of re-embedding, we show how the current strains on the normative underpinnings of environmental governance are mutually reinforced by underlying tendencies toward fragmentation in its institutional architecture. This tendency began with the failure of the United Nations Environment Programme (UNEP) to centralize international environmental governance and control. Once the trend toward fragmentation became institutionalized, it created path dependencies that militated against consolidation. The trajectory of global environmental governance since Rio reinforced these path dependencies, as described below.

THE FRAGMENTATION OF ENVIRONMENTAL GOVERNANCE

Contemporary governance architecture for international environmental issues originated with the establishment of UNEP as a result of the 1972 Stockholm Conference. The key premises of the institutional negotiations were that "the work in the field of environment needed a common outlook and direction" and that "a central co-ordinating mechanism [was necessary] to provide political and conceptual leadership in the United Nations system"

(Rydbeck 1972). The goal was to avoid and reduce global environmental risks by providing necessary information, establishing joint norms and standards, and coordinating the environmental activities of existing organizations.

The global environmental governance system has, however, not lived up to the task of responding adequately to the problems for which it was designed. In the words of one prominent contributor, it is "an experiment that has largely failed" (Speth 2004, 2). It is weak, fragmented, lacking in resources, and short on authority (French 1992; Conca 2000; UN University 2002; Esty and Ivanova 2002).[6] UNEP, designed to be the "anchor" in this system, was expected to take the lead in addressing environmental concerns and threats and to provide the necessary institutional home as new issues emerged (UN 1972a, 1972b). It has, however, fallen short of this mandate. Although the reasons for UNEP's failure are open to debate (see Ivanova, forthcoming), without a center of gravity the system has grown increasingly complex and fragmented.

Hence, UNEP has become only one forum among many for negotiations on international environmental issues. More than a dozen other UN bodies over which UNEP possesses little authority share the environmental portfolio and vie for the same political attention and financial resources—the Commission on Sustainable Development (CSD), the World Meteorological Organization (WMO), the International Oceanographic Commission (IOC), the UN Educational, Scientific and Cultural Organization's (UNESCO) Man and Biosphere Program, and the Food and Agriculture Organization (FAO), to name a few. The environmental financing mechanisms are also scattered among multiple institutions and conventions. For example, the Global Environment Facility (GEF) (established in 1991 as the primary funder of global environmental projects carried out by developing countries) operates independently from financing operations of its three implementing agencies—the World Bank, UNEP, and UNDP. Separate treaty-based funds such as the Montreal Protocol Multilateral Fund are also involved in environmental activities on a global scale, but coordination among these efforts is minimal. In contrast, other international issues such as trade, health, or labor have relatively well-developed and coherent governance structures centered in an anchor international organization (the WTO, World Health Organization, and International Labor Organization respectively).

The independent secretariats to the numerous environmental conventions provide an additional layer of environmental bureaucracy. There are more than two hundred multilateral environmental agreements (MEAs), many with their own independent secretariats (UNEP 2001a). As new agreements emerged, often through processes led by UNEP, new organizational structures sprang up in Geneva, Bonn, Montreal, and elsewhere to house their management functions and secretariats. Coordination among MEAs has been difficult, if not impossible, as UNEP has little if any formal authority over the conventions and is geographically far removed from the independent secretariats (von Moltke 2001b). No incentives exist for integrated activities between the conventions and UNEP. Efforts have been "piecemeal rather than the result of a deliberate, overarching strategic choice" (UNEP 2001a) and, as one convention secretariat put it, "considerable lip service is paid to the synergies paradigm but, when it comes to implementation, each convention continues to be inward-looking and afraid of sharing or giving away part of their sovereignty" (UNEP 2001a, Appendix 2, 62).

Fragmentation of the MEAs presents a serious operational challenge and undermines UNEP's coordination role. For example, UNEP staff must travel on average approximately 3,777 miles from Nairobi to UNEP-hosted convention secretariats while other international organizations, including the International Maritime Organization, the International Labor Organization, and the UN Economic Commission for Europe, provide an institutional home for the conventions that have emerged under their aegis.

Overlaying the organizational fragmentation are potentially competing and conflicting mandates, which reflect how liberalizing trends in environmental governance post-Rio have empowered economic institutions. Rules are written and policies formulated in a context where institutions designed for other purposes limit and direct the types of practices deemed appropriate or acceptable for the environment. For example, ostensibly economic organizations including the World Bank, UNDP, OECD, United Nations Conference on Trade and Development (UNCTAD), and WTO have become important policy nodes that directly or indirectly address global environmental issues. Moreover, the goals of environmental agreements and organizations increasingly intermingle with economic goals. While this has the potential to contribute to global equity and development, the practical effect is often to weaken environmental priorities either owing to the institutional power and dominance of economic concerns within these institutions or because existing rules in the international political economy more broadly favor corporate and investor rights and freedom. Thus, the fate of environmental quality is not unlike other noneconomic goals increasingly being addressed under a neoliberal framework, where the rosy "win-win" scenarios painted by institutions such as the World Bank (World Bank 1992) and globalization advocates frequently fail to materialize.

An added pressure in the environmental case is that new rules must attempt to work with market forces and be carefully formulated to not run afoul of international trade rules. Despite being a priority area for the WTO Committee on Trade and the Environment (CTE) since its creation in 1994, the CTE has made virtually no headway on the reconciliation of trade rules and multilateral environmental treaties (Eckersley 2004). In combination with increasing fears of legal challenges under the WTO and worries about the acceptability of environmental trade measures, the resultant "chill" and "self-censorship" has affected multilateral environmental negotiations, including the Cartagena Biosafety Protocol and the Stockholm Convention on Persistent Organic Pollutants (Eckersley 2004, 27).[7] Moreover, concern about compatibility with trade rules is increasingly on the minds of organizers of even non-state certification systems (Bernstein and Cashore 2006; interviews New York, May 2004).

Fragmentation versus Integration: A False Dichotomy?

It is difficult at this time to imagine an environmental organization as an integrating body in this context of numerous entities with environmental mandates at all levels of governance and a strong caucus of economic institutions with environmental impacts. Yet, as Rosenau argues in this volume, integration and fragmentation are two sides of the same coin rather than diametric opposites. Global environmental issues provide a stark example of the apparently contradictory tendencies toward order and fragmentation in contemporary politics, a phenomenon that Rosenau calls "fragmegration." Fragmegration refers to the inextricable linkage between the simultaneous devolution of power from the state to subnational and non-state actors (local authorities, nongovernmental organizations, and corporations) and to the concentration of power within supranational institutions and organizations.

On the one hand, environmental concerns are locally manifested and require tailored responses, making decentralization an absolute condition for effective problem solving. The proliferation of agreements, agencies, partnerships, and alternative forms of governance at multiple scales therefore bodes well for the environment. On the other hand, from some ecological perspectives, all environmental problems are global as every person, plant, animal, and nonanimate object on the planet is part of one interconnected system. Some problems, moreover, are particularly complex and difficult to address through traditional governance systems as they may originate in one locality while their effects manifest in a jurisdiction thousands of miles away (as in the case of persistent organic pollutants) or in the global commons (such as the atmosphere or the oceans). Thus, while there is a pervasive need for multiple activities at the local level, some kind of integrated response is necessary internationally.

Although most analysts agree on the need for an international response to environmental issues, especially those of transboundary character, there is much disagreement over the need for fragmentation in environmental governance in order for the system to be effective, legitimate, and just (von Moltke 2001a; Haas 2004). Peter Haas, for example, argues that "some degree of redundancy is actually desirable in the international system, as it provides insurance against the decline of any individual international institution and fits better with an ecological institutional design vision of requisite diversity" (3). Environmental problems are indeed characterized by complexity, scientific uncertainty, and, frequently, a lack of fit between the ecosystems involved and the territorial and hierarchical institutions of nation-states charged with their resolution.

Even when intergovernmental cooperation can be achieved, the nature of sovereign-state diplomacy often reproduces the problem by reinforcing states' sovereign control over resources within their borders, and over environment and development policies. These norms are well entrenched in international law and practice (Bernstein 2001, 46–47, 101–102, 208–209). Designing an effective institutional architecture that not only responds to these constitutive aspects of global environmental problems, but also responds to the political and economic forces that militate against centralized coordinated responses, poses a daunting challenge.

Seen in this light, fragmentation, if understood as multiplicity of agencies active in an issue area, is not inherently deleterious. No one organization—national or international—possesses sufficient authority, resources, and knowledge to turn policy intentions into policy practice. Rather, the concerted efforts of multiple actors are required, all possessing significant capabilities but each dependent on many others to solidify policy intention and convert it into action. Complex, multi-actor processes thus emerge for the identification, definition, and resolution of problems, and for the implementation of policy (Imperial 1999).

The problem, however, is that each agency tends to adopt parochial solutions that rely on policy instruments over which they have direct control, with no guarantee that these solutions will combine to produce desired policy outcomes (Imperial 1999). Even the United Nations has openly recognized the need for greater integration of the work of numerous environmental agencies since "the flourishing of new international institutions poses problems of coordination, eroding responsibilities and resulting in duplication of work as well as increased demand upon ministries and government" (United Nations 1998). The result is confusion of responsibility and authority, poor use of existing information and resources, inconsistency of policies across and between governance levels, and, most importantly, an inability to successfully tackle global environmental problems.

Fragmentation may not only limit effectiveness, but legitimacy and equity as well. The conflicts among international agencies, overlaps of activities and overload of national-level authorities responsible for implementation, and indeterminate rules disproportionately affect developing countries. The scattering of environmental activities across many international organizations creates high costs for attending intergovernmental sessions to negotiate environmental agreements and treaties, both in terms of direct economic expenses and opportunity costs of days away from already understaffed environmental ministries. Countries with limited diplomatic and financial resources have been forced to choose not only which conferences they can afford to attend or not attend, but even which sessions to attend in single negotiations where simultaneous activities and negotiations are common (Kelly 1997). Such physical challenges are exacerbated by limited capacity and a knowledge divide on many levels, which limits the effectiveness of developing countries in negotiations and implementation (Karlsson 2002).

Developing countries stand to benefit most from reform in the current system for global environmental governance and any move toward a more coherent and rule-based institutional structure. A more streamlined and effective system for environmental governance would ensure that developing countries' priorities—poverty eradication and development—figure more prominently and are embedded within environmental policies. A set of clear and enforceable rules would also better ensure that fairness and equity in terms of benefit and burden sharing are built in and that decision making is based on democratic principles.

INSTITUTIONAL ARCHITECTURE

In light of normative, structural, and institutional constraints, what governance architecture is most appropriate for the scale and scope of contemporary global environmental problems? We argue that continuing along the trajectory of simply adapting to the global marketplace—what we termed embedded liberalism in reverse—would be detrimental. If we do not address governance failures, our stewardship of the environment will continue to be ineffective and inequitable, with little chance of finding a path toward sustainability. Improved processes, institutions, and organizations are necessary to reduce our collective environmental impact and ensure a fairer distribution of costs and benefits. The legitimacy and sustainability of a renewed compromise, however, will require significant trade-offs. While the prospects of a radical reordering of the international political economy may not be realistic,[8] our argument is that the institutional basis should be created to facilitate a greater embedding of the economic order in environmental purposes.

Below we discuss three broad alternatives for global environmental governance reform that have received the most attention in the literature. We then suggest a fourth that we argue better takes into account the opportunities and constraints we have identified, and thus might form the institutional basis of a renewed compromise in environmental governance.

Refinement of the Status Quo

Some commentators (von Moltke 2001a; Najam 2003) believe that the most feasible way to improve global environmental results is to revitalize the existing regime centered on UNEP. They argue that the current system suffers from lack of political will, not from any inherent flaws in the institutional arrangements. These conservative reform proposals, which only aim to fine-tune the status quo, include elevating UNEP's status within the UN system from a program to a specialized agency, strengthening its funding, and increasing its responsibility for managing the proliferation of multilateral environmental agreements.

Proponents of a refined status quo approach argue that any broader gauge reform to consolidate global-scale environmental responsibilities will fall flat politically, and might diminish the effectiveness of the system. They note that the range of problems that require attention is diverse, which makes a decentralized structure of multiple international organizations and treaty secretariats a virtue. In their most aggressive proposals, experts in this camp have argued for a "clustering" of the various pieces of the existing environmental regime so as to improve policy coherence, tighten potential cross-issue linkages, and avoid the duplication of effort that comes from full decentralization (UNEP 2001b, 2001c; Oberthür 2002; von Moltke 2001b; Najam 2003).[9] Such analyses, however, fail to identify the root causes behind UNEP's inability to serve as the leading international environmental organization and ensure a coherent environmental governance system. Instead, they emphasize the difficulty of carrying out fundamental changes within the UN system and point to the likely bureaucratic obstruction and fierce turf battles that would be triggered by any wholesale restructuring.

However, current reform efforts within UNEP, which since 1997 has been engaged in a major effort to strengthen international environmental governance at large, have also so far yielded very little. The International Environmental Governance (IEG) initiative, which UNEP launched in 2001, resulted in a weak declaration with a large number of priorities and little in terms of a plan of action. Having received only perfunctory attention at the WSSD in 2002, UNEP downgraded the initiative considerably.

The two potentially most significant reforms pre-date that initiative: the creation of the Environmental Management Group (EMG) and a new Global Ministerial Environmental Forum, both approved by the UN General Assembly in 1999 (UNGA 1999). The EMG is a forum for UN agencies, convention secretariats, the Bretton Woods organizations, and the WTO, under the chairmanship of the UNEP Executive Director. It aims to "promote inter-linkages, encourage timely and relevant exchange of data and information on specific issues and compatibility of different approaches to finding solutions to those common problems, and contribute to the synergy and complementarity among and between activities of its members in the field of environment and human settlements" (UNEP-EMG 2005). The EMG largely avoids turf wars in its role as coordinator of UN activities on the environment, but should not be seen as a centralizing decision-making body of global environmental governance.

Since its first meeting in 2001, its activities have included the establishment of an issue management group to harmonize biodiversity-related reporting, as well as system-wide consultations on the implementation of the UN's water agenda, focusing on environmental aspects including clean water, sanitation, and human settlements. Its 2004 activities focused on coordinating capacity building efforts. Although the EMG is potentially a major innovation in the coordination of international environmental governance, it marks a minimal reform in practice as long as governments show little inclination to grant it significant authority. High-level political commitment has been difficult to attract because of parallel UN forums putting excessive demands on the time and resources of top management. The EMG is still perceived as an instrument for UNEP's control rather than as a crosscutting mechanism for mutually beneficial collaboration. Furthermore, the EMG's severely limited capacity (two professional staff and an annual budget of $0.5 million) prevents the institution from taking bold initiative and effectively performing coordination activities. In its early years, UNEP devoted 30 percent of its annual budget to the activities of other organizations. Currently, more than 90 percent of the $0.5 million budget of the EMG is devoted to staff salaries and internal operations. Thus, it is rendered virtually ineffective though it has the institutional and structural potential to serve as the foundation for a clearinghouse mechanism (Ivanova, forthcoming).

The Global Ministerial Environment Forum was designed to raise UNEP's profile by including a ministerial-level meeting of Governing Council members at its regular biannual meetings and at a special session in off years to annually review important and emerging policy issues in the field of the environment. However, militating against increasing UNEP's authority, its mandate is co-terminus with UNEP's and the resolution creating it explicitly recognizes "the need to maintain the role of the Commission on Sustainable Development as the main forum for high-level policy debate on sustainable development" (UNGA 1999). Addressing its weaknesses in financing, UNEP launched a new voluntary contribution initiative to its Environment Fund. The contribution levels in 2002, however, averaging US$ four hundred thousand, are still well below the 1993–1994 all-time high average of US$ nine hundred thousand per country.[10] While partly due to the increased number of participating countries, the overall level of financing has fallen from over US$ sixty million in 1993 in the Environment Fund to about US$ fifty million in 2002 (UNEP 2002).

The only recent innovation in governance of significance is the Bali Strategic Plan for Technology Support and Capacity Building, developed in 2004 and adopted by the Governing Council in 2005 to improve UNEP's capacity building efforts. The Bali Plan addresses problems of fragmentation by focusing on coordination. Its strategic premise is that efforts should build on existing institutions and be "coordinated, linked, and integrated with other sustainable development initiatives through existing coordination mechanisms" (UNEP 2005). The plan underlines the need for improved interagency coordination and cooperation based on transparent and reliable information. It does not, however, clarify the respective roles for UNEP, UNDP, and the World Bank, which have become more like competitors than partners. For some, the strategy in the Bali Plan marks the return of an issue-based philosophy and a shift from a function-based organizational structure and priorities. For others, it is the only means to enhance UNEP's profile and create a brand name and reputation for the leading organizations in the environmental domain. Comprehensive in its nature, it addresses many of the most important challenges facing UNEP in the core areas of its mandate; however, it offers few concrete solutions. In sum, the Bali Plan marks UNEP's improved commitment to its coordination role in global environmental governance, but it takes a conservative "refined status quo" approach to needed broader reforms, and tangible implementation of the plan is yet to be seen.

Redirecting Efforts to the National Level

A second camp argues that energies put into changing the international architecture are misplaced. The priority should be to strengthen domestic environmental capacity (Juma 2000). This position reflects a false dichotomy. Whereas strengthening national and local capacity is required for effective governance, the issue at the global level is whether the institutional architecture will support and reinforce such efforts. This is especially the case for developing countries, something governments explicitly acknowledged in the Bali Plan (UNEP 2005).[11]

Efforts on major global problems will require local responses, but international institutions often set the agenda and provide normative leverage for such change. They also can ensure that the normative and material incentives internationally work for positive action on environmental problems, not against them. For example, in the absence of either reform of international economic institutions to support local, national, and regional environmental efforts, or the creation or strengthening of environmental institutions to counteract rules that systematically favor economic over environmental values (for example, within the World Bank or WTO), national environmental policies will continue to be evaluated and encouraged as much from the perspective of their effects on trade or investment as on the environment, and will continue to be subject to legal challenges under institutions such as the WTO dispute settlement system.

In other words, if the status quo remains more or less intact in the environmental area, improvement will depend on system-wide reform within existing institutions, including the WTO and regional trade agreements such as NAFTA. This is not out of the question. In the abstract, the WTO and

NAFTA accept the idea that trade and sustainable development can be mutually supportive. The door is thus open to environmental demands that trade agreements take into account the environmental consequences of trade and the effect of trade rules on the natural environment and environmental regulations. However, the institutionalization of this linkage to date subordinates environmentalism by posing potential conflicts as challenges to free trade, instead of to the environment. For example, Rio Principle 12, based on the trade norm of nondiscrimination, reinforces a binary view of all trade-related measures as either liberalizing or protectionist by imposing the burden of proof on national environmental regulations to show they are not discriminatory, when it states that "trade policy measures for environmental purposes should not constitute a means of arbitrary or unjustifiable discrimination or a disguised restriction on international trade" (UN 1992). Nowhere does it say nondiscrimination or open markets should not constitute an unjustifiable restriction on environmental protection or ecosystem health. This normative environment makes trade-offs difficult between efficiency, economic growth, corporate freedom, and environmental protection, and thus risks justifying inaction if tough regulatory choices, which imply trade-offs with market values, are necessary to get the desired ecological effects.

As Gaines (2003) has argued, the real issue is whether, and what type of, institutional reform can "bridge the cultural gap between the worlds of environmental policy and trade policy" (325). More broadly, can we rebalance the norms and goals of the environment and economy in a more sustainable direction rather than privileging liberal economic goals? Gaines, like others in the national focus camp, argues that the creation of a counterorganization to the WTO is wrongheaded since it might be ignored by more powerful economic institutions rather than facilitate dialogue. Instead, given the normative and power configuration, we should "persist in the arduous process of attitudinal change and policy integration" within trade institutions and, especially, in powerful national governments to better integrate environmental policy into trade and other economic policies (Gaines 2003, 326). Those who argue for major structural reform and the creation of a World Environment Organization (WEO) contend that such reform within existing economic institutions is necessary but not sufficient to prevent the environmental agenda from being subsumed within the trade, investment, or finance agendas.

Fundamental Structural Reform

Proposals for major structural reform derive from a conclusion that the existing global-scale environmental architecture is deeply dysfunctional and structurally flawed, making a fresh start easier than reform along the margins. A growing number of politicians (Chirac 2001; Gorbachev 2001; Ruggiero

1998; Panitchpakdi 2001) and academics and analysts (Runge 2001; Esty 1994, 2000; Biermann 2000; Whalley and Zissimos 2002; Charnovitz 2002; Zedillo Commission 2001; Speth 2004) support this view. Beyond the difficulties of trying to fix a failed structure, those arguing for this approach often note that the existing regime was designed for a preglobalization era before the full spectrum of worldwide environmental problems was understood and prior to the current depth of economic integration. Moreover, globalization has changed the political landscape away from intergovernmentalism toward fragmented authority and the ascendancy of markets, conditions that reveal the limitations of national regulation and the need for social regulation of the global marketplace.

The case for a major overhaul of the environmental regime rests on several premises: (1) a "public goods" logic that requires collective action be organized at the scale of the problem to be addressed (Olson 1965); (2) the potential of a new body to overcome the fragmentation of the current structure, obtain synergies in addressing problems, and take advantage of opportunities for better issue prioritization, budget rationalization, and bureaucratic coordination; (3) the need for an organization to serve as a counterpoint and a counterweight to the WTO, the World Bank, and other international economic institutions, especially given the judicial powers of the WTO; and (4) the need for an authoritative international environmental body with a first-rate staff, a reputation for analytical rigor, and the capacity to take on tasks such as dispute resolution.

The political prospects for wholesale reform in the short to medium term, however, appear slim. A 2003 proposal of French President Jacques Chirac for the creation of a World Environment Organization has been downgraded considerably to fit with the existing political constraints. The French and German governments now advocate the establishment of a United Nations Environment Organization (UNEO), which essentially upgrades UNEP into a UN specialized agency with the aim to ensure more financial resources and bureaucratic independence. The proposed UNEO, however, fails to significantly upgrade UNEP from the status quo—even keeping its headquarters in Nairobi—and overlooks underlying problems and institutional faults of the existing architecture (Ivanova, forthcoming). Yet, the UNEO proposal is gaining increasing attention and is emerging as the only serious political option for institutional reform.

AN INSTITUTIONAL COMPROMISE:
A GLOBAL ENVIRONMENTAL MECHANISM

We argue for a fourth option that builds on Esty and Ivanova's (2002) proposal for a Global Environmental Mechanism (GEM) centered on a structure that can deliver the *functions* needed at the global level. Whereas this option avoids the pitfalls and poor prospects of a new World Environment Organization, it recognizes that shoring up a failing governance structure will not suffice given path dependencies in UNEP's operation and location, as well as its lack of authority to engage the broader global governance system. This option offers the best hope for a renewed compromise that successfully re-embeds liberalism within broader social purposes that include environmental purposes. Our argument depends on making the realist case that such a structure can facilitate the necessary principled dialogue within the liberal economic order and existing institutions, neither of which show signs of disappearing any time soon. Thus, below we attempt to bring our argument full circle, linking the institutional and normative elements required to revitalize what the compromise of liberal environmentalism promised, but could not deliver.

Institutionally, a GEM attempts to capture the middle ground of governing under conditions of "fragmegration," by acknowledging the diversity and dynamism of environmental problems and the need for specialized responses. No single bureaucratic structure can build an internal organization with the requisite knowledge and expertise to address the wide-ranging, dynamic, and interconnected problems we now face (Esty and Ivanova 2002). The issues demanding immediate attention arise on various geographic scales, requiring a multi-tier response structure (Esty 1999; Karlsson 2000; Ostrom 1990; Vogler 2000). They demand capacities in multiple areas, including ecological sciences, public health, risk assessment, cost-benefit analysis, performance measurement, and policy evaluation, as well as a sound ethical foundation. Today's global environmental governance challenge thus requires a more virtual structure built on a multi-institutional regime capable of drawing in a wide array of underlying disciplines through governments, NGOs, and global public policy networks.

The core governance functions required under these conditions include: (1) provision of adequate information and analysis to characterize problems, track trends, and identify interests as well as monitoring and reporting on performance; (2) creation of a "policy space" for environmental negotiation and bargaining; and (3) sustained buildup of capacity for addressing issues of agreed-upon concern and significance.

Consequently, a GEM would comprise: (1) a global information clearinghouse with mechanisms for data collection, assessment, monitoring, and analysis to reveal the nature of the problems; (2) a global technology clearinghouse with mechanisms for technology transfer and identification and dissemination of best practices to help build capacities where needed; and (3) a negotiation forum to elucidate values, bring forth ethics and justice concerns, and facilitate agreements that improve environmental quality and reconcile the interests of different parties. Rather than formal bureaucratic structures, these elements are more likely to take the form of networks that would build on the expertise of existing institutions, only creating new mechanisms where key functions are nonexistent or inadequate. Nonetheless, building on a proposal by the Norwegian environment minister, we do envisage the possible evolution of an office akin to the UN High Commissioner for Human Rights to add needed moral authority and agenda-setting capacity (Brende 2004). This office might, for example, evolve out of the Environmental Management Group in Geneva.

The information clearinghouse could contribute to the creation of a common vision and encourage long-term thinking by providing timely, relevant, and reliable data on environmental issues, risks, and trends on the global scale. Better and more accessible data, science, and analysis could shift assumptions, highlight preferences, and sharpen policies. Moreover, information on how similar problems are solved in various national contexts can aid national-level administrations in adopting best practices and learning. Comparative performance analysis across countries could provide greater transparency and encourage positive competition.

The technology clearinghouse would focus on problems of inadequate capacity. Although most multilateral environmental agreements contain provisions related to technology transfer as part of the incentive packages for developing countries to meet their obligations, most technologies are owned by private companies not governments. Thus, incentives need to be devised to motivate the private sector to disseminate technological advances optimally. An effective environmental technology clearinghouse could support North-South and public-private partnerships and provide a forum for coordinating financial assistance to developing countries. It would contain information on best practices around the world and facilitate technology development and continuous learning.

The real test for such a GEM, however, is whether it can facilitate reform of existing institutions to sufficiently address environmental purposes that are increasingly recognized as necessary for the stability of global liberalism. In this regard, the negotiation forum component of this proposal is absolutely essential, linked to something akin to a high commissioner's office. Together, they can facilitate a high-level political forum to try to catalyze the necessary dialogue within existing institutions such as the WTO's Committee on Trade and Environment, the Commission on Sustainable Development, the Global Compact, and even non-state governance schemes, as well as provide a forum for multilateral and bilateral bargaining. The new Environmental Management Group is already a step in this direction, and might be enhanced if states were to agree to let it evolve a more political role. In addition to what EMG already does, this office would facilitate learning and coordination across the full range of environmental governance institutions, as well as provide a high-profile office to promote environmental norms and develop new ones, promote national environmental infrastructure, and stimulate action on the environment. While more modest than a WEO, such an office would significantly raise the profile of environmental issues and provide a focal point to move the agenda forward where negotiations within existing institutions have been stalemated.

For example, it might do better in moving the trade-environment agenda forward than the WTO's Committee on Trade and Environment, because it would be outside that institutional environment. The CTE has proven unable to make any significant progress on its core mandates, such as when deviations from nondiscrimination for environmental protection are permissible, the reconciliation of WTO rules and environmental treaty provisions, or the question of eco-labeling. Instead, discussions reflect the subordination of environmental protection to trade and development rather than balancing or integrating the three goals. A Global Environmental Mechanism would not be a replacement or competitor with the CTE, which is institutionally best suited to deliberate on the trade-environment relationship and to influence trade rules. However, a more coherent and authoritative environmental voice would be present along with individual treaty secretariats, to which the CTE currently grants observer status. A GEM could similarly promote dialogue and mutual learning within regional trade agreements, other international economic organizations, national governments, and civil society, in all cases helping ensure that development, trade, and environmental goals are on more of an equal footing. Working with existing institutions and networks avoids the risks associated with expecting a WEO to counter the WTO, since its likely relative weakness could allow members of the trade community to "evade the difficult choices facing it and simply dump the trade-environment problem in the lap of the [WEO], or blame the policy impasse on the recalcitrance of its environmental counterpart" (Gaines 2003, 361).

While we believe that such a redesign is possible, the prospects will be considerably dimmer without the political engagement of the major powers, especially the United States. As Ruggie notes in his chapter, the administration of George W. Bush demonstrated little interest in even a modest centralization of authority of this sort. It prefers complete control over its own domestic environmental agenda, working in limited ways with existing institutions, and bilateral engagement or coalition building with countries willing to adapt to its policy preferences rather than working multilaterally.[12] Nonetheless, the normative conditions and ideational resources within existing institutions, global civil society, and even some segments of the global marketplace, are already available to draw upon to make the case for such a reform, if leaders are willing to seize them.

Any reform of global environmental governance, however, needs to be based on a holistic assessment of the strengths and weaknesses in the current system. An independent external review of (1) the system of global environmental governance and (2) UNEP's role and performance within the system would help to clarify the mandates of existing organizations, reveal their comparative advantage, and provide a vision for reduced competition and a productive division of labor. A strategic review will systematically assess the history and performance of the anchor institution for the global environment, outline current and future needs, and define scenarios for action based on sound assessment of progress to date, constraints, and opportunities. Designing a feasible and functional blueprint for a GEM, or other reform proposals, will hinge on such a learning experience (Ivanova, forthcoming).

CONCLUSION

The advent of sustainable development was a major accomplishment in global governance. It succeeded in bringing the environment onto the international agenda in a new, creative, and productive way that provided a solid basis for a global compromise between environment and economy. But attempts to institutionalize sustainable development in international institutions and agreements also produced the unintended consequences of embedding environmental governance too firmly in the emerging hyperliberalism of the late twentieth century. When combined with path dependencies in the institutional architecture, this liberal environmentalism was a recipe for governance failure. Indeed, the strongest argument for reform is that the legitimacy of that liberal order, as is increasingly understood within the major liberal economic institutions, will depend in part on at least the modest success of an environment-economy compromise.

Our argument has been that change is needed in both the norms and institutions of global governance, although perhaps less fundamental change than some environmentalists advocate. In the case of norms, the thinking that adapted environmentalism to the liberal economic order needs correction to allow greater consideration of how to leave policy space for local environmental protection. In other words, a correction that brings the compromise closer to the embedded liberalism ideal. Such a shift might, for example, elevate the Precautionary Principle—which suggests erring on the side of caution when there is risk of severe ecological harm—from its current economistic interpretation, as merely a justification for various methods of incorporating environmental risks into prices, to a more ecological footing that allows greater policy space to assess health and environmental risks on their own terms. At the same time, simply leaving policy space for national governments is insufficient given the global scope of some problems and the effects of globalization on national autonomy. Moreover, globalization has brought environmental consciousness to the global level and embedded it in a variety of networks that eschew clear spatial and political boundaries, and from which local solutions increasingly draw ideas and resources.

The normative changes, we argue, are unlikely to occur absent institutional change. One main element of institutional reform is to create the necessary basis for dialogue and greater moral authority for the environment. Greater coherence is also needed, even if some fragmentation and decentralization is a virtue. If environmental governance is to be effective, it requires clearer guiding principles, a strong voice to influence economic institutions and thinking, information, and resources, as well as a forum in which to make bargains, both large and small.

All this does not require a new grand compromise. But it would represent an important expression in our own time of the original promise of embedded liberalism.

NOTES

1. World Trade Organization (1994). The preamble to the Agreement Establishing the WTO includes a similar understanding of the trade/environment relationship.

2. On the project, see http://www.malampaya.com/web/index.html.

3. See also Thérien (this volume).

4. See, for example, Ruggie (this volume), and references therein to current activities and assessments of the Global Compact.

5. For a broader discussion of such governance systems, see Bernstein and Cashore (2006); Cashore (2002); Gereffi et al. (2001).

6. Our claim is simply that governance has performed poorly as measured by its own terms of reference and goals, with only a few notable exceptions such as international action to prevent depletion of the Earth's ozone layer. We cannot here independently assess the state of the world's environment.

7. See also Conca (2000).

8. For what such an ecological order might look like, see Helleiner (1996).

9. Three approaches to clustering have been identified: (1) at the thematic level (of issue-specific MEAs such as the biodiversity related conventions, chemical conventions, etc.); (2) at the functional level (harmonized reporting, capacity building, issues management, trade related issues, etc.); and (3) at the regional level (UNEP 2001d).

10. The contributions range from $1,100 for Bhutan to $6.5 million for the United Kingdom and the United States (UNEP 2002).

11. This discussion somewhat mirrors a similar discussion in the WTO. Any "grand" compromise in global governance must confront the problem of technical assistance and capacity building across the board, although the debate over what these entail is complex and ongoing. Some developing countries and development experts worry that technical assistance, for example, has been geared more toward socializing developing countries into the fold of existing regimes that favor Northern interests

than toward building indigenous knowledge, expertise, and capacity that would enable them to develop stronger negotiating positions and arguments or innovative solutions to problems facing their countries (Helleiner 2001; Adler and Bernstein 2005).

12. For example, at UNEP's Governing Council Meeting in March 2004, the US delegation either opposed or sought to delay discussion of any proposed institutional reform, including EU proposals for an Intergovernmental Panel on Global Change and proposed universal membership for UNEP's Governing Council (IISD 2004).

Works Cited

Abdelal, Rawi. 2007. *Capital rules.* Cambridge: Harvard University Press.

ACCA (Association of Chartered Certificate Accountants). 2004. Towards transparency: Progress on global sustainability reporting 2004. Retrieved September 16, 2004, from http://www.corporateregister.com.

Act Up New York. 2002, July 10. AIDS activists protest Coke's deadly neglect of workers with AIDS in developing countries. Act Up New York Press Release. Retrieved August 14, 2004, from http://www.actupny.org/reports/bcn?BCN-coke.html.

Adelman, Carol C. 2003. The privatization of foreign aid. *Foreign Affairs* 82, no. 6: 9–14.

Adler, Emanuel, and Michael Barnett. 1998. *Security communities.* Cambridge: Cambridge University Press.

Adler, Emanuel. 2002. Constructivism and international relations. In *Handbook of international relations,* ed. Walter Carlsnaes, Thomas Risse, and Beth Simmons. Thousand Oaks: Sage Publishers.

Adler, Emanuel, and Steven Bernstein. 2005. Knowledge in power: The epistemic construction of global governance. In *Power in global governance,* ed. Michael Barnett and Raymond Duvall. Cambridge: Cambridge University Press.

Alt, James E. 2002. Comparative political economy: Credibility, accountability, and institutions. In *Political science: State of the discipline,* ed. Ira Katznelson and Helen V. Milner. New York: Norton.

Altman, Lawrence T. 2002, July 13. Former presidents urge leadership on AIDS. *New York Times,* 5.

Anglo American. 2003. Anglo American plc supporting HIV and AIDS awareness. Retrieved August 14, 2004, from http://www.angloamerican.co.uk/hivaids/ourresponse/policy.asp.

Annan, Kofi A. 1999, January 31. A *compact for the new century.* UN, SG/SM/6881.

———. 2000. "*We the peoples*": The role of the United Nations in the 21st century. New York: United Nations.

———. 2001, November 9. *Message of the UN Secretary-General.* Doha Ministerial Conference of the WTO.

Archer, Clive. 2001. *International organizations.* 3rd edition. London: Routledge.

Arend, Anthony. 2003. International law and the preemptive use of military force. *Washington Quarterly* 26(2): 89–103.

Aylott, Nicholas. 2001. The Swedish Social Democratic Party. In *Social democracy and monetary union,* ed. T. Notermans. New York: Berghahn.

Ball, Jeffrey. 2003, April 16. Global warming threatens health of companies. *Wall Street Journal.*

Balls, Andrew. 2005, June 29. Aid will not lift growth in Africa, warns IMF. *Financial Times.*

Baradat, Leon P. 1997. *Political ideologies: Their origins and impact.* 6th edition. Upper Saddle River: Prentice-Hall.

Barnett, Michael, and Martha Finnemore. 2004. *Rules for the world: International organizations in global politics.* Ithaca, NY: Cornell University Press.

Barrett, Diana, and Daniella Ballou. 2003. Heineken International: Workplace HIV/AIDS programs in Africa. *Harvard Business School Case # 9-303-063.* Cambridge: Harvard Business School Press.

Baudot, Jacques, ed. 2000. *Building a world community: Globalization and the common good.* Copenhagen: Royal Danish Ministry of Foreign Affairs.

Bayne, Nicholas. 2005. Overcoming evil with good: Impressions of the Gleneagles Summit, 6–8 July 2005. Retrieved August 8, 2005, from: www.g8.utoronto.ca/evaluations/2005gleneagles/bayne2005-0718.html.

Beck, Ulrich. 2002a. Living your life in a runaway world: Individualisation, globalization, and politics. In *Global capitalism,* ed. Will Hutton and Anthony Giddens. New York: New Press.

———. 2002b. World risk society revisited. *Theory, Culture and Society* 19(4): 39–55.

Becker, Elizabeth. 2005, May 12. Low cost and sweatshop-free—Cambodia's garment makers hold off a vast Chinese challenge. *New York Times.*

Becker, Elizabeth, and Robert Pear. 2004, July 12. Trade agreement may undercut importing inexpensive drugs. *New York Times,* A-1.

Bergsten, Fred. 1999, April 22. Dollarization in emerging-market economies and its policy implications for the United States. Statement Before the Joint Hearing of the Subcommittee on Economic Policy and the Subcommittee on International Trade and Finance Committee on Banking, Housing and Urban Affairs, US Senate.

Bernstein, Steven. 2001. *The compromise of liberal environmentalism.* New York: Columbia University Press.

———. 2004. The elusive basis of legitimacy in global governance: Three conceptions. Globalization and Autonomy working paper series. Institute for Globalization and the Human Condition, McMaster University.

Bernstein, Steven, and Benjamin Cashore. 2006. Can non-state global governance be legitimate? A theoretical framework. Manuscript under review.

Biermann, Frank. 2000. The case for a world environment organization. *Environment* 42(9): 22.

Birchall, Jonathan. 2003, August 13. Companies face UN scrutiny on human rights. *Financial Times*.

Blustein, Paul. 2001. *The chastening*. New York: Public Affairs.

Blyth, Mark. 2002. *Great transformations: Economic ideas and institutional change in the twentieth century*. New York: Cambridge University Press.

Bøås, Morten, and Desmond McNeill, eds. 2004. *Global institutions and development: Framing the world?* London: Routledge.

Bobbio, Norberto. 1996. *Left and right: The significance of a political distinction*. Chicago: University of Chicago Press.

Boli, John, and George M. Thomas. 1999. *Constructing world culture: International non-governmental organizations since 1875*. Stanford: Stanford University Press.

Bolton, John R. 2000. Should we take global governance seriously? *Chicago Journal of International Law* 1(2): 205–22.

Bourdieu, Pierre. 1982. *Ce que parler veut dire. L'économie des échanges linguistiques*. Paris: Fayard.

Brainard, Lael, Carol Graham, Steven Radelet, Nigel Purvis, and Gayle Smith. 2003. *Global poverty and the millennium challenge account*. Washington, DC: Brookings Institute.

Braithwaite, John, and Peter Drahos. 2000. *Global business regulation*. Cambridge: Cambridge University Press.

Brende, Børge. 2004, February 13–15. Statement on international environmental governance. 7th Special Session of UNEP Governing Council/Global Ministerial Environment Forum, Cartegena.

Broad, Robin, ed. 2002. *Global backlash: Citizen initiatives for a just world economy*. Lanham, MD: Rowman and Littlefield.

Buira, Ariel, ed. 2003. *Challenges to the World Bank and the IMF: Developing country perspectives*. London: Anthem Press.

Busby, Josh, and Alexander Ochs. 2004. From Mars and Venus down to Earth: Understanding the transatlantic climate divide. In *Beyond Kyoto: Meeting the long-term challenge of global climate change*, ed. David Michel. Washington, DC: Center for Transatlantic Relations, School of Advanced International Studies, Johns Hopkins University.

Bush Bans Imports of "Blood Diamonds." 2003, July 29. *CNN.com*. Retrieved July 29, 2003, from http://www.cnn.com/2003/US/07/29/bush.diamonds.ap/index.html.

Carr, Edward Hallett. 1946. *The twenty years' crisis*, 2nd ed. New York: Harper and Row.

Cashore, Benjamin. 2002. Legitimacy and the privatization of environmental governance: How non-state market-driven (NSMD) governance systems gain rule-making authority. *Governance* 15(4): 502–29.

Castles, Francis G., and Peter Mair. 1984. Left-right political scales: Some "expert" judgements. *European Journal of Political Research* 12(4): 73–88.

Cederman, Lars-Erik. 2001. Nationalism and bounded integration: What it would take to construct a European demos. *European Journal of International Relations* 7(2): 139–74

Center for Business and Government, Kennedy School of Government, Harvard University. 2003. HIV/AIDS and business in Africa and Asia: Building sustainable partnerships. Retrieved August 14, 2004, from http:// www.ksg.harvard.edu/cbg/hiv-aids/home.htm.

Center for Civic Society Studies. 1999. *Global civil society: Dimensions of the non-profit sector*. Baltimore: Johns Hopkins University.

Charnovitz, Steve. 2002. A world environment organization. *Columbia Journal of Environmental Law* 27(2): 323–62.

Chernilo, Daniel. 2002. The theorization of social coordinations in differentiated societies: The theory of generalized symbolic media in Parsons, Luhmann, and Habermas. *British Journal of Sociology* 53(3): 431–49.

Chirac, Jacques. 2001, May 5. Jacques Chirac s'empare de l'écologie. *Le Monde*.

Chriszt, Michael. 2000. Perspectives on a potential North American monetary union. *Economic Review (Federal Reserve Bank of Atlanta)* 85(4): 29–38.

Chung, Joanna, and Alex Halperin. 2004, July 24–25. Arab attitudes to US hardening. *Financial Times*, 5.

Claude Jr., Inis L. 1966. Collective legitimization as a political function of the United Nations. *International Organization* 20(3): 367–79.

Clausing, Kimberly A. 2001, January. The behavior of intrafirm trade prices in U.S. international price data. U.S. Department of Labor, Bureau of Labor Statistics. *BLS Working Paper* 333: 1–41.

Clavin, Patricia. 2003. "Money talks": Competition and cooperation with the League of Nations, 1929–1940. In *Money doctors: The experience of international financial advising 1850–2000*, ed. Marc Flandreau. London: Routledge.

Cohen, B. J. 2002. US policy on dollarization: A political analysis. *Geopolitics* 7(1): 63–84.

Coicaud, Jean-Marc, and Veijo Heiskanen, eds. 2001. *The legitimacy of international organizations*. Tokyo: United Nations University Press.

Coleman, William D., and Anthony Perl. 1999. Internationalized policy environments and policy network analysis. *Political Studies* 47(4): 691–709.

Collado, Emilio. 1940. An economic program for the Americas, June 10, 1940. In United States Department of State, *Foreign relations of the United States, diplomatic papers 1940 Volume 5*. Washington, DC: US Government Printing Office.

Commission on the Private Sector and Development. 2004. *Unleashing entrepreneurship: Making business work for the poor: Report to the secretary-general of the United Nations*. New York: UNDP.

Conca, K. 2000. The WTO and the undermining of global environmental governance. *Review of International Political Economy* 7(3): 484–94.

Cooper, Andrew F., John English, and Ramesh Thakur, eds. 2002. *Enhancing global governance.* Tokyo: United Nations University Press.

Cortese, Amy. 2002, August 18. As the Earth warms, will companies pay? *New York Times.*

Cox, Kevin R. 1997. *Spaces of globalization: Reasserting the power of the local.* New York: Guildford.

Cox, Robert W. 1992. Multilateralism and world order. *Review of International Studies* 18(2): 161–80.

Cox, Robert W., with Michael G. Schechter. 2002. *The political economy of a plural world: Critical reflections on power, morals, and civilization.* London: Routledge.

Cutler, A. Clair, Virginia Haufler, and Tony Porter, eds. 1999. *Private authority and international affairs.* Albany: State University of New York Press.

D'Arista, Jane. 2001. *Dollarization: Critical U.S. views.* Financial Markets Center.

de Jonquières, Jon Guy. 2004, July 14. Survey shows cautious public support for global trade. *Financial Times,* 6.

Deacon, Bob, with Michelle Hulse and Paul Stubbs. 1997. *Global social policy: International organizations and the future of welfare.* London: Sage.

Dell, Sidney. 1990. *The United Nations and international business.* Durham-London: Duke University Press.

Devetak, Richard, and Richard Higgott. 1999. Justice unbound? Globalization, states, and the transformation of the social bond. *International Affairs* 75(3): 483–98.

Dicken, Peter, Philip F. Kelly, Kris Olds, and Henry Wai-Chung Yeung. 2001. Chains and networks, territories and scales: Towards a relational framework for analysing the global economy. *Global Networks* 1(2): 89–112.

Dickerson, Kitty. 1999. *Textiles and apparel in the global economy.* 3rd edition. Upper Saddle River: Merrill.

Distlerath, Linda. 2002. African comprehensive HIV/AIDS partnership. Retrieved August 14, 2004, from: http://www.ksg.harvard.edu/cbg/hiv-aids/ksg/Distlerath_presentation.pdf.

Doran, Peter. 2002, October 3. World summit on sustainable development: An assessment for IISD. Briefing paper. Winnipeg: International Institute for Sustainable Development.

Drake, Paul. 1989. *The money doctor in the Andes: The Kemmerer missions 1923–1933.* Durham: Duke University Press.

Drake, William J. 2001. Communications. In *Managing global issues,* ed. P. J. Simmons and Chantal de Jonge Oudraat. Washington, DC: Carnegie Endowment for International Peace.

Eckersley, Robyn. 2004. The big chill: The WTO and multilateral environmental agreements. *Global Environmental Politics* 4(2): 24–50.

Eichenberg, Richard C., and Russell J. Dalton. 1993. Europeans and the European Community. *International Organization* 47(4): 507–34.

EKOS. 2003. Canadian attitudes to international trade: Survey findings. EKOS Research Associates. Retrieved January 21, 2004, from http://www.queensu.ca/cora/polls/2003/May6–DFAIT-International_Trade.pdf.

Emmerij, Louis, Richard Jolly, and Thomas G. Weiss. 2001. *Ahead of the curve? UN ideas and global challenges*. Bloomington: Indiana University Press.

Environics International. 2002. The world economic forum poll: Global public opinion on globalization. Executive Briefing. Retrieved from www.globescan.com/brochures/WEF_Poll_Brief.pdf.

Esty, Daniel C. 1994. The case for a global environmental organization. In *Managing the world economy: Fifty years after Bretton Woods*, ed. Peter Kenen. Washington, DC: Institute for International Economics.

———. 1999. Toward optimal environmental governance. *New York University Law Review* 74(6): 1495–1574.

———. 2000. The value of creating a global environmental organization. *Environment Matters* 6 (12):13–15.

Esty, Daniel C., and Maria H. Ivanova. 2002. Revitalizing global environmental governance: A function-driven approach. In *Global environmental governance: Options and opportunities*, ed. Daniel C. Esty and Maria H. Ivanova. New Haven: Yale School of Forestry and Environmental Studies.

Europe Energy. 2001, March 30. Statoil signs agreement with ICEM. *Europe Energy*.

European Commission. 2003, November. Globalisation. *Flash Eurobarometer 151b*.

Finnemore, Martha. 1996. *National interests in international society*. Ithaca: Cornell University Press.

Fomerand, Jacques. 2002. Recent UN textbooks: Suggestions from an old-fashioned practitioner. *Global Governance* 8(3): 383–403.

Foucault, Michel, Graham Burchell, Colin Gordon, and Peter Miller. 1991. *The Foucault effect: Studies in governmentality: With two lectures by and an interview with Michel Foucault*. Chicago: University of Chicago Press.

Franck, Thomas M. 1990. *The power of legitimacy among nations*. New York: Oxford University Press.

Franda, Marcus. 2001. *Governing the internet: The emergence of an international regime*. Boulder: Lynne Rienner.

Frankel, Max. 2002, May 26. Sound of one saber rattling. *The New York Times Book Review*.

French, Hilary. 1992. Strengthening global environmental governance. In *State of the world 1992*, ed. Lester Brown. New York: Norton.

G7. 2005, February 4–5. *Statement of G7 finance ministers and central bank governors*. London, UK.

G77. 2005, June 12–16. *Second South Summit: Doha Declaration*. Doha, Qatar.

Gabel, Matthew J. 1998. *Interests and integration: Market liberalization, public opinion, and European union*. Ann Arbor: University of Michigan Press.

Gaines, Sanford E. 2003. The problem of enforcing environmental norms in the WTO and what to do about it. *Hastings International and Comparative Law Review* 26: 321–85.

Galbraith, John Kenneth. 1956. *American capitalism: The concept of counterveiling power*. Boston: Houghton Mifflin.

Galtung, Fredrik. 2000. A global network to curb corruption: The experience of Transparency International. In *The third force: The rise of transnational civil society*, ed. Ann M. Florini. Washington, DC: Carnegie Endowment for International Peace.

Gamble, Andrew, and Gavin Kelly. 2001. The British Labour Party and monetary union. In *Social democracy and monetary union*, ed. Ton Notermans. New York: Berghahn.

Garcia-Johnson, Ronie. 2000. *Exporting environmentalism: U.S. multinational chemical corporations in Brazil and Mexico*. Cambridge: MIT Press.

Gardner, Lloyd. 1964. *Economic aspects of New Deal diplomacy*. Madison: University of Wisconsin Press.

Garrett, Geoffrey. 1998. *Partisan politics in the global economy*. Cambridge: Cambridge University Press.

———. 2000a. Globalization and national autonomy. In *The political economy of globalization*, ed. Ngaire Woods. New York: St. Martin's Press.

———. 2000b. Capital mobility, exchange rates, and fiscal policy in the global economy. *Review of International Political Economy* 7(1): 153–70.

Garrett, Geoffrey, and Deborah Mitchell. 2001. Globalization, government spending, and taxation in the OECD. *European Journal of Political Research* 39(2): 145–77.

Gereffi, Gary. 1999. International trade and industrial upgrading in the apparel commodity chain. *Journal of International Economics* 48(1): 37–70.

———. 2001. Shifting governance structures in global commodity chains. *American Behavioral Scientist* 44(10): 1616–37.

Gereffi, Gary, Ronie Garcia-Johnson, and Erika Sasser. 2001. The NGO-Industrial Complex. *Foreign Policy* 125(July–August): 56–65.

Gereffi, Gary, John Humphrey, and Timothy Sturgeon. 2005. The governance of global value chains. *Review of International Political Economy* 12(1): 78–104.

Giddens, Anthony. 1979. *Central problems in social theory*. London: Macmillan.

———. 1991. *Modernity and self-identity*. Stanford: Stanford University Press.

———. 2000. *The third way and its critics*. Cambridge: Polity Press.

———, ed. 2001. *The global third way debate*. Cambridge: Polity Press.

Goodman, John B., and Louis W. Pauly. 1993. The obsolescence of capital controls? *World Politics* 46(1): 50–82.

Gorbachev, Mikhail. 2001, April 27. The American and Russian people don't want a new confrontation. *Newsweek*.

Gore, Charles. 2000. The rise and fall of the Washington consensus as a paradigm for developing countries. *World Development* 28(5): 789–804.

Gosovic, Branislav. 2000. Global intellectual hegemony and the international development agenda. *International Social Science Journal* 52(166): 447–56.

Government of Canada. 1998, March. *Voluntary codes: A guide for their development and use*. A joint initiative of the Office of Consumer Affairs, Industry Canada, and the Regulatory Affairs Division, Treasury Board Secretariat. Retrieved August 14, 2004, from http://strategis.ic.gc.ca/SSG/ca00863e.html.

Grande, Edgar, and Louis W. Pauly, eds. 2005. *Complex sovereignty: Reconstituting political authority in the twenty-first century*. Toronto: University of Toronto Press.

Granovetter, Mark. 1992a. Economic action and social structure: The problem of embeddedness. In *The sociology of economic life*, ed. Mark Granovetter and Richard Swedberg. Boulder: Westview.

———. 1992b. Economic institutions as social constructions: A framework for analysis. *Acta Sociologica* 35(1): 3–11.

Gwin, Catherine. 1995. A comparative assessment. In *The UN and the Bretton Woods institutions: New challenges for the twenty-first century*, ed. Mahbub ul Haq, Richard Jolly, Paul Streeten, and Khadija Haq. New York: St. Martin's Press.

Gwyn, Richard. 1996, December 27. Annan shows he's much more than "the U.S. choice." *Toronto Star*, A31.

Haas, Ernst B. 1990. *When knowledge is power*. Berkeley: University of California Press.

Haas, Peter M. 2004. Addressing the global governance deficit. *Global Environmental Politics* 4(4): 1–15.

Habermas, Jürgen. 1998. *Between facts and norms: Contributions to a discourse theory of law and democracy*. Translated by William Rehg. Cambridge: MIT Press.

Hall, Rodney Bruce, and Thomas J. Biersteker, eds. 2002. *The emergence of private authority in global governance*. Cambridge: Cambridge University Press.

Hays, Jude C., Sean D. Ehrlich, and Clint Peinhardt. 2005. Government spending and public support for trade in the OECD. *International Organization* 59(2): 473–94.

Heisbourg, Francois. 2003. A work in progress: The Bush doctrine and its consequences. *Washington Quarterly* 26(2): 75–88.

Held, David, and Anthony McGrew, eds. 2002. *Governing globalization: Power, authority, and global governance*. Cambridge: Polity Press.

Helleiner, Eric. 1996. International political economy and the Greens. *New Political Economy* 1(1): 59–77.

———. 2003a. *The making of national money: Territorial currencies in historical perspective*. Ithaca: Cornell University Press.

———. 2003b. Dollarization diplomacy: US policy towards Latin America comes full circle? *Review of International Political Economy* 10(3): 406–29.

Helleiner, Gerald K. 2001. Markets, politics, and globalization: Can the global economy be civilized? *Journal of Human Development* 2(1): 27–46.

Herman, Barry, Federica Pietracci, and Krishnan Sharma, eds. 2001. *Financing for development: UNU Policy Perspectives No. 6*. Tokyo: United Nations University Press.

Herman, Barry. 2002. Civil society and the financing for development initiative at the United Nations. In *Civil society and global finance*, ed. Jan Aart Scholte and Albrecht Schnabel. Tokyo: United Nations University Press.

Heywood, Andrew. 1992. *Political ideologies: An introduction*. New York: St. Martin's Press.

Hill, Martin. 1946. *The economic and financial organization of the League of Nations: A survey of twenty-five years' experience*. Washington, DC: Carnegie Endowment for International Peace.

———. 1978. *The United Nations system: Coordinating the economic and social work*. Cambridge: Cambridge University Press.

Hochschild, Arlie Russell. 2002. Global care chains and emotional surplus value. In *Global capitalism*, ed. Will Hutton and Anthony Giddens. New York: New Press.

Hoekman, Bernard. 2005. Operationalizing the concept of policy space in the WTO: Beyond special and differential treatment. *Journal of International Economic Law* 8 (2): 405–24.

Hollingsworth, J. Rogers, and Robert Boyer. 1997. Coordination of economic actors and social systems of production. In *Contemporary capitalism: The embeddedness of institutions*, ed. Hollingsworth and Boyer. Cambridge: Cambridge University Press.

Houlder, Vanessa. 2003, July 14. Climate change could be next legal battlefield. *Financial Times*.

Howe, Paul, and David Northrup. 2000. Strengthening Canadian democracy: The views of Canadians. *Policy Matters* 1(5).

Howse, Robert, and Kalypso Nicolaidis. 2003. Enhancing WTO legitimacy: Constitutionalization or global subsidiarity? *Governance* 16(1): 73–94.

Hurd, Ian. 1999. Legitimacy and authority in international affairs. *International Organization* 53(2): 379–408.

Ikenberry, John G. 2003. Is American multilateralism in decline? *Perspectives on Politics* 1(3): 533–50.

Immelt, Jeffrey. 2005, June 19. A consistent policy on cleaner energy. *Financial Times*.

Imperial, Mark T. 1999. Institutional analysis and ecosystem-based management: The institutional analysis and development framework. *Environmental Management* 24(4): 449–65.

International Federation of Chemical, Energy, Mine, and General Workers' Unions (ICEM). 2002. Historic first for mining in Africa – Anglo Gold signs global labour agreement. Retrieved August 12, 2004, from http://www.icem.org/update/upd2002/upd02-36.html.

International Institute for Sustainable Development (IISD). 2004. Summary of the eighth special session of the United Nations Environment Programme's Governing Council/Global Ministerial Environment Forum: 29–31 March. *Earth Negotiations Bulletin* 16 (35).

International Labor Organization (ILO). 2001, November 18. *Statement by Director-General Juan Somavia to the sixty-fourth meeting of the development committee*. Ottawa.

IMF, OECD, UN, and World Bank. 2000. *A better world for all*. Washington, DC: Communications Development.

International Monetary Fund (IMF). 1946, September 10. IMF Executive Board Document No. 46, rev. 1. IMF Archives.

———. 1951, February 21. Memorandum from IMF general counsel to deputy managing director. IMF Archives.

———. 2000a. *Annual report 2000*. Washington, DC: IMF.

———. 2000b. Köhler says surveillance and crisis prevention should be at the centre of IMF activities. *IMF Survey* 29(19): 303–305.

———. 2002, 28 January. *Working for a better globalization*. Remarks by Managing Director Horst Köhler at the Conference on Humanizing the Global Economy. Washington, DC: IMF.

———. 2003a, March 9. *The role of the IMF in a globalizing world economy*. Remarks by Managing Director Horst Köhler at the Fourth Annual Conference of the Parliamentary Network on the World Bank, Athens.

———. 2003b. *IMF Survey* 32, no. 8: 126–27.

———. 2004a. *IMF Survey* 33, no. 9: 160.

———. 2004b. *Report of the Executive Board to the International Monetary and Financial Committee (IMFC) on quotas, voice, and representation*. Washington, DC: IMF.

———. 2005a. *Factsheet: Debt relief under the heavily indebted poor countries (HIPC) initiative*. Washington, DC: IMF.

———. 2005b, 9 May. *'Tis not too late to seek a newer world: What globalization offers the poor*. Address by Anne O. Krueger, First Deputy Managing Director, to Oxford Union, Oxford.

———. 2005c, 9 June. *The time is always ripe: Rushing ahead with economic reform in Africa*. Lecture by Anne O. Krueger, First Deputy Managing Director, to the Economic Society of South Africa.

———. 2005d, 23 February. *Global imbalances and global poverty—Challenges for the IMF*. Remarks by Rodrigo de Rato, Managing Director, at Columbia University, New York.

Ivanova, Maria. Forthcoming. Assessing UNEP as anchor institution for the global environment. In *UNEO—Towards an international environmental organization: Approaches to a sustainable reform of global environmental governance*, ed. Andreas Reckhemmer. Baden-Baden: Nomos Verlagsgesellschaft.

Jolly, Richard et al. 1995. *The UN and the Bretton Woods institutions*. London: MacMillan.

Jolly, Richard, Louis Emmerij, Dharam Ghai, and Frédéric Lapeyre. 2004. *UN contributions to development thinking and practice*. Bloomington: Indiana University Press.

Jolly, Richard, Louis Emmerij, and Thomas G. Weiss. 2005. *The power of UN ideas: Lessons from the first 60 years*. New York: United Nations Intellectual History Project.

Jones, Charles. 1996. E. H. Carr: Ambivalent realist. In *Post-realism: The rhetorical turn in international relations*, ed. Francis Beer and Robert Hariman. East Lansing, MI: Michigan State University Press.

Jordan Valley Declaration: Time for mobilizing in the South. 2003, January 14–15. In South Centre, *South Centre High Level Policy Forum, Dead Sea, Jordan*. Geneva: South Centre.

Josselin, Daphne. 2001. Trade unions for EMU: Sectorial preferences and political opportunities. *West European Politics* 24(1): 55–74.

Juma, Calestous. 2000. The perils of centralizing global environmental governance. *Environment Matters* 6 (12):13–15.

Kagan, Robert. 2002. Power and weakness. *Policy Review* 113(June/July): 3–28.

———. 2004. America's crisis of legitimacy. *Foreign Affairs* 83(2): 65–87.

Kahler, Miles. 1995. *International institutions and the political economy of integration*. Washington DC: Brookings Institute.

Karlsson, Sylvia. 2000. *Multilayered governance: Pesticides in the south—Environmental concerns in a globalised world*. Linkoping: Department of Water and Environmental Studies, Linkoping University.

———. 2002. The North-South knowledge divide: Consequences for global environmental governance. In *Global governance: Options and opportunities*, ed. Daniel C. Esty and Maria H. Ivanova. New Haven: Yale School of Forestry and Environmental Studies.

Kell, Georg, and David Levin. 2003. The Global Compact Learning Network: An historic experiment in learning and action. *Business and Society Review* 108(2): 151–81.

Kelly, Michael J. 1997. Overcoming obstacles to the effective implementation of international environmental agreements. *Georgetown International Environmental Law Review* 9(2): 447–88.

Kemmerer, Edwin. 1916. *Modern currency reforms*. New York: MacMillan.

Keohane, Robert O. 1984. *After hegemony: Cooperation and discord in the world political economy*. Princeton: Princeton University Press.

Khagram, Sanjeev, James V. Riker, and Kathryn Sikkink, eds. 2002. *Restructuring world politics: Transnational social movements, networks and norms.* Minneapolis: University of Minnesota Press.

Knight, Andy W. 2000. *A changing United Nations.* London: MacMillan.

———, ed. 2001. *Adapting the United Nations to a postmodern era.* London: Palgrave.

Ko, Haksoo. 1998. Uncompetitive deal. *Far Eastern Economic Review* 161, no. 33: 34.

Kobrin, Stephen J. 1998. The MAI and the clash of globalizations. *Foreign Policy* 112: 97–110.

———. 2002. Economic governance in an electronically networked global economy. In *The emergence of private authority in global governance*, ed. Rodney Bruce Hall and Thomas J. Biersteker. New York: Cambridge University Press.

KPMG. 2002. International survey of corporate social responsibility reporting 2002. De Meern, Netherlands: KPMG Global Sustainability Services.

Krasner, Stephen. 1985. *Structural conflict.* Berkeley: University of California Press.

Kratochwil, Friedrich. 2000. Constructing a new orthodoxy? Wendt's "Social Theory of International Politics" and the constructivist challenge. *Millennium* 29(1): 73–101.

Krauthammer, Charles. 1990/1991. The unipolar moment. *Foreign Affairs* 70(1): 23–32.

Kull, Steven. 2004, April 7. Election year politics and American attitudes toward the global economy. Columbia University Business School, APEC Study Center.

———. 2005. It's lonely at the top. *Foreign Policy* 149 (July/August): xx.

Laponce, J. A. 1981. *Left and right: The topography of political perceptions.* Toronto: University of Toronto Press.

Lee, Jennifer. 2003, October 19. The warming is global but the legislating, in the US, is all local. *New York Times*, A20.

Leipziger, Deborah. 2001. *SA 8000: The definitive guide to the new social standard.* London: Financial Times/Prentice-Hall.

Lind, Michael. 2004, June 1. How a superpower lost its stature. *Financial Times*, 11.

Lindsay, Robert Ahomka. 2003, February 20–21. The Coca-Cola Africa Foundation/Coca-Cola bottlers in Africa HIV/AIDS program. *Workshop on HIV/AIDS and business in Africa and Asia: Building sustainable partnerships.* Center for Business and Government, Kennedy School of Government, Harvard University. Retrieved February 20, 2003, from http://www.ksg.harvard.edu/cbg/hiv-aids/workshop_ksg.htm/.

Luhmann, Niklas. 1982. *The differentiation of society.* New York: Columbia University Press.

Mack, Connie. 2000. Dollarization and cooperation to achieve sound money. Presentation at the conference hosted by the Federal Reserve Bank of Dallas entitled, *Dollarization: A common currency for the Americas*, March 6, Dallas. Retrieved from http://www.dallasfed.org/news/latin/oodollar_mack.html.

Martin, Pierre, and Michel Fortmann. 2001. Public opinion: Obstacle, partner, or scapegoat? *Policy Options* 22(1): 66–72.

McClure, Wallace. 1933. *World prosperity as sought through the economic work of the League of Nations*. New York: Macmillan.

McIntosh, Malcolm, Sandra Waddock, and Georg Kell, eds. 2004. *Learning to talk: Corporate citizenship and the development of the UN Global Compact*. Sheffield, UK: Greenleaf Publishing.

McKinsey and Co. 2004. Assessing the Global Compact's impact. United Nations Global Compact Initiative. Retrieved August 12, 2004, from http://www.unglobalcompact.org.

McTeer, Bob. 2000. Concluding comments. Presentation at the conference hosted by the Federal Reserve Bank of Dallas entitled, *Dollarization: A common currency for the Americas*, March 6, Dallas. Retrieved March 7, 2000, from http://www.dallasfed.org/htm/dallas/events/mack.html.

Mead, Walter Russell. 2004. *Power, terror, peace, and war: America's grand strategy in a world at risk*. New York: Knopf.

Mendelsohn, Matthew, and Robert Wolfe. 2001. Probing the aftermyth of Seattle: Canadian public opinion on international trade, 1980–2000. *International Journal* 56(2): 234–60.

———. 2003. *Values and interests in attitudes toward trade and globalization: The continuing compromise of embedded liberalism*. School of Policy Studies, Queen's University: unpublished manuscript.

Mendelsohn, Matthew, Robert Wolfe, and Andrew Parkin. 2002. Globalization, trade policy, and the permissive consensus in Canada. *Canadian Public Policy* 28(3): 351–71.

Meyer, John W., John Boli, George M. Thomas, and Francisco O. Ramirez. 1997. World society and the nation-state. *American Journal of Sociology* 103(1): 144–81.

Mingst, Karen A., and Margaret P. Karns. 2000. *The United Nations in the post-cold war era*. 2nd edition. Boulder: Westview.

Mittelman, James H. 2004. What is critical globalization studies. *International Studies Perspectives* 3(4): 219–30.

Mkandawire, Thandika. 2000. Preface. In United Nations Research Institute for Sustainable Development (UNRISD), *Visible hands: Taking responsibility for social development*. Geneva: UNRISD.

Monroe, Alan D. 1998. Public opinion and public policy, 1980–1993. *Public Opinion Quarterly* 62(1): 6–28.

Moravcsik, Andrew. 2000. Conservative idealism and international institutions. *Chicago Journal of International Law* 1(2): 291–314.

Munton, Don, and Tom Keating. 2001. Internationalism and the Canadian public. *Canadian Journal of Political Science* 34(3): 517–49.

Murphy, Craig. 1994. *International organization and industrial change: Global governance since 1850*. New York: Oxford University Press.

———. 2000. Global governance: Poorly done and poorly understood. *International Affairs* 76(4): 789–803.

Mutume, Gumasa. 2001. What Doha means for Africa: Compromises at WTO trade talks bring some gains, but at an uncertain cost. *Africa Recovery* 15(4): 3.

Najam, Adil. 2003. The case against a new international environmental organization. *Global Governance* 9(3): 367–84.

Nelson, Jane. 2000. *The business of peace: The private sector as a partner in conflict prevention and resolution*. London: Prince of Wales International Business Leaders Forum.

New York Times. 2005, July 22. Green light for bomb builders.

Nossal, Kim Richard. 1998–1999. Pinchpenny diplomacy the decline of "good international citizenship" in Canadian foreign policy? *International Journal* 44(1): 88–106.

Notermans, Ton, ed. 2001. *Social democracy and monetary union*. New York: Berghahn.

Nye, Joseph Jr. 2002. *The paradox of American power: Why the world's only superpower can't go it alone*. New York: Oxford University Press.

Oberthür, Sebastian. 2002. *Clustering of multilateral environmental agreements: Potentials and limitations*. Tokyo: United Nations University, Institute of Advanced Studies.

O'Brien, Robert, Anne Marie Goetz, Jan Aart Scholte, and Marc Williams. 2000. *Contesting global governance: Multilateral economic institutions and global social movements*. Cambridge: Cambridge University Press.

Olson, Mancur Jr. 1965. *The logic of collective action*. Cambridge: Harvard University Press.

Onuf, Nicholas. 1989. *World of our making*. Columbia, SC: University of South Carolina Press.

Organization for Economic Cooperation and Development (OECD). 2000. *The OECD guidelines for multinational enterprises: Revision 2000*. Paris: OECD. Retrieved August 14, 2004, from http://www.oecd.org/dataoecd/56/36/1922428.pdf.

———. 2001. *Corporate responsibility: Private initiatives and public goals*. Paris: OECD.

Ostrom, Elinor. 1990. *Governing the commons: The evolution of institutions for collective action*. 10th ed. New York: Cambridge University Press.

Ostry, Sylvia. Forthcoming. The post Doha trading system. In *Autonomy, democracy, and legitimacy in an era of globalization*, ed. Steven Bernstein and William Coleman. Vancouver: UBC Press.

Page, Benjamin, and Robert Shapiro. 1992. *The rational public: Fifty years of trends in America's policy preferences*. Chicago: University of Chicago Press.

Panitchpakdi, H. E. Supachai. 2001. Keynote address: The evolving multilateral trade system in the new millennium. *George Washington International Law Review* 33(3): 419–49.

Parkin, Andrew. 2001, April. Trade, globalization, and Canadian values. Centre for Research and Information on Canada. *CRIC Papers 1*.

Pauly, Louis W. 1997. *Who elected the bankers? Surveillance and control in the world economy*. Ithaca: Cornell University Press.

———. 2002. Global finance, political authority, and the problem of legitimation. In *The emergence of private authority in global governance*, ed. Rodney Hall and Thomas Biersteker. Cambridge: Cambridge University Press.

———. 2005. The political economy of international financial crises. In *Global political economy*, ed. John Ravenhill. Oxford: Oxford University Press.

Pearson, Lester B. 1969. *Partners in development. Report of the Commission on International Development*. New York: Praeger.

Pekkarinen, Jukka. 2001. Finnish social democracy and EMU. In *Social democracy and monetary union*, ed. T. Notermans. New York: Berghahn.

Pitruzzello, Salvatore. 2004. Trade globalization, economic performance, and social protection: Nineteenth-century British laissez-faire and post-World War II U.S.-embedded liberalism. *International Organization* 58(4): 705–44.

Polanyi, Karl. 1944. *The great transformation: The political and economic origins of our time*. Boston: Beacon Press.

Porter, Roger et al., eds. 2001. *Efficiency, equity, and legitimacy: The multilateral trading system at the millennium*. Washington, DC: Brookings Institution Press.

Porter, Tony. 2002a. *Technology, governance, and political conflict in international industries*. London: Routledge.

Porter, Tony, and William D. Coleman. 2002. Transformations in the private governance of global finance. Paper prepared for presentation at the International Studies Association Annual Meeting, New Orleans, March 25.

Rabkin, Jeremy. 1998. *Why sovereignty matters*. Washington, DC: American Enterprise Institute.

———. 2000. Is EU policy eroding the sovereignty of non-member states? *Chicago Journal of International Law* 1(2): 273–90.

———. 2005. *Law without nations? Why constitutional government requires sovereign states*. Princeton: Princeton University Press.

Radelet, Steven. 2003. Bush and foreign aid. *Foreign Affairs* 82(5): 104–17.

Revkin, Andrew C., and Neela Banerjee. 2001, August 1. Energy executives urge voluntary greenhouse gas limits. *New York Times*, C1.

Rhodes, Martin. 2002. Why EMU is—or may be—good for European welfare states. In *European states and the euro*, ed. K. Dyson. Oxford: Oxford University Press.

Risse, Thomas. 2000. The power of norms versus the norms of power. In *The third force: The rise of transnational civil society*, ed. Ann M. Florini. Washington, DC: Carnegie Endowment for International Peace.

Rodrik, Dani. 1997. *Has globalization gone too far?* Washington, DC: Institute of International Economics.

Rosamond, Ben. 2003. What do policy-makers know about "globalisation" and why do they know it? Paper delivered to the International Studies Association, Portland, Oregon, February 25–March 1.

Rosenau, James N. 1990. *Turbulence in world politics: A theory of change and continuity.* Princeton: Princeton University Press.

Rosenau, James N., and Ernst-Otto Czempiel, eds. 1992. *Governance without government.* Cambridge: Cambridge University Press.

Rosenau, James N. 1997. *Along the domestic-foreign frontier: Exploring governance in a turbulent world.* Cambridge: Cambridge University Press.

———. 2003. *Distant proximities: Dynamics beyond globalization.* Princeton: Princeton University Press.

Rosenberg, Emily. 1985. Foundations of US international financial power: Gold standard diplomacy, 1900–1905. *Business History Review* 59(2): 169–202.

———. 1999. *Financial missionaries to the world: The politics and culture of dollar diplomacy 1900–30.* Cambridge: Harvard University Press.

Rowe, David M. 1995. Politicians, voters, and trade. *Mershon International Studies Review* 39(2): 302–304.

Ruggie, John Gerard. 1982. International regimes, transactions, and change: Embedded liberalism in the postwar economic order. *International Organization* 36(2): 379–415.

———. 1992. Multilateralism: The anatomy of an institution. *International Organization* 46(3): 561–98.

———, ed. 1993a. *Multilateralism matters: The theory and praxis of an institutional form.* New York: Columbia University Press.

———. 1993b. Territoriality and beyond. *International Organization* 47(1): 139–74.

———. 1996. *Winning the peace: America and world order in the new era.* New York: Columbia University Press.

———. 1998a. What makes the world hang together? Neo-utilitarianism and the social constructivist challenge. *International Organization* 52(4): 855–85.

———. 1998b. *Constructing the world polity.* London: Routledge.

———. 2000, November 20. Globalization and global community: The role of the United Nations. The J. Douglas Gibson Lecture, School of Policy Studies, Queen's University, Kingston.

———. 2002. The theory and practice of learning networks: Corporate social responsibility and the global compact. *Journal of Corporate Citizenship* 5: 27–36.

———. 2003a. The United Nations and globalization: Patterns and limits of institutional adaptation. *Global Governance* 9(3): 301–21.

———. 2003b. Taking embedded liberalism global: The corporate connection. In *Taming globalization: Frontiers of governance,* ed. David Held and Mathias Koenig-Archibugi. Cambridge: Polity Press.

———. 2003c. The United Nations and globalization: Patterns and limits of institutional adaptation. *Global Governance* 9(3): 301–21.

———. 2004. American exceptionalism, exemptionalism, and global governance. In *American Exceptionalism and Human Rights*, ed. Michael Ignatieff. Princeton: Princeton University Press.

Ruggiero, Renato. 1998. *A global system for the next fifty years, address to the Royal Institute of International Affairs*. London: Royal Institute of International Affairs.

Runge, C. Ford. 2001. A global environment organization (GEO) and the world trading system. *Journal of World Trade* 35(4): 399–426.

Rydbeck, Olof. 1972. Statement by Ambassador Olof Rydbeck in the Preparatory Committee for the United Nations Conference on the Human Environment, Fourth Session. New York: Permanent Mission of Sweden to the United Nations.

Sandbrook, Richard, ed. 2003. *Civilizing globalization: A survival guide*. Albany: State University of New York Press.

Sassen, Saskia. 1995. When the state encounters a new space economy: The case of information industries. *American University Journal of International Law and Policy* 10(2): 769–789.

Scharpf, Fritz W. 1997. Economic integration, democracy and the welfare state. *Journal of European Public Policy* 4(1): 18–36.

———. 2000. Interdependence and democratic legitimation. In *Disaffected democracies: What's troubling the trilateral democracies?*, ed. Susan J. Pharr and Robert D. Putnam. Princeton: Princeton University Press.

Schechter, Michael G., ed. 2001. *United Nation–sponsored world conferences*. Tokyo: United Nations University Press.

Scheve, Kenneth F., and Matthew J. Slaughter. 2001. *Globalization and the perceptions of American workers*. Washington, DC: Institute for International Economics.

Scholte, Jan Aart. 1998. The IMF meets civil society. *Finance and Development* 35(3): 42–45.

Scholte, Jan Aart, and Albrecht Schnabel, eds. 2002. *Civil society and global finance*. London: Routledge/Warwick Studies in Globalisation.

Schuler, Kurt. 2000. *Basics of dollarization*. Washington, DC: United States Senate, Joint Economic Committee, US Senate.

Schuler, Kurt, and Robert Stein. 2000. The Mack dollarization plan: An analysis. Paper presented at conference, Dollarization: A Common Currency for the Americas? Federal Reserve Bank of Dallas, March 6.

Short, Michael. 2004, May 14. Model city sets pace for globe. *Australian Financial Review*.

Sikkink, Kathryn. 2002. Restructuring world politics: The limitations and asymmetries of soft power. In *Restructuring world politics: Transnational social movements, networks, and norms*, ed. Sanjeev Khagrram, James V. Riker, and Kathryn Sikkink. Minneapolis: University of Minnesota Press.

Sinclair, Timothy. 2000. Reinventing authority: Embedded knowledge networks and the new global finance. *Environment and Planning C: Government and Policy* 18: 487–502.

Sindzingre, Alice 2004. The evolution of the concept of poverty in multilateral financial institutions: The case of the World Bank. In *Global institutions and development: Framing the world?*, ed. M. Bøås and D. McNeill. London: Routledge.

Skidelsky, R. 2003. Keynes's road to Bretton Woods: An essay in interpretation. In *International financial history in the twentieth century*, ed. M. Flandreau, C.-L. Holtfrerich, and H. James. Cambridge: Cambridge University Press.

Smith, Jackie. Forthcoming. Contested globalizations: Social movements and the struggle for global democracy. In *Autonomy, democracy, and legitimacy in an era of globalization*, ed. Steven Bernstein and William· Coleman. Vancouver: UBC Press.

Smith, Jackie, and Kathryn Sikkink. 2002. Infrastructure for change: Transnational organizations, 1953–93. In *Restructuring world politics: Transnational social movements, networks, and norms*, ed. Sanjeev Khagrram, James V. Riker, and Kathryn Sikkink. Minneapolis: University of Minnesota Press.

Smouts, Marie-Claude. 1995. *Les organisations internationales*. Paris: Armand Colin.

Sniderman, Paul, and Thomas Piazza. 1993. *The scar of race*. Cambridge: Harvard University Press.

Social Movements International Secretariat. 2003, January 27. *Call of Porto Alegre 2003*. Porto Alegre.

Soederberg, Susanne. 2004. American empire and "excluded states": The Millennium Challenge Account and the shift to pre-emptive development. *Third World Quarterly* 25(2): 279–302.

Soros, George. 1998. *The crisis of global capitalism*. New York: Public Affairs.

Spero, Joan E., and Jeffrey A. Hart. 2003. *The politics of international economic relations*. 6th edition. Belmont: Wadsworth/Thompson Learning.

Speth, James Gustave. 2003. Perspectives on the Johannesburg Summit. *Environment* 45(1): 24–29.

———. 2004. *Red sky at morning: America and the crisis of the global environment*. New Haven: Yale University Press.

Spiro, Peter J. 2000. The new sovereigntists: American exceptionalism and its false prophets. *Foreign Affairs* 79(6): 9–15.

Stamler, Bernard. 2001, July 5. Companies are developing brand messages as a way to inspire loyalty among employees. *New York Times*.

Steffek, Jens. 2003. The legitimation of international governance: A discourse approach. *European Journal of International Relations* 9(2): 249–75.

Steger, Manfred B. 2002. *Globalism: The new market ideology*. Lanham: Rowman and Littlefield.

Stevenson, Richard W. 2003, July 10. Bush promotes his plan to help Africa. *New York Times*.

Stiglitz, Joseph. 2000, April 17–24. The insider: What I learned at the world economic crisis. *The New Republic*.

———. 2002. *La grande désillusion*. Paris: Fayard.

Strange, Susan. 1954. The economic work of the United Nations. *Yearbook of world affairs: 1954*. London: Stevens and Son.

Suchman, Mark C. 1995. Managing legitimacy: Strategic and institutional approaches. *Academy of Management Review* 20(3): 571–610.

Summers, Larry. 1999, April 22. Deputy Treasury Secretary Lawrence H. Summers Senate Banking Committee, Subcommittee on Economic Policy and Subcommittee on International Trade and Finance. Retrieved from http://www.ustreas.gov/press/releases/pr3098.htm.

Tarnoff, Curt, and Larry Nowels. 2004. Foreign aid: An introductory overview of U.S. programs and policy. Congressional Research Service, Library of Congress.

Tanzi, Vito, and Ludger Schuknecht. 2000. *Public spending in the 20th century*. New York: Cambridge University Press.

Task Force on the United Nations. 2005. *American interests and UN reform*. Washington, DC: United States Institute of Peace.

Taylor, Paul. 2000. Managing the economic and social activities of the United Nations system: Developing the role of ECOSOC. In *The United Nations at the millennium*, ed. Paul Taylor and A. J. R. Groom. London: Continuum.

Tesner, Sandrine, with Georg Kell. 2000. *The United Nations and business: A partnership recovered*. New York: St. Martin's Press.

The Pew Research Center for The People and The Press. 2003. *Views of a changing world: War with Iraq further divides global publics*. Washington, DC: The Pew Research Center for The People and The Press.

Thérien, Jean-Philippe. 1999. Beyond the North-South divide: The two tales of world poverty. *Third World Quarterly* 20(4): 723–42.

Thérien, Jean-Philippe, and Alain Noël. 2000. Political parties and foreign aid. *American Political Science Review* 94(1): 151–62.

Thérien, Jean-Philippe. 2002. Multilateral institutions and the poverty debate: Towards a global third way? *International Journal* 57 (2): 233–52.

Thérien, Jean-Philippe, and Vincent Pouliot. 2006. The global compact: Shifting the politics of international development? *Global Governance* 12(1): 55–75.

Thomas, Caroline. 2000. *Global governance, development, and human security: The challenge of poverty and inequality*. London: Pluto Press.

———. 2005. Poverty, development, and hunger. In *The globalization of world politics: An introduction to international relations*, 3rd edition, ed. John Baylis and Steve Smith. Oxford: Oxford University Press.

Thrift, Nigel, and Andrew Leyshon. 1994. A phantom state? The de-traditionalization of money, the international financial system, and international financial centres. *Political Geography* (13)4: 299–327.

Townsend, Peter. 1993. *The international analysis of poverty*. London: Harvester-Wheatsheaf.

ul Haq, Mahbub, Inge Kaul, and Isabelle Grunberg, eds. 1996. *The Tobin tax: Coping with financial volatility*. New York: Oxford University Press.

United Kingdom Department of Trade and Industry. 2004, May. Company law: Draft regulations on the operating and financial review and directors' report—A consultative document. Retrieved August 14, 2004, from http://www.dti.gov.uk/cld/condocs.htm.

United Nations. 1971, December 17. Consolidated document on the United Nations and the human environment. UN Doc. A/CONF.48/12. New York: United Nations.

———. 1972a, January 10. International organizational implications of action proposals. UN Doc. A/CONF.48/11. New York: United Nations.

———. 1972b, January 10. International organizational implications of action proposals. UN Doc. A/CONF.48/11/Add1. New York: United Nations.

———. 1992, August 12. Report of the United Nations Conference on Environment and Development, Rio De Janeiro, June 3–14. Annex 1, Rio Declaration on Environment and Development. UN Doc. A/CONF.151/26 (Vol. 1). New York: United Nations.

———. 1998, October 6. Agenda item 30: Environment and human settlements—Report of the secretary-general, 53rd Session. UN Doc. A/53/463. New York: United Nations.

———. 2001a, August 28. Cooperation between the United Nations and all relevant partners, in particular, the private sector: Report of the secretary-general. UN Doc. A/56/23, New York: United Nations.

———. 2001b. *2001 report on the world social situation*. New York: United Nations.

———. 2002a, March 22. Final outcome of the International Conference on Financing for Development. UN Doc. A/CONF.198/1. New York: United Nations.

———. 2002b. *Financing for development: A critical global collaboration*. New York: United Nations.

———. 2004. A more secure world: Our shared responsibility. Report of the high level on threats, challenges, and change. New York: United Nations.

———. 2005a. *In larger freedom: Towards development, security, and human rights for all*. UN Doc. A/59/2005. New York: United Nations.

———. 2005b. *Report on the world social situation 2005: The inequality predicament*. New York: United Nations

———. 2005c, July 6. Millennium development goals have unprecedented political support, secretary-general says at London event. Address by UN Secretary-General Kofi Annan to the St. Paul's Cathedral Event on the Millennium Development Goals, London.

———. 2005d, March 21. *In larger freedom: Towards development, security, and human rights for all.* Report of the secretary general. New York: United Nations.

———. 2005e, June 1. *The Monterrey consensus: Status of implementation and tasks ahead.* Report by the secretary general. New York: United Nations.

UN Commission on Human Rights (UNCHR). 2005, April 15. Promotion and protection of human rights. (E/CN.4/2005/L.87). New York: United Nations.

United Nations Conference on Trade and Development (UNCTAD). 2000a. *Bilateral investment treaties, 1959–1999.* New York: United Nations.

———. 2000b. *The least developed countries: 2000 report.* New York-Geneva: United Nations.

———. 2001. *World investment report.* New York: United Nations.

———. 2002a. *From adjustment to poverty reduction: What is new?* New York-Geneva: United Nations.

———. 2002b. Statement by Mr. Rubens Ricupero, secretary-general of UNCTAD to the IMF and World Bank meetings, Washington, 19–21 April.

———. 2002c. *The least developed countries report 2002: Escaping the poverty trap.* New York-Geneva: United Nations.

———. 2002d. *Trade and development report 2002.* Geneva: United Nations.

UN Daily News Digest. 2005, June 29. *As UN Development Council opens session, Annan says growth not enough.*

United Nations Department of Public Information. 2002. *Highlights of commitments and implementation initiatives.* Johannesburg Summit, 26 August-4 September. Retrieved August 12, 2004, from http://www.un.org/events/wssd/pressreleases/highlightsofsummit.pdf.

United Nations Development Programme (UNDP). 2001. *Development effectiveness: Review of evaluative evidence.* New York: Evaluation Office of the UNDP.

———. 2002a, January 16. *Statement by UNDP administrator Mark Malloch Brown at the Conference on the Review of Poverty Reduction strategy papers.* Washington, DC.

———. 2002b, June 27. *Meeting the millennium challenge: A strategy for helping achieve the United Nations Millennium Development goals.* Address by UNDP Administrator Mark Malloch Brown, Berlin.

———. 2003a, April 13. The United Nations, the World Bank, and the Millennium Development goals: A new framework for partnership. Address by UNDP Administrator Mark Malloch Brown to the International Monetary Fund-World Bank Development Committee, Washington, DC.

———. 2003b. *Human development report 2003: Millennium Development goals: A compact among nations to end human poverty.* New York: Oxford University Press.

———. 2004, June 15. Summary of press briefing by UNDP Administrator Mark Malloch Brown. Geneva.

United Nations Environment Programme (UNEP). 2001a. *International environmental governance: Report of the executive director.* Nairobi: UNEP.

———. 2001b. *International environmental governance: Multilateral environmental agreements (MEAs).* Bonn: UNEP.

———. 2001c. *Improving international environmental governance among multilareral environmental agreements: Negotiable terms for further discussion: A policy paper.* Bonn: UNEP.

———. 2001d. *Proposal for a systematic approach to coordination of multilateral environmental agreements.* Bonn: UNEP.

———. 2001e, April 18. Multilateral environment agreements: Summary (UNEP/IGM/1/INF/1). Open-ended intergovernmental group of ministers or their representatives on international environmental governance first meeting, New York. Retrieved December 9, 2005, from http://www.unep.org/dpdl/IEG/docs/MEA_full/INF3_MEA_Add.doc.

———. 2002. *UNEP Annual report.* Nairobi: UNEP.

———. 2005. Bali strategic plan for technology support and capacity building. Retrieved December 9, 2005, from http://www.unep.org/GC/GC23/documents/GC23-6-add-1.pdf.

United Nations Environment Programme—Environmental Management Group (UNEP-EMG). 2005. Environmental Management Group. Retrieved December 5, 2005, from http://www.nyo.unep.org/emg3.htm.

United Nations General Assembly (UNGA). 1997, December 18. Global partnership for development: High-level international intergovernmental consideration of financing for development. U.N. Doc. A/Res/52/179. New York: United Nations.

———. 1999, July 28. UN reform: Measures and proposals. U.N. Doc. A/RES/53/242. New York: United Nations.

———. 2000, September 18. *United Nations Millennium Declaration.* U.N. Doc. A/RES/55/2. New York: United Nations.

———. 2002, January 30. *Monterrey consensus: Draft outcome of the international conference on finance for development.* New York: United Nations.

United Nations Office of the High Commissioner for Human Rights (UNOHCHR, February 12–23). 2001. Contribution of the UNOHCHR to the Second Session of the Intergovernmental Preparatory Committee for the High-level International Intergovernmental Forum on Financing and Development. New York.

United Nations Research Institute for Social Development (UNRISD). 2000. *Visible hands taking responsibility for social development.* Geneva: UNRISD.

United Nations University. 2002. *International environmental governance: The question of reform: Key issues and proposals.* Tokyo: United Nations University Institute for Advanced Studies.

United States Agency for International Development (USAID). 2003. *USAID senior staff speeches and testimony, 2003.* Retrieved July 19, 2004, from http://www.usaid.gov/press/speeches/2003/.

United States Department of State. 2003a, July 23. MCA *update No. 3*.

———. 2003b. *Aids fact sheet*. Retrieved August 14, 2004, from http://www.state.gov/g/oes/rls/fs/2003/23909.htm.

United States Department of State, Bureau of Democracy, Human Rights, and Labor. 2001, February 20. Voluntary principles on security and human rights. Retrieved August 14, 2004, from http://www.state.gov/g/drl/rls/2931.htm.

United States General Accounting Office. 1999. *International environment: Literature on the effectiveness of international environmental agreements*. Washington, DC: United States General Accounting Office.

United States Institute of Peace. 2005. *American interests and UN reform: Report of the task force on the United Nations*. Retrieved November 30 from: http://www.usip.org/un/report/usip_un_report.pdf.

United States Senate. 1999a, April 22. Hearing on official dollarization in emerging-market countries. Senate Committee on Banking, Housing and Urban Affairs, Subcommittee on Economic Affairs and Subcommittee on International Trade and Finance.

———. 1999b, July 15. Hearing on official dollarization in emerging-market countries. Senate Committee on Banking, Housing and Urban Affairs, Subcommittee on Economic Affairs and Subcommittee on International Trade and Finance.

Vaubel, Roland. 1986. A public choice approach to international organization. *Public Choice* 51(1): 39–57.

Védrine, Hubert. 2003. *Face à l'hyper-puissance. Textes et discours 1995–2003*. Paris: Fayard.

Veiden, Pal. 2001. The Austrian Social Democratic Party. In *Social democracy and monetary union*, ed. Ton Notermans. New York: Berghahn.

Verdier, Daniel. 1994. *Democracy and international trade: Britain, France, and the United States, 1860–1990*. Princeton: Princeton University Press.

Vogel, David. 2005. *The market for virtue: The potential and limits of corporate social responsibility*. Washington, DC: Brookings Institution Press.

Volcker, Paul A. 2000. The sea of global finance. In *Global capitalism*, ed. Will Hutton and Anthony Giddens. New York: New Press.

Vogler, John. 2000. *The global commons: Environmental and technological governance*. 2nd edition. Chichester: J. Wiley and Sons.

von Moltke, Konrad. 2001a. The organization of the impossible. *Global Environmental Politics* 1(1): 23–28.

———. 2001b. *On clustering international environmental agreements*. Winnipeg, Canada: International Institute for Sustainable Development.

Wallach, Lori, and Patrick Woodall. 2004. *Whose trade organization? A comprehensive guide to the WTO*. New York: The New Press.

Wallich, Henry. 1950. *Monetary problems of an export economy: The Cuban experience 1914–1947*. Cambridge: Harvard University Press.

Walter, Andrew. 2001. NGOs, business, and international investment: The multilateral agreement on investment, Seattle, and beyond. *Global Governance* 7(1): 51–73.

Wapner, Paul. 2003. World summit on sustainable development: Toward a post-Jo'burg environmentalism. *Global Environmental Politics* 3(1): 1–10.

Welles, Sumner. 1940. Statement to be made orally by Mr. Welles at the Meeting of the Inter-American Financial and Economic Advisory Committee of July 11, 1940. In United States Department of State, *Foreign Relations of the United States, Diplomatic Papers 1940 Volume 5*. Washington: U.S. Government Printing Office.

Wendt, Alexander. 1999. *Social theory of international politics*. Cambridge: Cambridge University Press.

Whalley, John, and Ben Zissimos. 2002. Making environmental deals: The economic case for a world environment organization. In *Global environmental governance: Options and opportunities*, ed. Daniel C. Esty and Maria H. Ivanova. New Haven: Yale School of Forestry and Environmental Studies.

White House. 2002. *National security strategy of the United States of America*. Washington, DC.

White, David. 2003, October 6. Chad starts scheme to track oil cash. *Financial Times*, 6.

White, Nigel D. 2002. *The United Nations system: Toward international justice*. Boulder: Lynne Rienner.

Who Cares Wins: Connecting Financial Markets to a Changing World. 2004. The United Nations Global Compact Initiative. Retrieved August 14, 2004, from http://www.unglobalcompact.org/irj/servlet/prt/portal/prtroot/com.sapportals.km.docs/ungc_html_content/NewsDocs/WhoCaresWins.pdf.

Wolfe, Robert, and Matthew Mendelsohn. 2004. Embedded liberalism in the global era: Would citizens support a new grand compromise? *International Journal* 59(2): 261–80.

———. 2005. Values and interests in attitudes towards trade and globalization: The continuing compromise of embedded liberalism. *Canadian Journal of Political Science* 38(1): 45–68.

Wolfe, Robert. 2005. See you in Geneva? Legal (mis)representation of the trading system. *European Journal of International Relations* 11(3): 339–65.

Wolfensohn, James D., and François Bourguignon. 2004. *Development and poverty reduction: Looking back, looking ahead*. Washington, DC: World Bank.

Woods, Ngaire. 2001. Making the IMF and the World Bank more accountable. *International Affairs* 77(1): 83–100.

World Bank. 2001. *Globalization, growth, and poverty: Building an inclusive world economy*. Washington, DC: Oxford University Press.

———. 2002. *The role and effectiveness of development assistance: Lessons from World Bank experience*. Washington, DC: World Bank.

———. 2003, March 27. Poverty reduction: The future of global development and peace. Keynote Address delivered by the president of the World Bank, James D. Wolfensohn, at the University of Pennsylvania, Philadelphia.

———. 2004, July 28. The Chad-Cameroon development and pipeline project. World Bank. Retrieved August 14. 2003, from http://www.worldbank.org/afr/ccproj.

World Commission on Environment and Development (WCED). 1987. *Our common future*. Oxford: Oxford University Press.

World Commission on the Social Dimension of Globalization. 2004. *A fair globalization: Creating opportunities for all*. Geneva: International Labour Office.

World Economic Forum. 2003. GHI case studies and supporting documents. Retrieved from http://www.weforum.org/site/homepublic.nsf/Content/Global+Health+Initiative%5CGHI+Business+Tools%5CGHI+Case+Studies+and+Supporting+Documents.

World Trade Organization. 1994, April 15. *Decision on trade and the environment*. Adopted by ministers at the meeting of the Uruguay Round Trade Negotiations Committee in Marrakech. Retrieved July 19, 2004, from http://www.wto.org/english/tratop_e/envir_e/issu5_e.htm.

———. 2002, November 1. Trade policies cannot work on their own, Supachai tells development seminar. Speech delivered by Director-General Supachai Panitchpakdi at the Second Integrated Framework Mainstreaming Seminar, Geneva.

———. 2005, April 13. Why trade matters for improving food security. Speech delivered by Director-General Supachai Panitchpakdi at the FAO High-Level Round Table on Agricultural Trade Reform and Food Security, Rome.

Zadek, Simon. 2004. The path to corporate responsibility. *Harvard Business Review* 82(12): 125–32.

Zaller, John. 1992. *The nature and origins of mass opinion*. New York: Cambridge University Press.

Zedillo Commission. 2001. *Report of the high-level panel on financing for Development*. New York: United Nations.

Zürn, Michael. 2000. Democratic governance beyond the nation-state: The EU and other international institutions. *European Journal of International Relations* 6(2): 183–221.

Contributors

STEVEN BERNSTEIN is an associate professor in the Department of Political Science, University of Toronto.

ERIC HELLEINER holds a CIGI Chair in International Governance and is an associate professor in the Department of Political Science, University of Waterloo.

MARIA IVANOVA is an assistant professor in the Department of Government, The College of William and Mary.

MATTHEW MENDELSOHN is currently Deputy Minister of Intergovernmental Affairs and Deputy Minister responsible for the Democratic Renewal Secretariat, Government of Ontario. He is on leave from Queen's University where he is an associate professor in the Department of Political Studies.

LOUIS W. PAULY holds a Canada Research Chair and is a professor in the Department of Political Science and Director of the Center for International Studies, University of Toronto.

TONY PORTER is a professor in the Department of Political Science, McMaster University.

JAMES N. ROSENAU is University Professor of International Affairs, George Washington University.

JOHN GERARD RUGGIE is Kirkpatrick Professor of International Affairs and director of the Mossavar-Rahmani Center for Business and Government, Kennedy School of Government, Harvard University; he is also the Special Representative of the United Nations Secretary-General for Business and Human Rights.

JEAN-PHILIPPE THÉRIEN is a professor in the Département de Science Politique, Université de Montréal.

ROBERT WOLFE is a professor in the School of Policy Studies and the Department of Political Studies, Queen's University.

Index

Africa, poverty, 82, Action Plan, 126
agency, 16, conceptions of, 17, global politics, 17, practice, 25, role of, 5
Albright, Madeleine, 32
Amnesty International, 34
Annan, Kofi, 24, 25, 39, 42, 76, 78, 79, 80, 84, 85, 92, 126, Global Compact, 25, 39, 42
anticorruption, 19, convention, 39, corporate sector, 80, 168, role of CSOs, 34
antiglobalization, 11, 28–30, 41, 139, agenda, 8, backlash, 11, 27, 125, 168, Battle of Seattle protesters, 24, movements, 139, neoliberalism, 25, public protest, 52
apparel industry, 41, 128, Multifibre Agreement, 48n.48, transnational networks labor standards, 119
Asian financial crisis, 3, 16, 80
authority, 97, 105, 125, 138–39, 171, 179, antiglobalization movements, 139, certification systems, 168, environment, 173, 180, 182, 184, globalizing economy, 95, governance, 35, 168, 170, 176, international institutions, 62, knowledge-based networks, 117, legitimate, 11, moral, 184, networks, 9, 17, private, 95, public, 20, 22, 95, regulation, 53, states, 8, 167, technical standards, codes, 110, values, 16

automobile industry, DaimlerChrysler, 37, GM, Toyota, Ford, and Honda, 128

BP (British Petroleum), 43
Bali Strategic Plan for Technology Support and Capacity Building, 176–77
Bangkok Consensus, 82
Bank for International Settlements, Committee on Payment and Settlement Systems, 123
bankruptcy court, 85
Bergsten, Fred, 153, 154, 158
Blair, Tony, 41, 81, 122, third way, 27
Blyth, Mark, 24
Bobbio, Norberto, 73
Bolton, John, 27–28, 126
Brazil, 39
Bretton Woods, 33, 158, agreements, 163, analysis of globalization, 83–84, decision-making procedures, 76, domestic conditions of development, 84, exchange rates, 143, financing for development, 14, hegemony of, 82, initiatives of, 16, General Agreement on Tariffs and Trade (GATT), 83, 163, institutions (*see also* IMF and World Bank) 8, 10, 78, 85, 92, 96, International Monetary Fund (IMF), 83, multilateral, 149, neoliberalism, 76, paradigms, 19,

Bretton Woods *(continued)*
    82–83, 86, partnership, 103, political authority, 93, poverty, 83, protests aimed at, 27, reforms at the global level, 85, role of, 75, shift in attitude, 80, social dimension of development, 77, UN agencies, 72, value systems, 83, World Bank, 83, World Trade Organization (WTO), 75, worldviews, 83
Brown, Mark Malloch, 81, 82
Brundtland Commission, 164–65
Bush, George W., 32, 41, 102, administration, 4, 7, 25, 27, 29, 30, 32, 100, 182, Kyoto Protocol, 43, unilateralism, 33

Canada, 13, 57–59, 60, 63, 65–66, 70n.9, 153, globalization, 68, 70n.8, public opinion, 28, 29, 52, trade, 68, water safety, 62
Canada-U.S. Free Trade Agreement, 57
Carr, E.H., 4
Cartagena Biosafety Protocol, 172
certification institutions, 36
Chad-Cameroon Pipeline, 38
chaos *(see also* political order), 9, 20, 136, 138, 139, 146, disorder, 5
chemical and pretroleum industry, Dupont, 128, Exxon Valdez spill, 36, Responsible Care standards for chemical safety, 120, Shell, 36, 167, Union Carbide's Bhopal disaster, 36, unsafe practices in, 36
China, 30, 42, 123, anti-retroviral treatment for its employees, 38, human rights violations, 63
Chirac, Jacques, 179
Chrétien, Jean, 81
citizens, autonomy of, 63, human rights, 63, mass opinion, 53, protections for, 109, values, 63
civil society, 7, 19, 79, 88
civil society organizations (CSOs), 66, dispute settlement, 65, global social organization, 25, Live 8 concerts, 56, multilateral agreement on investment, 129, OECD, 129, role of, 34, social responsibility of, 38, transnational networks of, 129, transnational organizations, 28
Claude, Inis, 95
Clinton, William J., 29, 32, 41, 81, 100, administration, 29, 41, third way, 27
Coca-Cola, 37, Africa, 37, anti-retroviral treatment, 37, 47n.38
cold war *(see also* war) 21, 94, 161
Collado, Emilio, 146
Commission on the Private Sector and Development, 80
communities, 30, 96, 111, norms, 15, 112
compromise *(see also* embedded liberalism), 82, 88, 110, 163, authority, 5, defined as, 131, environment, 163, 169, 174, 180, 183, globalizing economy, 106, grand, 86, key differences, 119, legitimation, 118–19, North-South, 165, order and fragmentation, 141, postwar, 28, reform, 84, Rio Summit, 166, standards and codes, 127, transnational networks, 115, 118, 127, 129
constructivism, 72–73, 97, 109
Copenhagen Consensus, 82
corporate sector, accountability, 44, environmental principles, 168, global embedded liberalism, 34, global governance gaps, 37, global rule making, 35, protecting and promoting human rights, 42, response to globalization within the UN system, 167, role in third way politics, 41, social responsibility, 34–37, 39, 40, 42, 44, 92, sweatshop suppliers, 36, unsustainable forestry practices, 36, workplace treatment programs, 37
corporations, 7, ethical, 66, role in conflict prevention, 38, transnational, 34
Cox, Robert, 88
crisis, Asian financial, 3, 80, debt, 101, fragmentation, 166, subordination of environmental goals to market principles, 166, underdevelopment, 104

INDEX

currencies, capital controls, 148, capital flows, 122, causes of crises, 152, Europe, 143, European Union, 143, exchange rate, 143, 148, gold or foreign exchange reserves, 148, government controls on, 122, national, 156, prospects for currency union, 144, supranational, 143, U.S. dollar, 143, 148

currency bloc, America, 143, creation of, 143, Economic and Monetary Union, 15, economic policy, 158, embedded liberal values, 158, Europe, 15, exchange rates, 143, floating exchange rates, 143, multilateral monetary order, 143, neoliberalism, 158, postwar world, 143, regional, 14, relations between Americas and Europe, 158, U.S. dollar, 143, 148

d'Alema, Massimo, 81
DaimlerChrysler, workplace treatment in Africa, 37
Davos World Economic Forum, 24
debt, external, 101, national, 105, reduction, 78, relief, 81, 99, 105, sustainable solution to, 87, unsustainable, 78
democracy, 138, decision making, 174, dilemma of, 140, economic, environmental and social agendas, 162, global, 13, guardianship, 65, international institutions, 65, 139, legitimacy, 10, 54, national governments, 65, order, 137, pluralistic order, 140, principles, 174, democratization, levels of, 64
Denmark, 55, 156
developed countries, 71, capitalist, 23, cost of protectionism, 79, markets, 87, Southern exports, 87
developing countries (*see also* Third World countries), 71, communist, 125, consultation, 103, development assistance, 125, economies, 13, effects of a liberalizing economy, 125, environmental governance, 174, environmental policies, 40, 174, financial challenges, 103, foreign aid, 125, global economic decision-making bodies, 78, globalization, 24, good practices by global firms, 35, knowledge of standards, 129, limits on, 173–74, microfinancing, 40, 127, multilateral environmental agreements, 181, new challenges of, 24, new globalizers, 84, New International Economic Order, 91, participation of, 78, poorly regulated, 42, poverty eradication and development, 174, private-public partnership projects, 40, self-responsibility in, 78, social development, 40–41, social welfare programs, 125, strategic importantance, 94, technology transfer, 181

development, compromise, 84, 87, competing paradigms, 19, domestic conditions of, 84, 98, 101, consensus fragmentary, 86, diplomacy, 86, economic performances, 88, financing for, 98, 125, global governance of, 87, globalization, 86, international financial resources for, 101, loans for, 147, multilateral consensus on, 87, policy commitments in Washington, 92, politics of, 86, private capital flows, 125, private capital markets, 94, 98, problem of, 83, reform of domestic policies, 98, reorient state policies, 125, systemic constraints on, 85, technical cooperation, 101, trading systems for, 101

development aid, 80, aid-as-entitlement, 80, compromise, 77, failures of, 166, financing, 77, 94, 102, 105, legal obligation, 85, national, 105, norms, 77, results-based management, 80

Doha Development Agenda (*see also* WTO), 66, Round of trade negotiations, 119

dollar bloc, Americas and U.S. opposition to, 158, convertibility, 26, response to euro zone, 151 dollarization, absence of an exchange rate, 153, antipoverty, 152, Argentina neoliberal support for, 152, benefits of, 153, critics of, 154, constraint on state policy, 153, countries, 154, domestic policy autonomy, 14, domestic monetary policy in, 154, exchange rate, 151, foreign economies, 153, impact on U.S., 154, Latin America, 14, 144, 150, 154, market discipline, 151, 153, nationalist opposition to, 152, opposition of, 153, pressure for, 14, prodevelopment policy, 152, social dislocation of, 153, supporters of, 153

dollarization diplomacy, 143, 152, currency bloc in the Americas, 143, discussions in Ecuador and El Salvador, 143, neoliberal advocates of, 151, 154, price stability, 154, U.S. dollar, 143, U.S. Federal Reserve Act, 154

domestic, autonomy, 61, economic security, 35, international collaboration, 61, policy frameworks, 35, political coalitions, 24, political distinction, 89n.4, political interventionism, 5, political issues, 62, political order, 28, post–New Deal, 28, 30, postwar compromise, 28, shift in role of the capitalist state, 27, social inclusion, 35, U.S. climate change policies, 42

Earth Summit, 161, 167, internationalize embedded liberalism, 162, global governance, 162

Eccles, Marriner, 149

economic efficiency, 93, forums voting procedures, 85, growth, 75, multilateralism (*see also* Bretton Woods institutions), 76, private flows, 77, role of norms, 111, social development, 77

economic institutions, authority, 17, interagency cooperation, 17, management, 67, social networks, 111

Economic Program for the Americas, 147

Economic Security Council, 85

economy, increasingly separate, 111–12, differentiated sphere in modern society, 111, socially embedded, 67

embedded liberalism, autonomous, 111, Canada, 29, challenges to, 7, 9, citizen support for, 13, compromise of, 163, concept of, 23, 53, 109, 115, constitutive rule, 69n.2, currency blocs, 20, 143, defined, 4–6, 51–52, dependence of interactions, 111, developing countries, 125, discretionary domestic monetary policy, 153, disembedding, 113, domestic policies, 15, 26, 121, elements of, 110, environment, 163, environmental governance, 183, era of, 43, euro, 15, exchange rate, 153, framework, 25, global, 20, 25, 55, globalization, 19, 21, governments role in, 23, in reverse, 15, 166, 174, institutional change, 19, institutional setting for, 17, institutional context, 111, institutional nexus of, 112, international economy, 24, international liberalization, 27, international organizations, 68, 96, international networks, 112–13, international technical systems, 114, key components of, 62, Keynesian monetary policy, 70n.9, laissez-faire, 18, legitimate, 8, 12–13, 69, Latin American governments, 153, legitimate social purpose, 9, 12, 16, 21, 53, liberal trade, 55, modernization, 111, multilateralism, 19, 55, 69n.1, natural environment, 164, networked forms of governance, 169, new institutional forms for, 43, norms, 114, 169, normative, 18, 25, open international order, 121, optimize social welfare, 153, order and fragmentation, 19, pillars of, 9, political foundations of, 51, popular legitimacy, 30, potential locations of, 17–18, postwar efforts, 9, 21, power and authority, 19, premise, 16, 24, principles of, 44, promise of, 184, principles of, 25, 29, principles in

Latin America, 149, public opinion in Canada, 54, shared knowledge and practices, 112, shared social purposes, 43, social movements, 115, social relations in premarket, 111, social security, 62, social solidarity, 55, state-led opting out of the global economy, 125, state policy, 122, technical knowledge paradigms, 114, transnational policy networks 115, welfare state, 55, 62, working conditions, 62

employment, 116, full, 156, income patterns, 8, social problem, 116, structural, 116

energy sector, 43, BP, 43, Enron, 43, Exxon Valdez, 36, General Electric, 43, greenhouse gas emissions limits, 43, Shell, 43

Enhanced Initiative for Highly Indebted Poor Countries, 78

environment, 7, 19, 27, 29, 34, agreements, 170–71, 173, animal and plant health, 163, authority for, 184, bureaucracy, 170, compromise, 18, conditions, 8, corporate sector, 168, costs, 165, degradation, 166, development, 165, disasters, 164, domestic policy, 163, Earth Summit, 161, eco-development, 165, economic goals, 165, 171, effect of trade rules on, 178, embedding in, 166, 174, GATT rules, 163, moral authority for, 184, movements, 164, natural resources conservation, 163, norms, 7, 183, normative, 18, 169, policy space, 180, private sector, 80, regulations, 178, role of CSOs, 34, standards, 19, social purpose, 35, 163–64, sustainable development, 161, 165, technology clearinghouse, 181, trade, 28–29, 166, 182, treaties, 173, 182

environmental governance, 9, 15, 19, 21, 162–69, 180, 182, 184, coherence, 21, compromise, 18, 162, eco-development, 165, fragmentation, 18, 21, 162, 167, 169, 172, Global Environmental Mechanism, 182, institutions, 181, institutional reform, 162, 179, 184, Johannesburg Declaration and Plan of Implementation, 166, liberalizing trends in, 171, normative foundations for, 18, 166, political compromise of, 166, protection, 168, 182, Precautionary Principle, 183, Rio Declaration on Environment and Development, 166, Stockholm Conference on the Human Environment, 169, sustainable development, 162, 165, 167, system for, 174, United Nations Environment Programme, 169, world society, 21, WTO Committee on Trade and the Environment, 171, 182

Environmental Management Group, 175–76, 181

environmental policies, 28, 164–65, 173, assess health and environmental risks, 183, developing countries, 165, 170, 181, eco-development, 165, institutional reform, 178, instruments, 165, national, 164, 177, international policy, 164, North-South compromise, 165, 181, Polluter and User Pays, 165, public-private partnerships, 167, 181, trade, 28–29, 163

environmental sustainability (*see also* Brundtland Commission), 11, 15, 27, 28, 36, 77, 88, 161, 164, eco-development, 165, promotion of, 88, Rio Principles on Environment and Development, 39, World Business Council on Sustainable Development, 40

equality, 89, 173, competing visions of, 76, ideal of, 73

Ethical Trading Initiative, 41

Europe, budget deficits and public debt, 155, Bundesbank, 157, Central Bank, 157, domestic wage and price flexibility, 156, Economic and Monetary Union, 15, 144, 155–58,

Europe (*continued*)
  embedded liberal values in, 144, 156, fiscal policies, 157, globalization, 68, 70n.8, multilateralism, 31, neoliberalism, 151, 155–56, price stability, 157, regional monetary union, 155, regulation, 70n.8, social democrats support for, 156, social protection measures, 157, Stability and Growth Pact, 155
European Central Bank, 154, 157, euro management of, 155, euro zone, 151, price stability, 155
European Economic and Monetary Union (EMU), currency bloc, 15, neoliberal shift in, 144
European Union, 31, 55, 100, 143, Cohesion Fund, 157, Commission, 59, currency, 20, 143, dollar, 151, euro, 143, 151, Economic and Monetary Union, 144, 156–58, embedded liberal goals, 157, employment rights, 157, governance, 27, intra-EU fiscal transfers, 157, liberalization of cross-border financial transactions, 122, public opinion, 59, social democracy, 27, 156–57, trade unions, 27, transatlantic energy policy, 43, transnational wage bargaining, 157
exchange rates, 24, 151, 155–56, fixed, 26
Exxon Valdez oil spill, 36

Fair Labor Association, 41
finance, arrangements in, 110, for development, 124, 130, rules and norms, 130, technical standards and codes, 130
financial crises, 3, 16, 80, 93, 95, 103–4, 122, 159n.7, Argentina, 153, 159, Asian, 3, 16, 80, 122, China national barriers, 123, compromises in public sector networks, 130, international, 122–23, Malaysian government's capital controls, 123, Mexico, 122, post-1945, 95, Russia, 122

Financial Stability Forum, 100, G7, 123
foreign aid (*see also* Millennium Challenge Account), 59, 79, 84, 92–93, 125, 164, U.S. foreign aid budget, 102
foreign policy, Canadian, 55, 59, EU, 55, U.S., 144
fragmegration, 139, 180, characteristic of, 138, concept of, 20, defined as, 136, 172, governance, 139, 172, 180
fragmentation (*see also* integration), 5, 9, 19–21, 135–36, 140–41, 173, 176, environmental governance, 18, 166–67, 169, 171–72, globalization, 163, political authority, 6, world affairs, 17, 135–36
free trade, 29, 51, 112, 146, 164, 178, Canada, 57–59, 65, 70n.9, environment, 166, 178, Free Trade Area of the Americas, 29, survey, 52, United States, 57
Free Trade Area of the Americas, 29
Funk, Walter, 146

G20, 95
G7, 94, financial liberalization, 123, Financial Stability Forum, 123, financial standards and codes, 123, liberalize economies, 86, promote private sector, 86, reform of the international financial architecture, 122, rules of global capitalism, 86
G77, 86
G8, 56, 78, 95, 126, Africa Action Plan, 126, aid commitments, 126, development assistance, 126, leaders, 126, Live 8 event, 56, 126, Make Poverty History campaign, 126, Millennium Development Goals, 126, standards to foster accountability with governments, 126, Summit, 56, 125
Garrett, Geoffrey, 26, 45n.7, 121
Gates, Bill, 79
Global Compact, 15, 19, 25, 39–40, 92, 167–68, Business Council on Sustainable Development, 40, Business for Social Responsibility

INDEX   221

Committee for Melbourne, 40, corporate social responsibility, 42, Global Reporting Initiative, 36, 40, health and safety standards, 40, labor rights, 40, multilateral form, 25, multi-stakeholder network, 80, national networks, regional and sectoral initiatives, 40, principles, 40, 47n.43, 48n.45, staff for, 48n.45, World Business Council on Sustainable Development, 40
General Electric, 43
generative grammar, 15, 52, 72–73
Germany, 145–46, Red-Green coalition government, 32
Giddens, Anthony, 73–74, 112, 113, 116
Gingrich, Newt, 33, 105
global capitalism, benefit from, 87, private authority of, 95, structures of, 95
global care chains, child-care programs, 116
global civil society, 7, 98, 131
global commons, 172, privatization of, 166
global compromise, 56, 161–63, 183
global economic integration, 83, 166, equitable, 77
Global Environment Facility, 170
global environmental governance, 5, 162, 170, 174, 182
Global Environmental Mechanism, 179, 182
global finance, 110, 112, 122
global governance, 5, 19, 27, 54–55, 64–67, 88, 109–10, 130, 138–39, 183, actors, 12, agency, 19, grand compromise, 51, 135, legitimacy, 11, 13, 54, Pearson Commission, 71, world economy, 25, 68
global justice movement (see also antiglobalization), 8
Global Ministerial Environment Forum, 175–76
Global Reporting Initiative, 36, 40
globalization, 3, 4, 8, 13–14, 23, 29, 39, 52, 54, 56, 66–67, 77, 171, attitudes toward, 29, backlash, 125, 168–69, citizens, 115, compromise of, 115, conflict resolution, 115, contributed to, 84, corporate social responsibility, 80, crisis, 6, critical studies, 4, definition of, 57–58, development, 8, 81, 86, 167, Earth Summit, 162, environment, 165, 183, failure of, 130, fragmentation, 163, glocalization, 112, immigration and foreign aid, 59, international institutions, 11, 24, 68, national autonomy, 183, negative consequences of, 115, poverty, 165, preglobalization era, 179, protectionism, 27, regulation, 8, 70n.8, reliance on technical knowledge, 119, role of non-state actors, 33, rolling back of, 21, social programs, 121, sustainable development, 168, systemic stability, 71, threat to social purpose and environment protection, 168, trade liberalization, 53, 58, values, 44, 58–59, 83,
globalized knowledge networks, 9, 110, 129
globalizers, Brazil, 84, China, 84, India, 84, Mexico, 84
glocalization, 112
gold standard, 145, 150, limitations of, 149
governance, 5, 15, 20, 102, 109, 170, 172, bilateralism, 8, certification systems, 168, corporate, 65, developing countries, 177, development, 20, 85, domestic, 53, environmental, 15, 162, 169, failures, 174, finance, 105, 112, fragmegration, 136, fragmentation, 163, gaps, 25, 35, 37, global, 15–16, 42, 69, 136, 177, intergovernmental regimes, 12, international organizations, 25, legitimacy of, 69, 86, 169, multilateral form of, 9, national, 177, networked forms of, 8, 169, non-state, 19, 168, plurilateralism, 8, social purposes of, 69, 169, social regulations, 53, state power,

governance *(continued)* 74, trade policy, 53, traditional systems, 172, UN agencies, 85, U.S. Millennium Challenge Account, 102

government, Center Left, 81, citizens, 129, democratic, 51, environmental policy, 178, globalization, 115, intergovernmental, 33, international problems, 33, market liberal, 121, national, 62, 178, negotiated market-sharing arrangements, 128, social democratic, 122, social protection, 127, Third Way, 122, trade, 127, treaties, 122, 129

grand compromise, global, 33, new, 25

Greenspan, Alan, 152

Growing Sustainable Business Initiative, 80

Gutt, Camille, 106n.1

Haas, Ernst, 95, 106

Halifax Summit, 122

health and safety standards, 40, 66

hegemonic power, 82, Bretton Woods institutions, 82, counter order, 88, form of, 82

Heineken, workplace treatment in Africa, 37

HIV/AIDS, Africa, 34, drugs pricing and intellectual property policies in poor countries, 37, global human resources policy, 38, U.S. Agency for International Development, 34, workplace treatment for employees, 37

human rights, 7, 28, business and corporate sector, 42, codes, 120, corporate sector, 168, legal obligation, 85, norms, 42, private sector, 80, private security forces, 41, public opinion on, 59, role of CSOs, 34, roles of states, 42, standards, 19, 42, transnational corporations, 42,

Human Rights Watch, 34

ideas, role of, 28, 72–74

Ikenberry, John, 10

Immelt, Jeffrey, 43

income distribution, 45n.11, disparities, 81, household inequality in, 45n.11, social dimension of development, 81, United States, 28

Indonesia, 36, 94, 99

industrialized countries (*see also* developed countries), good practices by global companies, 35, rise of, 127

integration (*see also* fragmentation), financial, 20, global environmental issues, 172, political institutions, 55, regulations, 68, welfare state, 68

International Accountings Standards Board, 123

International AIDS Society, 37

international community, 12, 76, norms, 36, solidarity, 78

International Conference on Financing for Development, 100

International Criminal Court, 30, 33

international economic order, building of, 145, Clearing Union proposal in, 146, decision making, 104, defined, 164–65, embedded liberal principles, 146, Europe, 146, Germany's New Order, 146, Keynesian liberalism, 164, legitimacy, 7, 26, liberalization, 109, negative effects of, 115, 118, protect citizens from, 118–19, regional context, 146, shared social objectives of, 26, sterling bloc, 146, U.S.–Latin American relations, 146, postwar, 146

International Environmental Governance, 175

International Federation of Accountants, 123

International Federation of Chemical, Energy, Mine and General Workers' Unions, 40

international financial institutions (*see also* International Monetary Fund, United Nations, World Bank, World Trade Organization), 60, 139, Bank for International Settlements, 123, capital controls, 123, Financial

Stability Forum, 100, 123, International Federation of Accountants, 123, multilateral standards and codes, 123, poverty reduction, 85, tax on, 85
international institutions, 8–9, 12, 65, 67, accountability of, 65, decision-making, 62, democratic values, 62, globalization, 11, managerial issues, 62, 65, need of reform, 106, promoting human rights, 62, public protests against, 11, sovereignty, 62
International Labour Organization, 29, 75, 100, 170–71, Fundamental Principles on Rights at Work, 39
international liberalism, framework of, 24, legitimacy, 9
International Maritime Organization, 171
International Monetary Fund, 86, 92, 96, 100, 102, articles of agreement, 26, capital control, 26, constitutive principles, 26, decision-making process, 85, development, 103, employment policies, 26, Enhanced Initiative for Highly Indebted Poor Countries (HIPC), 78, exchange rates, 26, financial liberalization, 123, interests of, 76, liberalization, 26, multilateral principles and practices, 26, payments crises, 99, Poverty Reduction Strategy Papers, 78, new international financial architecture, 85, regulatory role, 94, relationship with UN, 106n.1, representation, 85, role of intergovernmental institutions, 7, social safety nets, 26
international monetary policy, embedded liberal framework for, 154–55, instability on the domestic economy, 150, neoliberal arguments, 152
International Oceanographic Commission, 170
international politics, democratization of, 88
International Telecommunication Union, patents and standards, 35
Internet, International Corporation for Assigned Names and Numbers, 120

Johannesburg Declaration, 166
Johannesburg Summit (*see also* World Summit on Sustainable Development), 38, 167
Jordan Valley Declaration, 81
Jospin, Lionel, 81, 159n.8
justice, 97, distributive, 22, 71, 93, global, 55, social solidarity, taxes, 55

Kagan, Robert, 4, 31, 33
Kemmerer, Edwin, 145, 148, 149, 155
Keynes, John Maynard, 146
Keynesian, 149, international economic order, 164, liberalism, 164, macroeconomic policy, 24, midcentury policies of, 153, social-democratic views, 76
Köhler, Horst, 78
Krauthammer, Charles, 32
Kyoto Protocol, 30, 119, alternative energy technologies, 43, green brands, 43, greenhouse gas emissions limits, 43, U.S. rejection of, 43

labor, 24, 29, compromise, 121, corporate sector, 168, effects of global economic market forces, 27, international division of, 35, private sector, 80, standards, 7, 19, 28, 29, 80, 119, transnational networks, 119, unions, 122
Lange, Joep, 37
Latin America, autonomy of, 151, dollar bloc in, 15, dollarization, 157, dollarization diplomacy, 14, 143, domestic prices and wages in, 153, economic arrangements, 145, economic shocks, 153, Ecuador, 143, El Salvador, 143, economic development and industrialization, 149, fiscal position of supply-side reforms, 157, levels of real output, 153, limitations of gold standard, 149, monetary policies and systems, 147–48, 150, neoliberalism,

Latin America (*continued*)
156–57, social welfare, 144, unemployment, 153, U.S. policy on dollarization, 148, 150
legitimacy, 3, 5, 6, 12, 54, 68, 101, 106, 163, 173, 174, basis of, 20, compromise, 53–54, concept of sustainable development and environmental governance, 165, contemporary sources of, 117–18, crisis, 4, 11, 21n.1, 72, 168–69, governance, 11, 54, 86, international, 9, 33, 104, liberal order, 183, limits of, 67, market liberalism, 169, NAFTA dispute settlement, 65, plural system, 53, problem of, 5, reconfiguration of, 20, public-private partnerships for sustainable development, 167, shifting basis of, 163, social systems, 10, substantive, 12, 22n.11, sustainable, 55,
legitimation, collective, 95, decision processes, 64, democratic inputs and outputs, 64, framework of global organization, 97, global, 11, politics of, 32, values and policy objectives, 32
liberalism, global, 6, laissez-faire, 5, 18, 93, orthodox, 112
liberalization, 58, 69, 81, globalization, 53, monetary relationst, 26, trade 26, 53, U.S. financial firms, 123
Lie, Trygve, 106n.1
Long Term Capital Management, hedge fund, 99

Mack, Connie, 151–52
Malaysia, 42, 123
market, atomized rationalistic actors, 110, efficiency of, 52, free functioning of, 75, economy, 84, global development, 81, laissez-faire, 67, open, 23, 52, negative effects offset, 109, self-regulating, 67
Marrakech agreement on the implementation of the Kyoto Protocol on climate change, 119
Marshall Plan, 85
Martin, Paul, 80

mass opinion (*see also* public opinion), 54, relation to policy outputs, 69n.3, research on, 58, surveys, 54
McKinley, William, 32
Mead, Walter Russell, 43
Mexico, 94, 100, 153
Meyer, John, 97
Millennium Challenge Account, 92, 102, 126
Millennium Declaration 2000, 77, foundations for, 78
Millennium Development Goals, 77, 82, 88, 103–4, Africa Action Plan, 126, development goals, 81, funding, 88, G8 summit, 126, strategy, 81
Millennium Summit, 77
mining industry, Africa workplace coverage, 37, Anglo American, 37, Anglo Gold, 40, community-based treatment programs, 37, labor federation agreement applies to overseas operations, 40
Mitchell, George, 105
Mittelman, James, 4
Mkandawire, Thandika, 81
monetary automatism, 150, orthodox, 150
monetary union, common monetary unit, 148, German influence, 149, Pan-American, 148, pre-1931 era, 145, reforms, 145, regional, 157, U.S.-led, 145
Monterrey agreement, historic compact, 78, post-Monterrey system, 105
Monterrey Conference on Financing for Development, 77, 92, 101–3, 106, international cooperation for development through partnership, 103, UN General Assembly, 103
Monterrey Consensus, 82, 101, 105, objectives, 103, post-1945 intergovernmental cooperation, 102, U.S., 102
Monterrey Declaration, 77, foundations for, 78
Montreal Protocol Multilateral Fund, 170

moral authority, 181, 184
Moravcsik, Andrew, 28
Multilateral Agreement on Investment, opposition to, 34
multilateral institutions, against poverty, 74, development finance, 95, Left-Right Spectrum, 75–76, political authority, 74, political legitimacy, 75, promotion of development, 74, regional, 95, regional development banks, 94, role of, 86
multilateralism, 3–4, 102, adapted to, 9, compromise, 77, conceptions of interstate equality, 76, constraints of, 51, 53, cooperation, 61, 78, development system, 78, economic, 5, 89n.4, environmental agreements, 181, Europe, 31, globalized financial system, 123, global social organization, 25, ideological convergence among, 77, normative, 10, 76, political vs. economic, 76, 89n.4, poverty reduction, 77, principle of, 6, promotion of sustainable development, 167, social values, 69, standards and codes, 123, threat to, 7, trade and monetary affairs, 30, 167, U.S., 16, U.S. turn against, 30

national governments, consultation, 103, effects of globalization, 183, regulation, 179, role of social policy, 84, security, 28
nation-state, 97, 121, 141, 173
neoconservative, 28, 30, democratic imperialism, 31, new American sovereigntists, 27–28
neoliberal, 144, currency blocs, 158, economic orthodoxy, 24, 166, framework, 171, labor, 44n.6, monetary goals, 151, 157, monetary influence of Bundesbank, 157, noneconomic goals, 171, policy of dollarization, 151
neoliberalism (see also Washington consensus), 27, 30, 87, Bretton Woods institutions, 76, 152, champions of, 8, shift toward, 43

neorealist, 10–11, 16
Netherlands, 55
networks, new spheres of authority, 9, properties of, 117–18, standards and performance of, 117–18
New Deal, 23, 28, 30, 149
New Partnership for Africa's Development, 126
new sovereigntist, 7, 8, 25, 27
Nike, 35, 36, 37
nongovernmental organizations (NGOs), 34, 97, 100, 127, Freedom House, 127, Heritage Foundation, 127, Institutional Investor, 127, network, 100
norms, 4, 7, 18, 24, 31, 36, 42, 73, 77, 86, 88, 109, 111, 183, constitutive function of, 109, embedding of, 113–15, 119, 129–30, global market, 111, nonterritorial knowledge-based networks, 119, social, 111, strength of market, 166, system of, 169
North American Free Trade Agreement (NAFTA), 57, 177, trade and sustainable development, 178
North American Treaty Organization (NATO), alliance relations with U.S., 31
North-South relations, 82, 86–88, convergence between the Bretton Woods institutions and the UN agencies, 72, 77–78, 83, 86–87, diplomacy, 161, future of, 72, Global Third Way, 87, North-South politics, 78, perspective of conflict, 11
Nye, Joseph, 33

oil shocks, 127
opinion polls, American structure of, 56, Canadian structure of, 56, Centre for Research and Information on Canada, 56, le Centre de recherche en opinion publique, 56, European, 59, globalization, 58, mass, 53, September 11, 2001, 59, structure of, 55, survey, 54, 56, trade, 58, values, 58

order and fragmentation, 9, 17, 135, 136, 141, 163, methodological problems, 140
Organization for Economic Cooperation and Development (OECD), 78, 86, 100, 120, Polluter and User Pays, 165, voluntary guidelines for multinational enterprises, 41
Oxfam, 34

Panitchpakdi, Supachai, 78
peace, 6, 32, 68, 78, 138
Pearson Commission, 71
PharmAccess, anti-retroviral treatment program, 37
pharmaceutical sector, 37, anti-retroviral treatment programs, 37–38, Botswana, 37, China, 38, Gates Foundation, 37, Merck, 37, Novartis, 38
pluralism, 136, 138, institutions, 139
Polanyi, Karl, 5, 15, 18, 44n.2, 67, 69
political authority, capitalist countries, 31, characteristic of modernity, 117, foundations of, 5, fracturing of, 3, fragmented, 6, 25, global, 5, governmentality, 117, international organizations, 93, multilateral institutions, 74
political economy, changing demands of, 162, develop global currency blocs, 143, dominant role in, 145, global, 98, 145, 162, hyper-liberal, 162, international, 171, 174, reordering of, 174, rules in, 171, U.S., 145
political order (*see also* chaos), 10, 20, 28, financial integration, 20
political parties, 27, declining role of, 56
postwar, compromise, 5, 21, 24, 93, capital controls, 146, corporatist wage bargaining structures, 156, domestic, 24, European economy, 146, exchange rates and free trade, 146, global, 24, international economic order, 146
postwar order, 33, 68, international, 51, 69, legitimacy of, 10, multilateralism, 6

poverty, 8, 71, 74, 78, 80, 83, 152, 165, 174, Africa, 82, 126, 138, Live8 event, 126, Make Poverty History campaign, 126, microfinancing and lending, 40, 127, new globalizers, 84, political support, 77, power, 109, reduction, 38, 77, 79, 81, 83–85, 87, 99, 103, 164, socio-economic strategies to reduce inequality, 83, third world countries, 87, World Bank, 79, 99, World Bank–IMF Poverty Reduction Strategy Papers (PRSPs), 78, 126
private enterprise, private-public partnerships, 38, public role of, 42
Program on International Policy Attitudes (PIPA), 56, sectors, 41
protectionism, 27, 68, 79, protectionist, 29
protest marches, 3, 8, global, 3, public, 59, spheres of authority, 139
public goods logic, 179
public opinion, 11, 28, 51, 54, 63, boundaries of, 55, Canada, 52, 54–59
public-private partnerships, 167, 181

Rabkin, Jeremy, 27, 28
realists, 4, 180, neorealists, 10, 16, political, 111, role of norms, 111, traditional, 96
regulation, authorities, 53, conflicting environments, 43, cross-border financial flows, 123, European Union, 43, financial standards for, 124, flow of capital, 62, fragmentation, 53, national, 179, political, 75, production process, 53, social, 53, 179, standards and codes, 120, structure, 123, transnational networks, 120, types of norms, 120
Rio Declaration on Environment and Development, 166
Russia, 23, 99, crises of, 122

Sachs, Jeffrey, 126
Santiago Consensus, 82

Schröder, Gerhard, 81
Schuknecht, Ludker, 26
Seattle conference (*see also* antiglobalization and World Trade Organization), 28, 79
security, 88, 104, collective, 3, failures of, 3, peacekeeping, 3, political coalitions of, 95, Somalia, 3, Rwanda, 3
semiconductors industry, 128, International Technology Roadmap for Semiconductors, 129, technical standards, 129, World Semiconductor Council, 128
September 11, 2001, 4, 59, 125
Shell, 36, Malampaya Deep Water Gas to Power Project, 167, Philippine government, 167
Sindzingre, Alice, 83
social compromise, 119, changes in, 111, character of, 111, contracts, 139, democracy, 87, justice, 75, new spheres of authority, 138
social responsibility (*see also* Global Compact), civil society organizations, 38, corporate, 19, 25, 34–40, 42, 44, 80, 92
social sector, 26, 42, foreign aid, 125, increases in spending, 121, Latin America, 14, 144, 153, New Deal state, 23, 30, privatize, 29, protection, 29, public spending, 26, 116, rolling back, 29–30, safety nets, 23, 26, security, 62, standards, 19, welfare, 54, 67, 125, 144, 153, 156
sovereignty, 6–7, 19, 27–28, 53, 60, 62, 171, clean drinking water, 62, defer to another country, 67, European Union, 7, international institutions, 62, national, 62, 137, new sovereigntists, 7–8, social programs, 62, state-centric world, 137, state diplomacy, 4, 173, support for, 62, unbundling of, 53, workplace, 62
Soviet Union, 30, 31
Special Representative for Business and Human Rights, 42
stagflation, 127

standards, 120, conduct, 117, decentralized arrangements, 123, development of, 123, financial systems, 124, knowledge networks, 125, networks of technical experts, 123, performance, 117, private sector, 123, social programs, 62, source of legitimacy for, 117, role of state, 120, voluntary, 120, workplace, 62
state, 6, 12, 23–24, 51, 85, 92, 118, authority, 9, 35, 167, citizens, 42, 123, compromise of, 123, domestic, 11, 26–27, economic role of, 28, 166, liberalization, 92, 123, market, 6, multilateralism, 20, national borders, 123, nation-state, 97, non-state actors, 7, 33–34, 110, 113, 167, 172, power, 9, 16, 25, 30, 93, social compromise, 119, sovereign, 19, 27–28, 173, territorial, 25, 33, 115, trade liberalization, 62, welfare, 6, 51–52, 54, 55, 58, 62, 67–68, 125, 156
Statoil, 40
steel industry, 128
Stockholm Conference on the Human Environment, 164, 169
Stockholm Convention on Persistent Organic Pollutants, 172
Summers, Larry, 152
sustainable development, 161, 162, 164, 176, Brundtland Commission, 165, concept, 165, developed and developing countries, 164, evolution of, 165, ideal of, 164, international institutions and agreements, 183, public-private partnerships for, 167
Sweden, 156
synthetic textile industry, 128, apparel industry, 36, 41, 119, 127–28, Dupont, 128, Ethical Trading Initiative, 41, Multifibre Agreement, 48n.48, multinational chemical companies, 128, WTO agreements, 127

Tanzi, Vito, 26
tariffs, 24, 53, 58, 79, General Agreement on Tariffs and Trade, 75

tax, 55, 156, cross-border financial flows, 123, employment-friendly schemes, 157, international financial transactions, 85, Tobin tax, 123
technical knowledge, 13, 114–15, 118–19, paradigms, 114, sustaining the continuity of norms, 114
terrorism, 25, 81, war against, 77, 102
textiles and apparel industry, globalized set of production networks, 128, standards for, 41
third world countries (*see also* developing countries), global governance of development, 88, integrate global economy, 88, Marshall Plan for, 85, promises to, 82, reducing poverty, 87
timber industry, unsustainable forestry practices, 36
trade agreement, 166–67, antidumping measures and countervailing duties, 127, environment, 166, 171, 178, 182, legitimating function for, 167, negotiations, 64–65, 99, 127, public opinion and values, 58–59, 58, softwood lumber disputes, 70n.11, support for, 29, 57, sustainable development, 178
trade liberalization, 67, attitudes toward, 57, Canadian support for, 54, globalization, 58, U.S. support for, 28
transatlantic power gap, 31
transnational activist networks, 34
transnational corporations (TNCs), 28, 33–37, 42, bilateral investment pacts, 35, corporate social responsibility, 35–37, domestic liberalization, 35, global embedded liberalism, 34, global rule making, 35, international financial institutions, 35, multilateral trade agreements, 35, rights, 35–37, world order, 137
transnational networks, 113, 118–19, compromise, 129–30, conflict resolution, 115, legitimacy, 16, norms in, 114, territorial spaces, 114
treaties, 30, 110, 122, 129, environmental, 171, 173

Triffin, Robert, 18, 149, 150, 151, 155
Turner, Ted, 79

unilateralism, 32–33, 88, Contract with America, 33, doctrinal, 32–33, economic issues, 88, U.S., 33, 44, 88, 95
Union Carbide, 36
United Nations, 14, 16, 30, 95, 97, 103, 161, *A Better World For All*, 78–79, A More Secure World study, 104, agencies, 14, 72, 75, 80, 82, 91, 96, analysis of globalization, 83–84, anticorruption convention, 39, authority, 96, business community, 80, Business Council, 100, Capital Development Fund, 80, certification scheme for blood diamonds, 41, collaborative authority, 105, conflict prevention, 40, convergence with Bretton Woods institutions, 72, 77–78, 83, 86–87, 105, debates on reform, 104, development, 81, 95, 98, Earth Summit, 161, economic and financial mandates, 92, 98, Food and Agriculture Organization, 170, global civil society, 98, governance of development, 85, HIV/AIDS Initiative, 92, ideological shift, 79, inequality, 83, international development cooperation, 82, legitimacy, 96, 104, Man and Biosphere Program, 170, market forces, 77, 79, Millennium Development Goals, 92, 103, multilateral conflict management, 3, New International Economic Order, 91, North-South diplomacy, 161, paradigm, 19, 75, 79, 82–83, 86, participation of NGOs and social actors, 98, peacemaking activities, 40, policies of interstate equality, 88, political authority, 93, postwar international economy, 93, power of, 30, private sector partnerships, 79–80, pro-market shift, 81, relationships with the IMF and the World Bank, 98, 106n.1, *Report on the World Social Situation*, 84, role of, 75, 91, 94, security, 104, social justice and equality,

83, U.S. financial accounts in, 92, U.S. foreign aid programs in, 92, value systems, 60, 83, voting system, 76, water agenda, 176, world affairs, 83, 88
United Nations Commission on Human Rights, 42
United Nations Commission on Sustainable Development, 170, 176, 181
United Nations Conference on Environment and Development (*see also* Earth Summit), 161
United Nations Conference on Trade and Development (UNCTAD), 75, 94
United Nations Department of Economic and Social Affairs (DESA), 92
United Nations Development Program (UNDP), 75, 80, 92, 105, 170, 177
United Nations Environment Programme (UNEP), 169, 173, Environment Fund, 176, Environmental Management Group, 175, Global Ministerial Environmental Forum, 175, proposal, 179, reform proposals, 175
United Nations Economic and Social Council (ECOSOC), 42, 75, 78, 92, 94, 101, collective security, 104, Committee on the Social and Economic Aspects of Security Threats, 104, debates on reform, 104, development cooperation forum, 104, forum for, 104, member-states, 94, Millennium Development Goals, 104
United Nations Economic Commission for Europe, 171
United Nations Educational, Scientific and Cultural Organization (UNESCO), 170, U.S. rejoins, 92
United Nations Environmental Management Group, 175–76
United Nations General Assembly, 100, 175

United Nations Global Compact, 15, 138, corporate social responsibility, 39, developing country companies, 39, initiative, 19, principles, 39
United Nations High Commissioner for Human Rights, 181
United Nations Millennium Project, 126
United Nations Millennium Summit, 71
United Nations Office of the High Commissioner for Human Rights, 85
United Nations Office of the Secretary-General, 104
United Nations Secretary-General, 92
United Nations Security Council, 33, 104
United Nations Universal Declaration of Human Rights, 39
United Kingdom, 26, 55, 125, 156
United States, 25, 26, 92, alliance relations, 31, currency, 20, 148, development, 34, 81, 95, 102, dollar in Latin America, 14, dollarization, 143–44, 152, domestic, 7, 26, domestic environmental agenda, 182, economic policies, 30–31, embedded liberal framework for, 154–55, Export-Import Bank, 147, Federal Reserve, 147, foreign aid, 92, 102, foreign policy, 4, HIV/AIDS Initiative, 34, 92, hyperpower of, 32, 81, independent central banks, 145, Inter-American Bank, 147, international policy making, 18, military, 31, 32, Millennium Challenge, 92, 102, monetary policy, 145, 149, 152, 154–55, National Security Strategy, 102, NATO alliance, 32, neoliberalism, 152, New Deal, 23, 30, 149, postwar economic order, 6, power asymmetry, 31, public opinion, 28, rejoined UNESCO, 92, security strategy, 30, 32, shift in foreign policy, 25, strategic restraint, 10, trade, 147, tariff concessions, 147, treatment of prisoners, 31, unilateralism, 32–33, 44, 88, 95, UN, 81, Uruguay Round, 120

United States Agency for International Development, 34, funding for HIV/AIDS in sub-Saharan Africa, 34
United States Federal Reserve System, 99, 147, 149, 152, 154, 159, New Deal, 149, price stability, 151
United States Institute of Peace, 105
United States International Monetary Stability Act, 150, 152, 154

values, 58–59, 116, authority, 117, order and justice, 86, properties of most knowledge-based networks, 117
Védrine, Hubert, 32
voting procedures, economic forums, 85

wage and price flexibility, 151, alternative adjustment mechanisms, 153, domestic, 156, Economic and Monetary Union, 155, Europe, 156, external shocks, 156, Latin America, 156, neoliberalism, 155
war, 69, Afghanistan, 31–32, cold, 93, International Security Assistance Force, 32, Iraq, 30–31, 139–40, post-1945 compromise, 92, post-international order, 30, post-World War II, 3, terrorism, 77, world, 68
Washington consensus (*see also* neoliberalism), 27, 85, 96, 99, 101, challenge of development, 102, developing countries, 122, post-Washington Consensus, 82
Weber, Max, 10, 53
welfare state, 68, characteristic of, 6, internationalism, 62, prevent cuts to, 156, role of, 68, security of, 52, social security, 62
Welles, Sumner, 147
White, Harry Dexter, 147
Wolfensohn, James, 79
women, 116–17, child-care programs, 116–17, social crisis phenomena, 116
workers, 29, 44n.6, 45n.11, 84, 151, 153, 155, safeguards for, 29, workplace standards, 40, workplace treatment programs, 37–38

World Bank, 76, 78, 92, 94, 100, 102, 170, 171, 177, alternatives to, 179, basic needs strategy, 77, debt relief, 99, good-policy countries, 85, international cooperation for development through partnership, 103, management of interdependence, 96, payments crises, 99, poor-policy countries, 85, poverty reduction, 99, role of intergovernmental institutions, 7
World Bank–IMF Poverty Reduction Strategy Papers, 126
World Business Council on Sustainable Development, 40
World Commission on the Social Dimension of Globalization, 84
World Environment Organization, 178–80
World Health Organization, 170
World Meteorological Organization, 170
world order, 3, 87, contradictory tendencies, 9, economic, 86, European Union model of, 7, legitimacy requirements of, 163, U.S. reconstruction of, 6
world politics, 113, globalized, 12, international organizations, 74, main actors, 87, process of, 113, production of new ideas, 74, restructuring, 113, role of non-state actors, 33–34, states, 87
world power, 16, 25, normative challenges in, 25, structural change in, 25, U.S. position, 16
world society, 15, 21, 97, 163, environmental governance, 21, 162–63, social purposes of, 162–63, 163
World Summit on Sustainable Development (*see also* Johannesburg Summit), 38, 162, 166
World Trade Organization (WTO) 76, 86, 88, 100, 170, 182, accelerating opening of markets, 85, adjudication, 66, agreements, 127, agriculture, 127, alternatives to, 179, antiglobalization protests, 24, 27,

apparel and textiles, 127, Battle of Seattle protesters, 24, collaboration with, 29, conflict, 88, developing countries, 13, dispute settlement system, 65, 177, eco-labeling, 182, environment, 28–29, environmental protection, 182, environmental treaty provisions, 182, external and internal transparency, 64–65, Hong Kong ministerial, 126, international cooperation for development through partnership, 103, intellectual property rights, 35, labor standards, 28, legitimacy crisis, 27, liberalization of cross-border financial transactions, 122, politics of, 64, poverty reduction, 79, Rio Principle 12, 167, role of transnational networks of civil society actors, 129, system, 14, trade and sustainable development, 177

World Trade Organization Committee on Trade and the Environment, 171, 181–82

World Trade Organization Doha Development Agenda, 66, agricultural export subsidies, 79

World Trade Organization Uruguay Round, 79, 120

World War II, 93, 95, 97, post–World War II institutional order, 125–27

World Wide Fund for Nature, 34

Zedillo, Ernesto, 80, 100

SUNY series in Global Politics
James N. Rosenau, Editor

LIST OF TITLES

American Patriotism in a Global Society—Betty Jean Craige

The Political Discourse of Anarchy: A Disciplinary History of International Relations—Brian C. Schmidt

Power and Ideas: North-South Politics of Intellectual Property and Antitrust—Susan K. Sell

From Pirates to Drug Lords: The Post–Cold War Caribbean Security Environment—Michael C. Desch, Jorge I. Dominguez, and Andres Serbin (eds.)

Collective Conflict Management and Changing World Politics—Joseph Lepgold and Thomas G. Weiss (eds.)

Zones of Peace in the Third World: South America and West Africa in Comparative Perspective—Arie M. Kacowicz

Private Authority and International Affairs—A. Claire Cutler, Virginia Haufler, and Tony Porter (eds.)

Harmonizing Europe: Nation-States within the Common Market—Francesco G. Duina

Economic Interdependence in Ukrainian-Russian Relations—Paul J. D'Anieri

Leapfrogging Development? The Political Economy of Telecommunications Restructuring—J. P. Singh

States, Firms, and Power: Successful Sanctions in United States Foreign Policy—George E. Shambaugh

Approaches to Global Governance Theory—Martin Hewson and Timothy J. Sinclair (eds.)

After Authority: War, Peace, and Global Politics in the Twenty-First Century—Ronnie D. Lipschutz

Pondering Postinternationalism: A Paradigm for the Twenty-First Century?—Heidi H. Hobbs (ed.)

Beyond Boundaries? Disciplines, Paradigms, and Theoretical Integration in International Studies—Rudra Sil and Eileen M. Doherty (eds.)

International Relations—Still an American Social Science? Toward Diversity in International Thought—Robert M. A. Crawford and Darryl S. L. Jarvis (eds.)

Which Lessons Matter? American Foreign Policy Decision Making in the Middle East, 1979–1987—Christopher Hemmer (ed.)

Hierarchy Amidst Anarchy: Transaction Costs and Institutional Choice—Katja Weber

Counter-Hegemony and Foreign Policy: The Dialectics of Marginalized and Global Forces in Jamaica—Randolph B. Persaud

Global Limits: Immanuel Kant, International Relations, and Critique of World Politics—Mark F. N. Franke

Money and Power in Europe: The Political Economy of European Monetary Cooperation—Matthias Kaelberer

Why Movements Matter: The West German Peace Movement and U. S. Arms Control Policy—Steve Breyman

Agency and Ethics: The Politics of Military Intervention—Anthony F. Lang Jr.

Life after the Soviet Union: The Newly Independent Republics of the Transcaucasus and Central Asia—Nozar Alaolmolki

Information Technologies and Global Politics: The Changing Scope of Power and Governance—James N. Rosenau and J. P. Singh (eds.)

Theories of International Cooperation and the Primacy of Anarchy: Explaining U. S. International Monetary Policy-Making After Bretton Woods—Jennifer Sterling-Folker

Technology, Democracy, and Development: International Conflict and Cooperation in the Information Age—Juliann Emmons Allison (ed.)

Systems of Violence: The Political Economy of War and Peace in Colombia—Nazih Richani

The Arab-Israeli Conflict Transformed: Fifty Years of Interstate and Ethnic Crises—Hemda Ben-Yehuda and Shmuel Sandler

Debating the Global Financial Architecture—Leslie Elliot Armijo

Political Space: Frontiers of Change and Governance in a Globalizing World—Yale Ferguson and R. J. Barry Jones (eds.)

Crisis Theory and World Order: Heideggerian Reflections—Norman K. Swazo

Political Identity and Social Change: The Remaking of the South African Social Order—Jamie Frueh

Social Construction and the Logic of Money: Financial Predominance and International Economic Leadership—J. Samuel Barkin

What Moves Man: The Realist Theory of International Relations and Its Judgment of Human Nature — Annette Freyberg-Inan

Democratizing Global Politics: Discourse Norms, International Regimes, and Political Community—Rodger A. Payne and Nayef H. Samhat

Landmines and Human Security: International Politics and War's Hidden Legacy—Richard A. Matthew, Bryan McDonald, and Kenneth R. Rutherford (eds.)

Collective Preventative Diplomacy: A Study of International Management—Barry H. Steiner

International Relations Under Risk: Framing State Choice—Jeffrey D. Berejikian

Globalization and the Environment: Greening Global Political Economy—Gabriela Kütting

Sovereignty, Democracy, and Global Civil Society—Elisabeth Jay Friedman, Kathryn Hochstetler, and Ann Marie Clark

United We Stand? Divide and Conquer Politics and the Logic of International Hostility—Aaron Belkin

Imperialism and Nationalism in the Discipline of International Relations—David Long and Brian C. Schmidt (eds.)

Globalization, Security, and the Nation State: Paradigms in Transition—Ersel Aydinli and James N. Rosenau (eds.)

Identity and Institutions: Conflict Reduction in Divided Societies—Neal G. Jesse and Kristen P. Williams

Globalizing Interests: Pressure Groups and Denationalization—Michael Zürn (ed., with assistance from Gregor Walter)

International Regimes for the Final Frontier—M. J. Peterson

Ozone Depletion and Climate Change: Constructing A Global Response—Matthew J. Hoffmann

States of Liberalization: Redefining the Public Sector in Integrated Europe—Mitchell P. Smith

Mediating Globalization: Domestic Institutions and Industrial Policies in the United States and Britain—Andrew P. Cortell

The Multi-Governance of Water: Four Case Studies—Matthias Finger, Ludivine Tamiotti, and Jeremy Allouche (eds.)

Building Trust: Overcoming Suspicion in International Conflict—Aaron M. Hoffman

Global Capitalism, Democracy, and Civil-Military Relations in Colombia—Williams Avilés

Complexity in World Politics: Concepts and Methods of a New Paradigm—Neil E. Harrison

Technology and International Transformation: The Railroad, the Atom Bomb, and the Politics of Technological Transformation—Geoffrey L. Herrera

Perils and Promise of Global Transparency: Why the Information Revolution May Not Lead to Security, Democracy, or Peace—Kristin M. Lord